Terry Laybourne's

Quest *for* Taste

Terry Laybourne's

Quest for Taste

Quest: Stewart Howson

Taste: Terry Laybourne

Photography: Duncan Davis

Design: flyingfish Design Consultants Limited
             www.flyingfish.co.uk
Editorial: Lindsey Shaw-Miller, Honeychurch Associates
Print: Printed in England by NB Group
             1st Edition (2004)

Terry Laybourne's text written with Helen Pickles

Published by Quest for Taste Publishing
© Copyright 2004 Quest for Taste Publishing
All images © Duncan Davis
Quest © Stewart Howson and Terry Laybourne

ISBN: 0-9548733-0-0

FOREWORD BY RICK STEIN

I think it was Leonardo da Vinci who said that when artists get together, the one thing they are most likely to discuss is the price of paint. Blow great concepts, it's the raw materials and, naturally, their cost that matter most. No chef I know is more serious about finding good quality local food and then cooking great dishes with it than Terry Laybourne. As he himself says, '90% of good cooking is good shopping.'

What could be a better subject for a cookery book than a series of leisurely journeys, a Quest for Taste, meeting all those local suppliers whose produce makes Terry's cooking so special. Take Anthony and Lucy Carroll, for example, who grow old varieties of potatoes at Carroll's Heritage Potatoes. I just know I'd get on with them after enjoying reading of Terry's visit to their farm, Tiptoe in the Till Valley in North Northumberland. Anthony, like so many small producers of food with flavour, has discovered a life of satisfaction. He gave up producing uniform sized potatoes with perfect, shiny skins and started growing varieties like Dunbar Rover, Pink Fir Apple and the lovely French variety La Ratte. The reason he says, 'I just realized that I wasn't enjoying producing stuff like that. I was selling to a co-op who sold on to pack-houses miles away in the south. I'd no idea whether anyone was getting any enjoyment out of what I produced – which would have given me some pleasure in producing'.

That comment speaks to me of why the sort of suppliers Terry is using sell food that is better. When I was making a TV series about small producers in Britain, I came to the conclusion that what made them different was a determination to consider the quality of what they were making of more importance than profit. They really care about what they're doing.

That dedication shines out in the recipes: Potted Craster Kippers, Casserole of Blackfaced Lamb from Northumberland Quality Meats, Mashed Potatoes made with Dunbar Rovers, Roast Middle White Pork Loin with Apple Stuffing from Ravensworth Grange Farm, or the Cheese Soufflé using Mark Robertson's prize winning Northumberland Cheese.

The recipes, the infectious trips to some great local producers and some very evocative photography by Duncan Davis go together to make a fabulous book about the cooking of a man who has stayed true to his roots.

And on the subject of the price of paint, every time I meet Terry we talk about beef, oysters and the price of cod.

Rick Stein

Contents

Terry Laybourne
Restaurateur

Café 21

...90% of good cooking
is good shopping

I have always resisted the desire to write a cookery book. 'I've got nothing meaningful to say,' has been my stock response to anyone who sought to persuade me. 'There's no need for yet another self-conscious, chefy recipe book. There are too many of those already.'

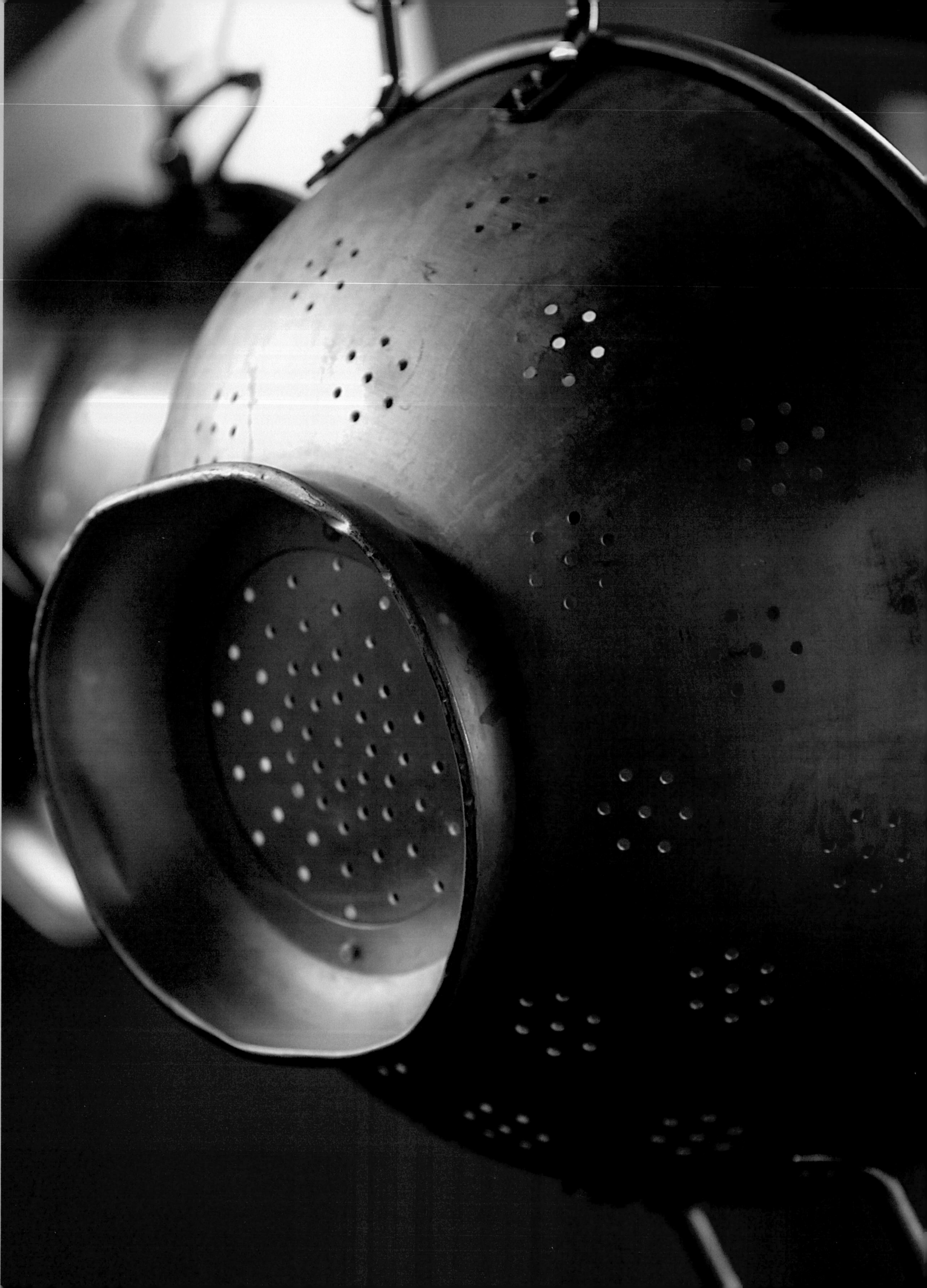

The last time a friend asked, I went further. 'Everyone assumes that the chef is an artist. Let me tell you something. If the guy who supplies my asparagus does his job properly, and it arrives in perfect condition, all I do is sling it in a pan of boiling salted water, take it out when it's ready, put it on a nice plate with a dish of melted butter and a wedge of lemon, and people fête me as a magician.

'On the other hand, if he doesn't do his job properly and produces second rate asparagus, which I cook in exactly the same way, put on a nice plate with a dish of melted butter and a wedge of lemon – what does the customer think? Exactly. He thinks I'm useless. Yet, I didn't do anything differently. Moral: ninety per cent of good cooking is good shopping, the other ten per cent is craft. You can argue the percentages but the facts are the facts. Write a book about the asparagus grower,' I said to my friend. 'He's the artist.' So we did.

I'm becoming someone who eschews the dramarama of *haute cuisine* for more simple pleasures. I don't know if this is in response to a general movement towards a simpler, less cluttered lifestyle, with its renewed appreciation of craftsmanship and authenticity, in which the organic vegetable box is almost a prerequisite of any thinking person's weekly shop. Or it could just be that I'm maturing as a cook. But I worry that food is becoming over sophisticated; too clever, too global – year-round asparagus is surely a contradiction in terms? And we're overlooking the fact that some of our finest food sources are on our doorstep, full of the flavour, texture and seasonality that make cooking such a joy.

If we can agree that good food needs to be two things, fresh and flavoursome, then it is logical that the freshest produce is not the produce that has travelled from the other side of

the world. Almost all commercially grown produce has had its seasons altered in order to meet year-round demand. This constant accessibility has depleted the deep, natural flavours as well as the textures of many of our more familiar fruits and vegetables. To ensure quality, buy the best of whatever is in season at the moment. Use your taste buds to determine substitutions when the produce called for is not available. When you have the opportunity, buy from local farmers or grow your own. Start with the freshest, most flavoursome produce available and you will be surprised at how little work is required to create a memorable meal.

Through improved communications and an obsession with food by the media, the last decade has brought us in touch with myriad cuisines from around the world. Sometimes this causes us to ignore what we have here in our locality: fantastic, native ingredients of which we really should be making more; sourcing not just the best, but the stuff with charismatic provenance. We should be getting to know the people who milk the cows, churn the cheese, fish the violent seas. That is what authenticity is all about: honest toil to the seasonal clock.

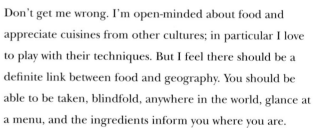

12

Don't get me wrong. I'm open-minded about food and appreciate cuisines from other cultures; in particular I love to play with their techniques. But I feel there should be a definite link between food and geography. You should be able to be taken, blindfold, anywhere in the world, glance at a menu, and the ingredients inform you where you are.

Here, in the north east, we have real craftsmen, working with nature to produce crops, seafood and meat bursting with flavour and freshness. This is a roundabout way of explaining what finally persuaded me to produce this book: I feel a desperate need to retain some sort of regional identity to (my) cooking, a sense of time and place.

Once you start to think in terms of seasons, and what is at its best, ninety per cent of the effort of thinking about what to cook for supper, or the next dinner party, or Sunday

"Recipes don't make things taste good; people do."

lunch, is removed. So, begin by learning about the and what they bring. If you live in the countryside, discover what the farmers and fishermen are producing. If you live in town, seek out farmers' markets. Here in the north east, I know that spring means asparagus, rhubarb and wild salmon; summer is the best time for heather-fed lamb or wild bilberries; autumn brings an abundance of wild mushrooms; and, in winter, there's a huge variety of top quality game.

Get to know your greengrocer, fishmonger and local butcher. They're a valuable source of information about what's coming into season, what's past its best and what you can use instead. Remember, good cooking comes from responding to ingredients – what's fresh, ripe, tasty – not from slavishly following the latest recipe. Recipes don't make things taste good; people do.

Using only seasonal, local produce can be restricting. On the other hand, you gain a far better understanding of ingredients and what works together. Mother Nature is no fool: blackberry and apple, salmon and asparagus, lamb and new potatoes. They aren't perfect combinations by accident: what grows together, goes together.

As for that book about the asparagus grower… my friend Stewart Howson, actor, playwright and rally driver, not only wrote about him but also about the dairy farmer, the corn miller, the herring smoker and the other unsung, craftsmen stars of our region and of this book. His words, at the start of each chapter, describe our quest and celebrate their skills.

Steve Ramshaw
Monkridge Hill Farm

Lamb

"What we're about here is using the best of old breeds with the best of modern science to produce unique flavour and texture in our product. The sheep here are the Scottish Blackfaced sheep that would have grazed these lands hundreds of years ago. They're a breed who like to graze extensively and here they're able to find themselves a varied diet, not just seasonal grasses but things like sphagnum moss, which is high in protein, or young heather roots, small sedges, bilberry, cotton-grass and various seed heads. All this goes toward contributing to the flavour and texture of the meat."

16

M onkridge Hill Farm is high up in Redesdale, in what was once the Debatable Lands. Seven hundred years ago, the Border Reivers raided, marauded and murdered here, and though much romanticized now, they were a mean bunch. Really the place was more a 'wild west Badlands', with no law or bad law, complete with crooked sheriff. The conflicts and blood feuds lasted for generations, until the new King James I of England, VI of Scotland (1603–25) no longer needed watchdogs on the borders of his newly united kingdom. So he summarily sorted them out with Jeddart Justice, a trial system which reversed the usual process by executing the sentence at the start. A hard place and hard times.

To reach Monkridge Hill you can go one of two ways. You can take the Jedburgh road from Newcastle and head for the Borders. If you're unlucky, you might find yourself stuck behind a military convoy heading for the firing ranges at Otterburn, site of the famous battle between the English and the Scots in 1388, much lauded in Border Ballads. More likely, you will encounter the Tyneside racing cyclists, wheeling at high cadence up to the village of Elsdon and the famous cyclists' Front Room Caff. There they'll load up on spaghetti on toast, before they make the final assault on the climb up to Winter's Gibbet. Or you could come over from Alnwick and take the Rothbury road past Cragside, with its amazing views and exhaust-crunching dips.

Whichever way you've come, you will have to follow me now as we turn off the main road and take a single-track lane, which winds its way over the hills. You stop to pass through the gates and then wend your way through the sheep, who stand there, totally disinclined to assist your progress. Beside his farmhouse on the hillside, with the lake beyond, stands Steve Ramshaw, a broad, ruddy, big-boned man, every inch a farmer. You imagine him to be part of a dynasty, hefted like his sheep to these Northumbrian hills for generations.

In fact, he was born in Newcastle on the infamous Scotswood Road, and brought up in the city's West End. Not so long ago, Steve was Senior Clerk of Works for Newcastle City Architects, and his speciality was quality control on building works, which came in handy for the building of that new farmhouse of his – the first entirely new farm to be built in Northumberland for a generation. He built the lake, too, part of the many conservation and environmental features on the farm, which include 30,000 new trees.

Wherever he's from, Steve really does look the part, which is why his picture's been used on the front cover of lots of rural life brochures.

Steve came to Monkridge Hill twenty years ago, and for ten years farmed here whilst still working at his day-job. He bought the bare land from a London development company and started from scratch. Stones grubbed up from the fields went to provide hardcore for the house, and much hard graft went into bringing in electricity and water. Without the local knowledge of a retired shepherd, Steve doesn't think they would ever have found the tiny spring that bubbles up and disappears again within feet. Mind you, finding it was still the easy part, compared to the mile of trenches they had to dig for the pipe-work back to the farm.

Previous generations of Steve's family had been farmers elsewhere, and he'd always been a lad with countryside interests, who dreamed of becoming a farmer. What Steve

lacks in lineage, he makes up for in his sheer passion for farming, particularly organic farming. This has led to him gaining the Soil Association Organic Food Awards, winning the Organic Beef and Sheep producer of the Year Award (2004), and to Monkridge Hill being cited by both the Soil Association and English Nature as a 'model farm'.

Yet in tandem with this he was also declared the NFU North East Farming Entrepreneur of the Year. That's a canny combination, for as Steve himself says, with a laugh, "I'm no beard-and-sandals man. Farming extensively the way we do here, dealing with the animals in the way we do just makes

Steve Ramshaw *Monkridge Hill Farm*

Lamb

perfectly good sense as far as I'm concerned. It's just common sense not to pressurize the environment and animals, just to provide more short term profit. It's a pet hate of mine that the long term, crippling financial costs of something like BSE aren't taken into account."

Steve does produce excellent organic beef from pedigree Aberdeen Angus, but in this chapter we're going to concentrate on lamb, so let's have a look at the lamb  produced at Monkridge Hill. "What we're about here," says Steve "is using the best of old breeds with the best of modern science to produce unique flavour and texture in our product. The sheep here are the Scottish Blackfaced sheep that would have grazed these lands hundreds of years ago. They're a breed who like to graze extensively, and here they're able to find themselves a varied diet, not just seasonal grasses but things like sphagnum moss, which is high in protein, or young heather roots, small sedges, bilberry, cotton-grass and various seed heads. All this goes toward contributing to the flavour and texture of the meat."

And those grasses?

"Well, with us being organic, we're not using any artificial fertilizers, no chemicals. We're not using modern, quick-growing grasses here and chucking nitrogen on 'em, so that the roots don't have to go down into the soil. No, we're using slow-growing varieties like Timothy, red fescue and sheep's fescue, which are getting their roots down into the soil, picking up those trace elements that are so important to the sheep.

Some of the lambs are finished on clover. After we've taken the off the silage (grass that is cut young and allowed to ferment in its own juices for feeding later), this forces a clover regeneration and the hill lambs are fed on the aftermath. Which means about a hundred lambs to a field of young, sweet clover, which again influences flavour."

Is it just the feeding that makes things different and better? No. For Steve it is also the choice of breed.

"For me, in terms of quality, it's important that you don't have the big, lean, double-muscled lamb that the big supermarkets present to their consumers as visually attractive. The Blackface is a smaller carcass, a smaller cut, but for me it's the periphery of fat that surrounds the meat that helps retain juices and tenderness of the joint or cut when cooking."

And then comes the *science*

"We're working hard on our breed index, which means ensuring the genetic ability of the animals to produce high-quality-carcass lamb. The breeding is very carefully monitored, rams being very carefully chosen, and selected for scrapie resistance, too. There's lots of time-consuming work logging a wealth of information about generations of sheep onto computer."

Those who do buy direct from Steve know that the information on the label ensures traceability, which means that Steve can tell you, not just about that individual animal, but about its grandparents.

And the *care*

"We treat our animals carefully here, staff know to handle animals carefully, dogs are trained not to 'grip'". The medical care of animals is different. There's no blanket treatment (ie preventative dosing of the whole flock). "If they don't need it, they don't get it!"

Sheep movement and housing are all thought about, as is the way they go to slaughter, as Steve emphasizes. "We always remember and emphasize to others that we're dealing with living things here, not objects. I use a local abattoir only half an hour away, with a good understanding about organic, and our animals are slaughtered to Soil Association conditions, which means they have access

to organic food and clean water. They are killed 'first up the line', which reduces stress, and after the kill they don't come in contact with non-organic meat, to avoid cross-contamination. Then it comes back to the modern butchers' premises on the farm, where our own two butchers will deal with it."

Steve believes that his lack of father-to-son farming experience has actually been something of an advantage. "When it comes to farming, I've been able to get outside of the box, look at it and question it". Well he must be doing something right, because people are beating a path to his door – some via the phone and the internet, some literally, rolling in past those cyclists, whilst Steve Ramshaw's vans are busy rolling out, their distinctive livery proudly proclaiming Northumbrian Quality Meats.

This strategy of selling direct, coupled with a strong belief in conservation, has shown Steve Ramshaw's Monkridge Hill Farm to be an outstanding example of rural renascence.

Lamb

22

When the year's first lambs arrive in our kitchens, something close to a cheer goes up. It's a tangible sign that the long, dark winter is over. Chefs are mercurial creatures. In winter, we long for spring with its tender lamb, English asparagus and sweet young vegetables. By the end of summer, we're fed up with quickly cooked food and can't wait for the first cold snap so we can start braising and stewing again. Thank God for the seasons, or there would be a lot of miserable chefs out there.

Although sheep have safely grazed on British pastures for centuries, lamb is a relatively recent meat. The first references to lamb in recipe books don't occur until after the Second World War. Historically, sheep were valued for their fleeces and the animals were allowed to mature. Correctly called mutton, their meat was strong and gamey and lead to such traditional dishes as Lancashire hot pot and Irish stew, which required long, slow cooking. While very tasty, these dishes are not so great for young lamb, whose delicate flavour would be overpowered by such robust treatment.

The first lambs of the season are from lowland pastures; pale, tender, sweet. What gets us really excited, however, are those that arrive in late June. These blackfaced hill sheep are upland grazers. Smaller than their lowland cousins, they have to work harder to find food, foraging on wild herbs, grasses and heather. As a result, they are leaner, their flavour more complex. Meat from a young lamb is characteristically pale pink and covered with a hard, almost white fat. Deeper red meat and yellowing fat indicates a more mature animal.

Early season lamb, I maintain, is far and away the best. Others say age gives flavour. It's a personal thing, but our menus predominantly feature lamb in spring and summer. By October, we generally avoid roasts, although we are happy to braise and stew. Having said that, a joint of more mature

lamb roasted with spices – cumin, turmeric, coriander, saffron – works well. These middle-eastern seasonings make a refreshing change from the traditional British accompaniments of mint sauce and redcurrant jelly, or the popular Provençal flavours of thyme, garlic and rosemary. Marinating a leg of lamb, boned into joints, in a selection of middle-eastern spices, olive oil and puréed onions, then grilling it over a barbecue will have your neighbours salivating.

Despite its small size, there is far more to lamb than roast leg or grilled cutlets. There are over ten different cuts and each benefits from a different style of cooking. For example, fillets can be steamed or poached, shanks can be braised and shoulders confit in their own fat. At home, as a kid, we often ate 'lap' – the belly – which my mother braised with barley and root vegetables. Not a lot of meat, but loads of flavour.

Irish stew was another favourite. I still love it and often cook it as an autumn lunch for the staff. I know I said this dish was designed for older animals. However, with judicious use of seasoning and careful attention to the cooking, it can work well with lamb. Choose a shoulder or shank – these joints have a higher gelatine content, so retain moisture better – and blanch in boiling water to get rid of excess fat. Use a good strong stock, rather than water, and be precise with the seasoning. Small, waxy potatoes are better than main crop, and shouldn't be added until twenty minutes before the end. This ensures they remain soft but not mushy. I also add a handful of carrots, which traditionalists would abhor.

One of the biggest revelations for me was discovering the sweet pleasure of eating lamb that was roasted pink. I first came across this when working in the ski resort of St. Moritz in Switzerland in 1975. Pink, let's make it clear, is not the same as rare. Lamb needs a certain amount of heat in the centre to release the juices and flavours. I would also argue that it needs a certain amount of fat. In the heyday of nouvelle cuisine there was a lot of chefy nonsense for stripping the meat of fat, cooking it rare and slicing it paper thin. The argument was that it looked nicer. A total nonsense. The meat ended up blood red, devoid of all flavour and, because of the way it was cut, cooled so quickly that after the first forkful it was stone cold.

To get a perfect pink roast, the golden rule is, don't mess about with it. Place a shoulder of lamb in a hot roasting tray along with a little flavourless oil and a broken head of garlic. The latter permeates rather than overpowers the meat. Beg some bones from the butcher and toss them in the tray as well. Once the meat is cooked, let it rest. Meanwhile, discard the excess fat from the tray, add a cup of water and scrape the tray contents like mad. Simmer for ten minutes, and there's your gravy. Thinly slice the lamb, serve with French beans and spoon the strained garlic gravy over the top. Sit down and eat and let the juices dribble down your chin.

Tips

Resting meat:

The high heat needed to roast meat seals the outside, trapping the juices inside. As the juices start to boil, they retreat from the outer surfaces of the meat to the centre through the network of blood vessels. As they are forced to the middle, pressure builds up in this more confined space. Carving the meat when the joint is taken from the oven would immediately release these juices. Resting allows the juices to filter back, the muscle fibres to relax and the meat to tenderize evenly. Place the meat on the back of an upturned plate which itself is sitting in a larger dish. This allows you to collect any juices that run out. Cover the meat lightly with foil (too tight and steam will collect and the meat stew) and place the dish on the open door of the oven. For a kilo of meat (enough for six people) allow 15–20 minutes.

On the bone:

Meat left on the bone has a better, sweeter flavour. However, it's harder to carve. If meat is boned, seasoning can be inserted and the easier carving makes for a better presentation. But there's no doubt in my mind that a leg of lamb roasted on the bone has a unique, sweet intensity.

Best end of lamb with olive crust

(Serves 4)

This is a twist on a traditional French preparation for a best end of lamb. Normally the crust, referred to as 'persillade', would include only breadcrumbs, garlic and herbs, and the lamb would be coated with Dijon mustard. In the restaurant we mess about with this technique quite often and I feel that this is one of the best variations.

1	best end of lamb (around 900g), trimmed of fat and bones and cleaned
	salt & pepper

Crust

4tbsp	olive oil
2	shallots
160g	pitted green & black olives
2tbsp	chopped parsley
160g	dried, white breadcrumbs
300ml	lamb stock
100ml	red wine

Preheat the oven to **180°c**.

Season the **lamb** with **salt and pepper**. Heat a roasting tray, put in the best end of lamb together with a little **olive oil**. Place in the hot oven and roast for 10minutes.

Meanwhile make the olive crust. Chop the **shallots** and **olives** finely and let them sweat in the remaining olive oil. Cook gently until soft and transparent before stirring in the **breadcrumbs** and **parsley**. Season with **salt** and **pepper**, remove from the heat.

After 10 minutes, remove the lamb from the oven and coat with a layer of the crust mixture. Return to the oven for a further 5 minutes, remove and allow to rest in a warm place.

Deglaze the roasting tin with the **red wine** and boil in order to reduce a little. Add the **lamb stock** and reduce a little more to a good sauce consistency. Check the seasoning and strain through a fine sieve.

Carve the lamb into thick cutlets. Serve with some potatoes roasted in olive oil and garlic, and good seasonal vegetables.

SPICED LAMB BURGER WITH GOATS CHEESE

(Serves 4)

4	soft bread rolls
700g	minced lamb
1 pinch	chilli powder
2 pinches	ground cinnamon
	salt and milled black pepper
2tbsp	chopped coriander
180g	soft goat's cheese
½ head	shredded iceberg lettuce

Yoghurt and cucumber sauce

240g	plain yoghurt
1tbsp	cumin seeds
½	cucumber (peeled, seeded and cut into 3mm dice)
pinch	of salt
pinch	of chilli powder

First make the sauce. Toast the **cumin seeds** very, very gently in a dry frying pan over a low heat, just until the seeds become aromatic. Transfer to a plate and allow to cool. Mix the **yoghurt, cucumber, salt, chilli powder** and **cumin seeds**. Refrigerate until needed.

Mix the **lamb, chilli powder** and **cinammon**, season with **salt and pepper**. Divide into 4 equal portions of 175g and roll into balls.

Mix the **coriander** into the **goat's cheese** and divide into 4 x 45g balls. Make an indentation in each ball of lamb and stuff 45g of goat's cheese into each. Close the indentation to cover the cheese mixture completely with the meat. Flatten gently into patties about 25–30mm thick. Grill on a hot barbeque, or a ridged, cast iron grill pan. 7–8 minutes should be long enough to give you beautifully pink lamb with a warm, melting goat's cheese centre.

Split the bread rolls and toast or grill lightly. Divide the **iceberg** between the bottom half of the rolls and spoon over a large spoonful of yoghurt and cucumber sauce. Place a lamb burger on top and finish with the bread roll lids.

BARBEQUED SPRING LAMB WITH MIDDLE EASTERN SPICES

(Serves 6)

1.2kg	boneless leg of lamb
2tsp	coriander seeds
1tsp	cumin seeds
6tsp	cardamom pods
1 small	chopped onion
60g	chopped ginger
6	crushed garlic cloves
2tbsp	vegetable oil
1tsp	turmeric
1tsp	ground cinnamon
½tsp	coarse sea salt
½tsp	dried chilli flakes

Gently heat the **coriander seeds, cumin** and **cardamom** in a dry frying pan until fragrant. Cool and grind with a pestle and mortar or an electric coffee mill. Purée the **onion, garlic** and **ginger** in a food processor with the **vegetable oil**. Add the ground spices, as well as the t**urmeric, cinnamon, salt** and **chilli**. Mix through, adding a little water if needed to produce a smooth purée. Spread the spice mixture evenly over the **lamb**, cover and marinate in the refrigerator for 4–6 hours.

Prepare the barbeque or preheat the oven to **180°c**.

Remove the lamb from the fridge and, using a firm brush, remove any excess marinade. Allow to come to room temperature, then barbeque over hot charcoal, or roast in the oven until cooked to your liking. Allow to relax in a warm place for 20–25 minutes before carving into thick slices.

Serve with a couscous salad, or maybe a tomato and mint salad, or even houmus and some grilled pitta bread.

FILLET OF LAMB WITH BASIL MOUSSE AND MEDITERRANEAN VEGETABLES

(Serves 6)

This may seem complicated on first reading, but don't be put off; it's a breeze really, once you've mastered the chicken mousse. Ensure that all the ingredients are thoroughly chilled before you start and you can't go wrong. Mint or tarragon could replace the basil if you wish. In winter we sometimes make a version using pork fillet rather than lamb, and a mousse flavoured with sage and onion. A cannon is the trimmed, barrel-shaped piece of meat taken from the lamb loin. Ask your butcher to prepare this for you.

6 x 120g	lamb cannons, trimmed of all fat and sinew
200g	chicken breast
2	egg yolks
¼ tsp	salt
1	small handful basil leaves
225ml	double cream
1	red pepper
1	yellow pepper
1	small aubergine
1	courgette
1	beef tomato
1	whole garlic clove
	extra virgin olive oil
250ml	reduced lamb stock
4tbsp	basil oil

Dice the **chicken breast** and chill thoroughly. Chill the **double cream**, the **egg yolks** and the bowl of the food processor. Cut both of the **peppers**, the **aubergine** and the **courgette** into neat dice. Blanch the **beef tomato** in boiling water for six seconds, then refresh it in iced water. Do the same with the **basil leaves** and then chop them. Remove the skin from the tomato, cut into quarters, remove the seeds and cut the flesh into neat dice.

When the chicken is thoroughly chilled, process it with a pinch of **salt** for 30 seconds, or until you have a smooth purée. Process again, pouring in the **cream** a little at a time as the machine runs. Stop the machine, remove the lid and scrape down the sides of the bowl with a plastic spatula. Switch the machine on again and run in the remaining cream. Remove the mousse to a bowl and chill thoroughly again. Stir in the remaining **salt** and **chopped basil**.

Season the **lamb** with salt and pepper and spread 50g mousse onto the top side of each lamb fillet. Invert onto a square of cling film and wrap tightly. Chill for 30 minutes.

Place a Chinese bamboo steamer over a pan of boiling water, place in the lamb fillets (still wrapped in cling film), cook for 8 minutes, or 12 if you prefer your lamb more cooked. Preheat the grill. While the lamb is cooking, sauté the **diced vegetables** in a little **olive oil** with a crushed **clove of garlic**. Cook gently over a low heat; the vegetables should not brown. When the other vegetables are tender, add the tomato dice to the pan.

Remove the lamb from the steamer when ready and set aside in a warm place to rest for 10 minutes. Heat the **lamb stock** in a small saucepan and boil to reduce to a sauce consistency. Remove the lamb from the cling film and place on a tray under the preheated grill. Lightly brown the basil mousse, then remove and trim the ends to expose the lovely pink flesh.

Serve the lamb on top of the vegetables, with the reduced lamb stock and basil oil spooned around.

CASSEROLE OF LAMB AND YOUNG VEGETABLES

(Serves 6)

1200g	lean lamb shoulder, cut into 50mm cubes
4	medium carrots, peeled and diced
2	medium onions, peeled and diced
3	ripe tomatoes, halved, seeds squeezed out and flesh chopped
6	garlic cloves, skinned and finely chopped
1 bunch	fresh thyme
1	bay leaf
	salt
1tbsp	unsalted butter
1tbsp	vegetable oil
2tbsp	flour
	milled white pepper

Vegetables

1 bunch	young carrots
1 bunch	young white turnips
225g	button onions
125g	small button mushrooms
450g	small new potatoes
225g	fine French beans
5tbsp	shelled peas
	salt and pepper
pinch	sugar
1tbsp	unsalted butter
1 bunch	flat parsley

Separate the *parsley leaves* from the stalks. Set the leaves aside and tie the stalks together with ⅔ bunch of *thyme* and the *bay leaf*. Preheat the oven to *130°c*.

Heat a large, heavy, cast iron casserole over a high heat. Season the *lamb* with *salt, pepper* and a pinch of *sugar*. Add the *butter and oil* to the casserole, followed by the diced *lamb*. Turn regularly with a spatula until seared, but only lightly browned. Remove to a plate with a slotted spoon and add *carrots* and *onions* to the casserole. Sauté over a medium heat until softened and lightly browned.

Remove the vegetables to the plate with the lamb.

Pour off the fat from the casserole and replace the meat and vegetables on the heat. Add *tomatoes* and *garlic* and cook for 3–4 minutes before adding the flour, stirring well. Add the *bouquet garni* and enough water just to cover the meat. Bring to the boil, cover with a lid and transfer to the oven for 40–50 minutes.

As the meat cooks, scrape the *young carrots and turnips*. Cook in boiling, salted water. Place the button onions in a non-stick frying pan with a pinch of *salt*, pinch of *sugar* and a knob of *butter*. Cover with water and cook until the water is reduced away and the onions are tender and caramelized.

Sauté the *mushrooms* in *butter*. Cook the *beans, peas* and *potatoes* separately in boiling, salted water. Remove the casserole from the oven and lift out the meat with a slotted spoon. Cover and keep warm. Strain the cooking juices through a fine strainer into a saucepan. Place over a medium heat, remove any grease that rises to the surface and reduce for 5 minutes or so. Separate the vegetables from the meat and discard, returning the meat to the sauce. Add the *vegetables* and the remaining *thyme sprig*. Check the seasoning and serve, sprinkled with *flat parsley* leaves.

Julia Nolan
Heatherslaw Mill

Flour

"To be a successful miller you have to have a feel for it. I have to use all my five senses here."
Remember Chaucer's miller, who 'had a golden thumb'?

"The miller's touch. That's where that comes from. You've got to have that feel for the quality of what you are grinding, got to be able to stick a hand under the spout and tell instantly."

We're heading out to the north of Northumberland again today, close to the border with Scotland. Near to the village of Branxton, we'll pass close by the site of the Battle of Flodden. If you decide to take a detour to see it, you'll find yourself winding your way through very narrow lanes, slipping past a sturdy church and through the tiny village itself.

Then, above you, there appears what seems to be a large, isolated, man-made mound, topped by a cross. If you stop at the car park and climb the steps, it's a surprise to find that you are not on the top of an artificial mound at all, but on the edge of a ridge – in exactly the position of the English army at the start of the battle – looking up, across the battlefield, to the heights where the Scottish army was assembled. The plaque by the cross gives a vivid account of the conflict, and of the sad disposal of the tens of thousands (mainly Scots) who were killed.

Rejoining our route north, we are stopped just short of the border by the brown signs for Ford and Etal. Interestingly, given their names, there's a ford at Etal and a castle at Ford! There's a Flodden connection with Ford Castle, too, for according to local legend, Lady Heron seduced King James

IV into a dalliance, which delayed the Scots and allowed the English army to slip around the back of them to the north.

Etal has a castle as well; ruined but worth a look. No talk there, though, of dalliances and secret passages between rooms. Etal also boasts The Black Bull, Northumberland's only thatched pub, indeed one of the very few thatched buildings in the county. At Ford there's the famous Lady Waterford Hall, on whose walls Lady Louisa Anna, the Victorian Marchioness of Waterford, painted pre-Raphaelite-style paintings of scenes from the Bible. You can also take a ride on the Heatherslaw Light Railway, or visit Heatherslaw Mill. All in all, Ford and Etal provide enough to see and do (and enough tea and scones) for a canny number of folk to stop off and spend a few hours, or even find it a perfect centre for a peaceful holiday.

Heatherslaw Mill is our destination today, so we turn off the main road and follow the waterwheel on the brown sign, which takes us across the river on a very narrow bridge indeed. So narrow I fear for the chrome on my door handles! The river is the Till, which looks benign today, but has something of a reputation, encapsulated in the old rhyme

> *Tweed said to Till:*
> *'What makes you run so still?'*
> *Till said to Tweed:*
> *'Tho' ye run with speed*
> *And I run slaw,*
> *Yet where you drown ae man*
> *I drown twa.'*

The Till is the only tributary of the river Tweed that is wholly in England, and it drains a large area of the Cheviots. At this point it tumbles over a shelf of rock, which makes it the perfect location to build a dam and a watermill.

There was a working mill here before 1300; an ancient document of 1306 records that the widow of Nicholas Graham held a watermill in Heatherslaw worth £4 a year. The mill went through several owners, some of them trustees for the Heron family, who owned the Ford Estate. There's no record of the mill during the centuries of trouble and strife 'twixt the Scots and the English (c. 1400–1603). There would have been constant raiding and carrying off of stock, and then periodically, conflict would break out on a larger scale, such as the Battle of Flodden. As late as 1678, barely a mile away at Crookham, there was a minor battle, which is

believed to have been the last affray between the Scots and the English to take place on English soil (discounting the Young Pretender's sally down to Derby in 1745).

With the arrival of more settled times, the mill emerged from obscurity. In the eighteenth century, Sir John Hussey Delaval bought the Ford Estate, and in 1768 he paid the enormous sum of £8,400 for 750 acres at Heatherslaw. The last part of the century saw an amazing period of prosperity for north Northumberland and a period of great development at Heatherslaw. Across the river, Sir John built a new forge mill for the manufacture of farming tools, and established a sawmill. At Heatherslaw, you can see a copy of an engraving of the complex in 1779. It seems strange to think that nowadays, people come here for a quiet holiday, where once there would have been a noisy, smelly, busy industrial place.

The mill continued into the nineteenth century, being altered *c*.1830 into the three-storey, double mill that it is today. Things seemed to be going well. Thomas and James Black operated both mills and appeared to be thriving, but then trade dwindled and was brought low by the great agricultural depression of the 1880s. A writer of the period, Reverend H. M. Neville, captures the scene of melancholy:

'To those who were accustomed to [the sound of the mill] its silence still seems like the stopping of the tick of the eight-day clock to the cottager, or the sudden ceasing of the engines on an ocean boat; a silence that may be felt, ominous of something wrong.'

From 1915–49 the mill was used by various tenants to mill pearl barley for human consumption, although a little grinding and crushing was undertaken for local farmers. It was then used as a grainstore until 1957, when even that

came to an end. Unused and abandoned, the mill rapidly became derelict and the river silt, washed in by the floods, choked the millraces. Demolition – the fate for many an old mill – seemed just around the corner for Heatherslaw.

So how come we're sitting here, in the working mill, in 2003, talking to the Head Miller, Julia Nolan? Julia explains.

"It had been hoped that the National Trust might take on the mill, but there wasn't enough money and that idea fell through, so to rescue the mill, The Heatherslaw Mill Trust was set up in 1972 by Lord Michael Joicey, whose family had owned the Ford and Etal estates since the early twentieth century. It took a great deal of work from the staff of the estates and local contractors. The silt had to be dug out by hand from the millraces. The massive millstones and waterwheels were renovated and all the complicated, heavy gear-wheels and shafts had to be realigned, so that they would run smoothly once again. It's not all working; remember, this place was actually two mills in one building. The upper mill is back in full working order, but the lower mill was left largely at it was before restoration. We were lucky we still had the last mill foreman, Jimmy Middlemiss, who was in his seventies, living nearby. He was the instruction book! We're a working museum now and our purpose is largely educational, but we do produce a good

34

amount of flour a year. There's a board of trustees now, chaired by Lord James Joicey, and the mill is the most northerly working water mill in England."

So how did Julia come to be Head Miller?

Heatherslaw are members of the Traditional Corn Millers Guild, and out of that membership only four have a woman as Head Miller, so she belongs to a very select group indeed.

"I started here eight years ago. I'd got three daughters and was trying to find a part-time job. My previous employer retired and her husband asked if I'd like to do two mornings here. So I came to do the bagging and packing, breaking down the big sacks into anything from 500g to 5kilo… hard work. Of course, there's more of it to be done these days. When I first started, other than our own shop on the premises, we supplied two shops and two bakeries; nowadays it's six dozen shops. People kept ringing up and wanting stuff delivering, so we came to an arrangement with a bakery and now our flour goes out on their vans. We do four farmers' markets too. We can go through 300 kilos in a morning these days. But back then, there I was bagging, and then started asking questions, so John Bradley, the Head Miller, who was looking to retire, saw I was interested and started to teach me."

I am about to ask another bread-and-butter question, about different kinds of grain, when I stop because I realize that

I am vibrating. So is the chair, the table and the floor. And then I hear a series of deep noises; groaning, rumbling and creaking, like someone starting to warm up a great church organ, or sound effects from a *Lord of the Rings* film. I forget my question, and Julia notices and smiles.

"She's just saying, 'Oh, is nobody taking any notice of me then?'"

"She?" I ask.

"Oh yes, the mill's a she, with a personality and mood swings. The miller's got to understand that it's a partnership. To be a successful miller, you have to have a feel for it. I have to use all my five senses here."

Remember Chaucer's miller, who 'had a golden thumb?' Julia makes that familiar finger-and-thumb, rubbing gesture that everybody understands as 'money'. "The miller's touch. That's where that comes from," she continues. "You've got to have that feel for the quality of what you are grinding, got to be able to stick a hand under the spout and tell instantly. You've got to be able, too, to feel the vibrations coming up through the floor. If something's not set right, then you should be able to feel the mill isn't right. This place has a set of unique noises, too, so you've got to be able to hear and understand them. You've got to be able to smell and taste when things are not right too. If you've set the stones wrong, if the gap between the two stones is too close, then you can burn the flour and there's a particular, acrid, almost chemical smell in the air."

Not only could you burn the flour, but a careless miller could also cause an explosion if things got too hot and the flour in the air went up with a bang.

"Contracts for mills often banned brewhouses in the same building," points out Julia. "You see, it was too much of a temptation otherwise. Well, you had all the ingredients for beer in a water mill. Then on a hot day, after a dry and dusty morning's work, the miller might be tempted to go and sit on the riverbank to cool off with a jug or two of beer. He then falls asleep with the mill running, it's a hot day so things expand, and maybe its humid, too, so they swell, which means that the millstones end up too close to each other, heating and burning the corn and then bingo! Bye bye mill, bye bye careless miller!"

In the past, a careful miller, one with 'the touch' and 'the golden thumb', could have made himself some money and a place in society. Julia enlightens me.

"There would have been the manor, the church and the mill, and sometimes the only one amongst them with any cash would have been the miller, and he often ended up as a money lender. If someone in the village had a letter, then they'd take it to either the vicar or the miller to be read… depending of course upon the subject matter.

Mills were handed down to sons, the secrets of milling would be kept in the family with nothing written down. If there were no sons, then the miller would take apprentices and the eldest daughter would be taught her three 'r's, reading, writing and reckoning up. She could then control the purse strings and the mill when she was married off to the best apprentice. So it wasn't unusual in mediaeval times to have a woman in control of a mill, although not doing the actual physical work."

Will Julia be handing on her miller's skills to the family? She laughs. "Well, my daughters spent so much time here as they grew up that there's a Heatherslaw standing joke that they probably could run the place… but no, not really. I will have to look for someone to train up though, 'cos my two 'lads' who both come in part time are in their sixties! Whoever it is will have to have the feel for it mind, there's still no manual."

What actually is being milled at Heatherslaw?

"Breadmaking flours, both stoneground and wholemeal flour from wheat and rye. The wheat is grown half a mile away, although the rye is bought in and comes on a longer journey. We do stock oat flakes, medium oatmeal and pinhead oatmeal, which is used for 'crumbing' fish and for porridge with a rougher texture. It's also used in the Scottish dessert Cranachan."

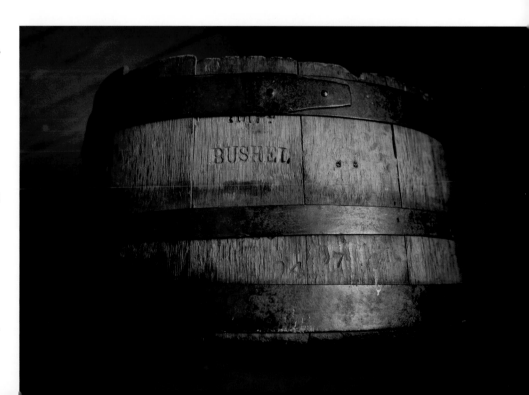

Julia warms to her subject.

"Breadmakers have got choosy, they want flavour in their flour and in their bread." Demand has shot up since the advent of the home bread-making machine, by the way. "Not only do they want 'nowt taken out', but they want 'nowt putting in' either. We add no stabilizers and no preservatives. What comes out of here is just pure flour.

When it comes to choosing the wheat I go out and see the farmer, exactly as the miller would have done in the past. I'm looking for bread-making quality with high gluten and high protein. We use only one variety of wheat per flour in this mill. If we tried to mix varieties then it would come out in layers, like one of those sand pictures.

Modern mills are able to mix wheats, so that they could combine one with a high yield but not 'strong' (i.e. not a high protein content), and mix in some lower yielding 'strong' wheat. It is also the practice to add acetic acid additives and enhancers to take borderline wheat up to the state where it is useable. We do nothing like that here. I go and visit the farmer and see what he recommends. Then I'll bring some samples back and mill them, and then hand it out to customers for a blind tasting. They'll give me feedback on flavour and texture and we'll choose one."

Talking about feedback, Julia loves talking to people out in the farmers' markets. "Customers are always ready for a chat and they'll be quick to let me know what they like and perhaps sometimes let me know that maybe something hasn't worked as good as others."

Heatherslaw are to be found at several farmers' markets throughout the north east and in Edinburgh. You can find them at shows and food festivals such as the Herring Festival and the Northumbria Food Festival at the Baltic Centre on the quayside in Newcastle. They do have a website and I'm sure would let you know how you could get hold of their product, should you phone them. The mill itself is well worth a visit; the ingenious mechanical systems that power and control the place would delight the most Fred Dibnahite of enthusiasts. The social history details on display are thought-provoking too. Thousands of people every year make their way through this fascinating place, some of them with milling experience, and Julia is very happy to listen to them and then pass on their knowledge to the children and young people who visit.

In questing for taste, we keep coming back to the importance of the human touch and the personal dimension in achieving a quality product. I didn't somehow expect it here, I don't quite know why. I'd just thought 'Well, a mill's a machine. You turn it on and away it goes." But I knew I was wrong when 'she' started vibrating and talking to Julia; when Julia's eyes came alive as she talked of her personal relationship with it, of the necessity for all her senses to play a part in the process, and of having 'the miller's thumb'. Then I recognized familiar territory. Julia Nolan is someone who loves what she does and puts an awful lot of herself into the job. It's no surprise that many of her customers know her by name, and know the quality of her product by its taste.

Flour

Give me an apprentice cook and I'll give him a bag of flour. It may sound old-fashioned, but I believe that learning to make pastry is one of the cornerstones of becoming a good chef. It's one of the few areas of cooking – bread is the same – where you genuinely work with very few basics – flour, fat, water. (Or, in the case of bread: flour, water, yeast and salt.) How the pastry or bread turns out is utterly dependent on how the cook handles those few ingredients. Careless measures, sloppy technique, a failure to understand the science, and you're in a mess. If a sauce is too thick, you can thin it. If a marinade is too sharp, you can sweeten it. If the steak is tough, you can blame the butcher. If pastry fails, you bin it. It's unforgiving. As a result, it is a fantastic reminder that cookery is a scientifically based craft, and you disrespect ingredients at your peril.

In our household, food was honest fuel rather than a labour of love, except when it came to baking. On Sundays, my mother and, later, my sister, had a baking marathon. I didn't join in, other than to scrape out the bowl, but I learnt to appreciate what good, simple, freshly made food can taste like. I also, although I didn't realize it at the time, saw the science of cookery at work. To me it was pure magic that flour, sugar and butter – three such different textures – could turn into something sweet and crunchy like a German biscuit. (Although, to this day, I'm still puzzled why two biscuits sandwiched together with jam, topped with water icing and decorated with a silver ball are considered to be German.)

So, the fewer ingredients a recipe has, the more it relies upon – or reveals – the skill of the cook. It should be equally obvious that the quality of those ingredients becomes paramount. Stoneground flour is, without doubt, the best. High-volume, commercial mills use steel rollers, which have a tendency to generate heat and scorch the wheat. Stone millstones grind more slowly and don't generate the same

heat. Be suspicious of any flour that's incredibly white; it could have been bleached. And don't make the mistake of thinking it will keep indefinitely. A bag of flour can change dramatically over a few months. Buy in small quantities and keep opened bags in air-tight containers. An easy test is to take a handful of flour and squeeze it lightly. It should 'cake' in your hand.

Ah, but what type of flour? To some extent that comes down to personal taste, but there are a few guidelines. All flour is good for you. White and brown flours have more calcium than wholemeal, but wholemeal has more fibre. There is no difference between wholewheat and wholemeal flour. Both contain the whole wheat grain.

Plain flour is all-purpose flour that won't let you down, although others may have a more interesting taste or texture. Broadly, it divides into hard (or 'strong') flour and soft (or 'weak') flour. Hard flour has a higher proportion of gluten (the elasticity in dough which helps to trap air) and is what you need for making bread, pasta and puff pastry. The lower proportion of gluten in soft flour makes it best for biscuits, cakes and shortcrust pastry. A useful tip, if you need softer flour, is to replace some of the plain flour with cornflour.

Lots of good cooks are nervous of making pastry. It really isn't difficult, providing you follow the rules. Start getting clever, and it can punish. Use stoneground flour and butter. Margarine can be used, but butter has a far better flavour. Make sure everything – ingredients, work surface, implements – is chilled. A stainless steel bowl and marble or granite work surface are best, but you can always chill a worktop with a bag of ice cubes. With small amounts of pastry (made with less than 500g of flour), a food processor is better than a mixer as it cuts rather than beats the flour, butter and water.

Your aim, when making pastry, is to work it as little as possible; over-handling encourages gluten to form, which will make it too elastic. Allow it to rest for half an hour in the fridge; again, this allows the gluten to relax. Roll out on a cold surface, with plenty of flour to prevent it sticking, and let it rest again before baking. Once baked, immediately remove it from the baking tray or dish – otherwise the heat will continue cooking it – and let it cool evenly on a wire tray. See, it wasn't that difficult.

Bread, mind you, is a different story. Not because it's difficult but because you will never, ever get people to agree on what makes the perfect loaf. Should it be crisp or chewy? Should it have a fine, dense texture or be loose and open? Should you use sour dough or yeast? And I haven't started on Ukrainian pumpernickel, Russian rye or Lebanese flatbread. Bread is, arguably, the most regionalized of products; developed from the native flour, adapted to local needs, customized to local tastes.

In the north east, of course, we have the stotty cake; confusing to the outsider, as it's neither sweet like a cake nor loaf-shaped like bread. A flat, white disc, it was traditionally made from leftover dough which was never sufficient to fill a tin, hence the low, flat shape. Cooked on the 'sole', or flat bottom, of a cooling oven, the lower temperature allowed the yeast to work longer and produce a chewier, denser bread with a floury crust. As for the name, apparently the baker would test whether it was cooked by 'stotting', or bouncing, the bread on the kitchen floor. If it bounced, it was done.

This isn't a bread to be neatly sliced. It's one to be roughly cut and eaten warm with butter and jam.

WHITE COUNTRY BREAD

(Makes two 350g cobs)

450g	strong, white, stoneground flour
1½tsp	fine salt
1tsp	caster sugar
300ml	still mineral water
10g	fresh yeast

Sift the *flour* and *salt* into a mixing bowl and make a well in the centre. Crumble the *yeast* into a small measuring jug. Heat the mineral water to 20°C. Add a little warmed water to the yeast, along with the *sugar*. Stir to make a smooth, loose paste then mix in the remaining water. Pour into the well in the flour and, with your finger, introduce a little of the flour into the liquid. Leave for 5 minutes or so until bubbles appear on the surface.

With one hand, roughly combine the ingredients and turn out onto a clean table. The dough will be quite sticky at this stage, but there should be no need to add more flour. Knead the dough by grabbing hold of one end and pushing it with the heel of your hand. Do this for 3–4 minutes until the dough has become smooth and silky.

Lightly oil a large mixing bowl, place the dough in the bottom and cover with a damp tea towel. Leave in a warm place to rise for 40 minutes for the first proving. Remove the towel, dust the risen dough lightly with flour and turn out onto the table. Press the dough down firmly with your hands, without further kneading, and divide it into two. Take each half in turn and bring the edges of the dough towards the centre, turn upside down and set on a floured baking tray.

Preheat the oven to *200°c*. Slide the tray into an oiled plastic bin liner and return to a warm place for about 50 minutes, to rise and double in volume. Remove the tray of risen dough from the bin liner and sift over a fine layer of flour. Slash the tops of the loaves with a sharp blade. Spray the inside of the oven with water from a plant sprayer and bake the cobs for 40 minutes, leaving the door ajar slightly for the last 10 minutes, which helps to achieve a crusty finish. Test the bread by tapping it sharply on the underside; it will sound hollow when baked. Cool on a wire rack.

MOZZARELLA PIZZA WITH BASIL

(Makes 4 individual pizzas)

I haven't met anyone who didn't like pizza. This dough is a little bit special, with the inclusion of honey in the recipe, which feeds the yeast and aids aeration, developing a nice, chewy, yeasty crust. Try to make the dough a day in advance and refrigerate; the flavour is noticeably better.

Pizza Dough

345g	plain flour
1tsp	fine sea salt
1tbsp	mild honey
2tbsp	olive oil
190ml	cold water
1pkt	active dry yeast
60ml	luke warm water

Tomato sauce

2 x 400g	tins plum tomatoes
2 pinches	salt
2 pinches	sugar
2tbsp	chopped oregano
½	medium onion, grated
2 balls	Mozzarella cheese
1 handful	fresh basil

Place the *flour* in an electric mixer with a dough hook. Combine the *salt, honey, olive oil* and *cold water* in a small bowl and mix well. Dissolve the *yeast* in the *warm water* and leave to prove for 10 minutes in a warm place (the mixture will become bubbly). Switch on the machine at low speed. Pour in the honey and salt mixture, followed by the dissolved yeast. Mix until the dough forms a ball (if sticky, add an extra sprinkle of flour). Transfer the dough to a lightly floured surface and knead until smooth. Place in an oiled bowl and cover with a tea towel to relax for 30 minutes.

Divide the dough into 4 pieces. Roll each piece into a smooth, tight ball. Place on a floured baking sheet, cover with a damp tea towel and refrigerate. Use the following day, if possible.

Drain the juice from the *tomatoes* and squeeze out any excess liquid. Force through a vegetable mill and stir in the other ingredients.

One hour before baking, preheat the oven to its highest setting and remove the dough from the fridge. Roll out the balls of dough and spread one heaped spoonful of tomato sauce on each one. Top with 5 or 6 thin slices of mozzarella and bake until crispy (a little charring around the edges is good and tasty). Remove from the oven and sprinkle with coarsely cut basil.

RYE AND SUNFLOWER BREAD

(Makes two 350g bloomers)

350g	strong, white, stoneground flour
100g	rye flour
1½tsp	fine sea salt
1tsp	caster sugar
250–300ml	still mineral water, heated to 20°c
10g	fresh yeast
50g	toasted sunflower seeds

Make by the same method as white bread, above. (*NB* Rye flour does not have the same absorption rate as white flour, so all of the 300ml water may not be needed.) Reserve a few *sunflower seeds* for decoration and add the remainder to the dough after the first proving, which will take about 60 minutes. Preheat the oven to *200°c*. Divide the dough into two and shape into ovals, spray with a little water and sprinkle with the reserved sunflower seeds before setting to rise again. Slash the tops and bake for 40 minutes.

There is no question that the making of pastry can be difficult and frustrating at times; however, with a little patience, care and perseverance it is possible to acquire a deft hand and a feel for the process quite quickly. Once the basic techniques are mastered, pastry making can become the most satisfying, even therapeutic practice. As with all cooking, the best way to understand the process properly is to have a go and make a few mistakes along the way. A few failures force the questions 'how?' and 'why?'. Inevitably, the quality of the ingredients has a direct bearing on the quality of the end result, so try to use the best where possible. Temperature is also important. Whenever possible, work in a cool environment; pastry doesn't respond well to hot, steamy kitchens.

PARMESAN SHORTBREAD

Very, very delicate and used generally in the making of canapés where its savoury qualities stimulate the appetite. They are delicious topped with a little soft goat's cheese, a cherry tomato and a dab of pesto. A crispy, deep-fried basil leaf adds another texture.

100g	cold, unsalted butter, diced
100g	grated white Cheddar cheese
100g	grated Parmesan cheese
100g	plain flour

Put everything together in the bowl of a food processor and run until just smooth. (Alternatively, rub the **butter** into the **flour**, quickly and lightly, and mix in the two **cheeses**.) Turn out onto a well-floured board and roll to a thickness of about 3mm. Cut into biscuits with a 25mm cutter and transfer to a baking tray. Chill for 20 minutes. Preheat the oven to **190°c**. Prick once with a table fork before baking for 15 - 18 minutes. Remove and allow to chill thoroughly before handling (these biscuits are very fragile).

SHORTBREAD

This pastry is very rich and can be difficult to handle, but the finished product is really exceptional. Work swiftly, in a cool environment, and most of the potential problems are eliminated.

200g	unsalted butter
100g	icing sugar
pinch	of salt
2	egg yolks
250g	plain flour, sifted
	a drop of vanilla extract

Process the **butter, sugar, salt** and **vanilla** in a food processor until light and creamy. (Alternatively, cream them together with a wooden spoon until light and fluffy.) Add the egg yolks and process (or mix) until smooth. Add the sifted flour and pulse, *watching the pastry like a hawk, until it just begins to combine (do not process until smooth)*. Tip out onto a cold, floured work surface, knead through 3 times with your hands.

Roll into a log, about 2" in diameter, wrap in cling film and chill for 1 hour. Preheat the oven to **200°c**. Unwrap and cut the pastry into 4 pieces. Working quickly and with liberal amounts of flour, roll out to 3mm thick. Cut out into biscuits, prick once and bake for 9 minutes.

You can make a really intense chocolate pastry by substituting 50g of the flour with 50g unsweetened cocoa powder. Use to line small patty tins and bake blind (see short pastry recipe). The tarts can then be filled with *ganache*, a rich chocolate cream, to make the most fantastic chocolate tart.

SHORT PASTRY

For savoury tarts, quiches etc.. At it's best, it is light,
delicate and crumbly.

1 pinch	caster sugar
½tsp	salt
140g	cold, unsalted butter
½	egg, beaten
2–3tsp	iced water

In the chilled bowl of a food processor, mix *flour, salt, sugar*
and *butter* until crumbly in texture. Add the *egg* and the *iced*
water and pulse until just incorporated (do not overwork or
your pastry will become elastic and ultimately tough).

Alternatively, rub the butter into the flour, salt and sugar
with your fingers, lifting the mixture high to incorporate air,
and handling the process quickly and lightly. Mix in the
egg and iced water by hand, again, working swiftly.
Do not overwork, it should just hold together.

Turn the pastry out onto a cold work surface (ideally
marble) and knead through two or three times with your
hands (don't worry if it doesn't look totally smooth at
this stage). Wrap in cling film and chill for at least 1 hour
in the fridge.

Work the pastry quickly with the palm of you hand to
soften it slightly, and then roll out to a thickness of about
3mm on a floured work surface. Use to line a 10" tart ring
with a removable base. Chill for 20 minutes. Preheat the
oven to *200°c.*

Lay 4 sheets of cling film on top of one another and then
place them over the pastry. Add enough baking beans, rice
or lentils to fill the tart (these will hold the pastry in place
during the initial baking). Place in the oven and bake for
15 minutes. Carefully remove the cling film and the beans
(this is easily done by bringing the loose corners of the
cling film together and lifting swiftly). Return to the oven
for 5 minutes more.

Your tart case is now ready to fill or can be stored in an
airtight container until a later date.

CHOUX PASTRY

Incredibly versatile, it can be used in sweet and savoury dishes,
and even deep-fried to produce fantastic cheese fritters. For a really
tasty, simple first course or supper dish, split some savoury choux
buns and fill them with cream cheese, grilled pancetta, sliced pickled
onions and rocket leaves.

125ml	water
125ml	milk
100g	unsalted butter
½tsp	salt
½tsp	sugar
150g	strong, plain flour, sifted
4	eggs, beaten
	(60g Gruyère cheese, diced, for a savoury pastry)

Put the *water, milk, salt, sugar* and *butter* into a saucepan.
Bring to a boil and, whilst stirring, add all of the *flour* in one
go. Return to the heat and beat vigorously until smooth.
Continue cooking over a medium heat for a minute or two
until the paste leaves the sides of the pan. Remove from the
heat and allow to cool for 3 minutes.

Weigh 200g of the *beaten eggs*. Begin adding the egg a little
at a time and beating well between each addition. The pastry
is now ready to use or could be covered with cling film to be
used later. The *Gruyère cheese* can be added at this stage if
you prefer a savoury pastry.

Preheat the oven to *200°c* and transfer the choux pastry to
a piping bag with a plain nozzle. Pipe out onto a greased
baking tray into small buns for profiteroles, or fingers if
you prefer éclairs. Don't make them too large, or put them
too close together. Bake for 10–15 minutes, depending on
the size of the pastries. They should be golden brown and
have tripled in size.

LEMON AND STRAWBERRY SHORTBREAD

(Serves 6)

Beat the *butter* and *icing sugar* together until white. Beat in the *egg yolks, salt* and *lemon rind* until smooth. Add the *flour* and work it in gently and quickly, forming a soft dough. Wrap in cling film and refrigerate for 1 hour.

After resting, roll it out quickly on a floured work surface to a thickness of about 2mm. Cut into neat triangles, with sides measuring approximately 75mm. Refrigerate once more for about 30 minutes.

Preheat the oven to *190°c.* When firm and chilled, stack the triangles into 6 piles (you will need 24 triangles in total, plus 4 extra in case of breakages). Then drill a hole through the centre of each pile with a bamboo skewer. Transfer the triangles to a baking tray lined with non-stick baking paper and bake until set and very lightly coloured (about 6–7 minutes). Remove and allow to cool.

Fold the *cream* and *curd* together gently and chill. Wash, hull and trim the *strawberries*. You need nine trimmed strawberry halves and one whole strawberry per portion. Liquidize any remaining strawberries and any trimmings with sugar to taste and a few drops of lemon juice. Strain though a fine sieve and reserve.

Assembly

Put 1 teaspoon of lemon curd mousse onto the centre of each plate. Lay a shortbread triangle on top. Arrange three strawberry halves on the shortbread followed by 1teaspoon of mousse (don't worry about spreading the mousse neatly, just dollop it on!). Continue building in this way until you have 4 layers of shortbread and 3 layers of strawberries. Dust the top of the shortbread with *icing sugar*, thread the reserved whole strawberry onto a skewer and push the skewer through the pre-drilled holes in the shortbread to fasten everything together. Drizzle the sauce around.

Lemon shortbread

250g	plain flour
200g	unsalted butter, at room temperature
100g	icing sugar
1 pinch	salt
2	egg yolks
½tsp	lemon rind

Lemon curd mousse

90g	lemon curd
90ml	double cream, whipped to soft peaks

Strawberries and sauce

420g	ripe strawberries, trimmed and halved lengthways, retaining 6 whole strawberries for garnish
	caster sugar
	lemon juice

SINGIN' HINNY

(Makes 4)

As well as being a term of endearment, a hinny is a large, round cake made of a scone mixture and baked on a girdle (or griddle), where it sings and fizzes as it cooks. In parts of Northumberland they are also know as 'small coal fizzers', since they were cooked over the small coals of the fire.

170g	plain flour
25g	ground rice
pinch	of salt
25g	sugar
1 heaped tsp	baking powder
25g	currants
25g	lard
	milk

Sift the **dry ingredients** into a bowl, add the **currants** and rub in the **lard**, not too finely. Mix with enough **milk** to make a soft but not sticky dough. Roll out very lightly to about ½" thick. Cut into a neat round and then into quarters. Cook on a hot griddle iron or in a non- stick, cast iron frying pan until nicely browned on either side and lightly risen (about 20 minutes). Serve hot, split and buttered.

PROFITEROLES WITH HOT CHOCOLATE SAUCE

(Serves 6)

Choux Pastry

Make choux pastry as in the recipe above. Preheat the oven to **200°c**. Spoon the choux pastry into a piping bag with a 12mm plain nozzle. Pipe out 18 profiterôles onto a greased baking sheet. Bake for 10 minutes, lower the heat to **140°c** and continue baking for a further 20 minutes. Remove from the oven and cool on a wire rack.

Chocolate Sauce

100g	best quality dark chocolate
75ml	milk
1tbsp	double cream
1tbsp	sugar
1tbsp	soft butter
1ltr	vanilla or pistachio ice cream

Melt the **chocolate** over a pan of hot water. Bring the **milk, cream** and **sugar** to a boil and pour onto the melted chocolate. Return to the pan and reboil for a second, remove from the heat and whisk in the **butter**. Keep warm.

Assembly

Cut each profiterôle in half, return to the oven for 3 minutes. Remove and divide the bottoms between serving plates, 3 pieces per portion. Place a ball of ice cream on each piece and top with the lids. Spoon over the hot chocolate sauce and serve immediately.

Anthony & Lucy Carroll
Carroll's Heritage Potatoes

Potatoes

"What a stunning location...high on a scarp looking down into the beautiful Till valley in North Northumberland. Old Egypt? A gypsy name for the quarry site that now provides the house's toehold on the slope. Tiptoe? derived apparently from the Latin for spur on the bend of a river."

W

e're going to get as close as we can today to the border between England and Scotland. From either direction, north or south, just head for Coldstream. If you are coming from the south, you can by-pass Alnwick and its tourists, all flocking to see the Alnwick Garden or the *Harry Potter* locations. If you're up here in the early autumn, the Northumbrian villages will all be advertising their agricultural or country shows, timed so that the farmers and shepherds can let their hair down after harvest. I suspect it wouldn't have been long ago that some of these shows would also have been 'hirings', where lads and lasses would have 'stood standing', waiting to strike a bargain for a year with the farmer who offered the best deal of a couple of shillings wages and their keep, known in these parts as 'taters found'. I've got potatoes on my mind today.

You can bypass the villages, though, and as we pass the town of Wooler, we move ever northwards towards the Scots border, ignoring the signs to the villages of Kirk Yetholm and Town Yetholm. A welcome end there to the Pennine Way for many a walker who strapped on their boots long ago in Derbyshire. Long ago, too, the Romany kings and queens lived in and around Yetholm and the gypsy influence can still be seen in the town's gala, which even now has its 'barri menushi' instead of a carnival queen.

Once past the road to the Yetholms, we encounter more brown tourist signs, this time for the villages of Ford and Etal.

Our quest paid them a visit in the last chapter, at Heatherslaw Mill, so today we head on up the road past the village of Branxton, where a mechanized unit is chugging away, harvesting a vast field of potatoes. We also pass the signs for the site of the Battle of Flodden, with its own more deadly harvest; one of the most melancholy spots on this earth. But today is not a day for gloom as we head north in sunshine, ignoring the main road's sweep over the Tweed into Scotland as we turn up and over the river Till and down the farm track to Tiptoe, where there awaits a warm and enthusiastic welcome.

50

Scotland is to the south and southwest of England? It is true of this location, a little finger of Northumberland that juts out, running east to west in this zig-zag border.

As I sit and drink my tea, admiring the view over the river, I realize that I'm in for one of those great experiences, when someone envelops you with such a blast of positive energy that you cannot help but be swept along on the torrent of enthusiasm. And what is Anthony Carroll's special subject?

Potatoes. Heritage variety potatoes.

Now there may be some sceptics amongst you thinking 'Taters? I've seen a potato and I know what one looks like. What on earth can be different about them?'

Well let me tell you that if you think that, you have certainly not visited Anthony Carroll. There're pink ones, red ones, blue ones, even a red, white and blue one. There're knobbly ones, flowery ones, flowery-named ones, mashers, steamers, roasters and delicate pink salad potatoes.

How did Anthony Carroll come to be such an enthusiast?

"I started farming here in 1985, in partnership with my grandmother, although the place has been in my family since the 1930s. Back then one of the family was an avid aviator and used to fly his bi-plane in from Newcastle. He had to buzz the sheep first to get them to move before he could land. Then they became used to the plane and wouldn't budge, so he had to phone ahead and have someone round 'em up". One paddock became known as 'aerodrome field' and Anthony remembers an old farm steward who referred to one wood as 'where the major tied his plane down'.

I'm sitting at Tiptoe drinking tea, outside Old Egypt, Anthony Carroll's delightful family farmhouse. Originally the house was two farm cottages, built at the turn of the nineteenth century and extensively redesigned by the architect Sir Basil Spence. It's reputed to be the first private house on which he worked. What a stunning location, high on a scarp looking down into the beautiful Till valley. Old Egypt? A gypsy name for the quarry site that provided the house's toehold on the slope. Tiptoe apparently derives from the Latin for spur on the bend of a river. Well yes, I can definitely see that below me.

I can see more than that on this sunny August morning, as there is an absolutely clear view over to the Muckle Cheviot, slumbering, surrounded by its attendant hills. Sitting here in England we turn, face north, and there lies Scotland. If we turn our eyes again to the south, there lies… Scotland. Wait a minute, there's an idea that most English people might find it hard to get their heads round.

Now it's Anthony and his wife Lucy Carroll at Tiptoe. She's been working on the marketing side of things, as well as thinking up the new recipes that are given away at farmers' markets as a way of inspiring people to use these extra special spuds. Lucy also gets roped into the sorting sheds to help hand-sort their wares. Storing and dispatching many varieties in an orderly fashion, as compared with having a shedful of one kind of potato, is just one of the ways in which Heritage potatoes are very labour-intensive.

So why go to the bother?

Anthony: " I grew disillusioned with the way I was farming potatoes and with the current potato trade generally. As a small producer, we weren't an important part of anybody's supply chain, and in a year of plenty we could

be left high and dry. I also felt that the wrong emphasis was being placed upon the growing of potatoes. What had become important was regularity. They all had to be of a uniform size with perfect, shiny skin and easily peeled. A great deal of this was due to the demand from supermarkets and also potato processors, for spuds that were easy to process into ready-meal croquets or products like that.

I've nothing against ordinary, modern potatoes, or those growing them, they do give a higher yield than the older varieties. But I just realized that I wasn't enjoying producing stuff like that. I was selling to a co-op, who sold on to pack-houses miles away in the south. I'd no idea whether anyone was getting any enjoyment out of what I produced – which would have given me some pleasure in producing. It was just a vague feeling, really, that I wanted to bring to market something that was different."

And the next step on from the "vague feeling", Anthony?

"I was visiting a British Potato Council event and saw these pre-1950 varieties. I didn't know that all these shapes and colours existed. I grew potatoes, but this was the domain of the organic grower and the allotment. I was amazed, but didn't do anything at that stage, just stored the idea somewhere in my head, where it went nag-nag-nag."

So there we have you, Mr Anthony Carroll, with a vague feeling and an idea nagging away. A lot of people get to that stage but don't do anything about it. What next?

"I saw a postcard produced by the Business Service Challenge for absolutely the situation I was in. (It's the one trying to nudge people into action with the cartoons of a bright light bulb fading to darkness as someone's brilliant idea fades with it.) "I thought, that's what'll happen to me," continues Anthony, "if I don't actually do something. I've got to go for it. So I planted some older varieties. It was an entire leap of faith, we didn't have a single order at that time. But the response was great. It took some time, of course, and lots of hard work, but we sold at the farmers' markets in Berwick and Edinburgh, and we built up our sales via farm shops, including the one at Chatsworth. There were steady orders from various direct customers, including of course Terry Laybourne, who was very supportive, for which we were very grateful. We also supply Gleneagles Hotel and, via a specialist wholesaler, we're now being marketed to prestige restaurants and hotels all over Scotland."

When Anthony says it took time and hard work, you have to remember that with some of the rarer varieties they worked from a very small amount of seed. As the rarer potatoes are grown from microtubers, it takes several seasons of multiplying the crop until there is enough for a commercial crop. This means several seasons of hand planting and hand picking. One of Tiptoe's varieties started as one row in the garden, and it was a real labour of love coaxing it along. Anthony's enthusiasm was so strong that his neighbours at Tiptoe became involved and still talk about the struggle to get that one row up and thriving.

Another reason that heritage varieties mean harder work is the fact that the older varieties are more susceptible to disease. This is why, of course, commercial producers abandoned them and turned to modern varieties, with more in-bred disease resistance, yield and regularity. Unfortunately the price paid is that they also bred out flavour and texture.

The problems with susceptibility to disease meant that, after careful consideration, Anthony felt it wasn't viable to try to farm these varieties organically on the scale they do at Tiptoe. The supply chain problems could be catastrophic. If blight struck and lots of orders were promised, then you'd be stuck with a lot of dissatisfied customers. The Carrolls decided to go down the path of LEAF which stands for Linking Environment And Farming. In terms of the use of fertilizers, this means carefully testing and monitoring the soil and then only applying fertilizer to remedy a specific deficiency. In terms of spraying for blight, then protectants and/or eradicants are used, depending on the blight pressure. The farm is linked to a weather station, and if a 'Smith period' is forecast (i.e. one where potato blight would be likely to flourish), then appropriate measures can be taken.

When it's time to kill the potato plant foliage, ready for picking the crop, it is burnt off with a flame rather than using sulphuric acid. "I wouldn't want any wildlife to be sprayed with something like that,"

says Anthony, who later, as we walk his fields, points with some pride to a covey of grey partridge which rises from his crop and takes flight.

When we take that walk in Anthony's fields of potatoes, I am struck by the lack of uniformity. There are plants of different heights and different colours of foliage – colours! I am really surprised by the colours, not just outside but inside the potatoes. Anthony digs up a few examples and then, taking out his knife, cuts them to reveal hues of dark blue and burgundy .

It really is rather startling. I did a little test and took an example of the blue variety and quizzed a pub table full of mates and none of them had any idea of what they were looking at. One of them managed to believe his nose and ventured, "It smells like a potato". The others just didn't believe him. (The landlord threw us out, he didn't believe we were sniffing potatoes either!)

So how do things stand for the Carrolls, now that Anthony's lightbulb of an idea is throwing lots of spotlight on the apparently humble potato?

Well, at Tiptoe you get the feeling that everything is in very good hands. They have a 'whole farm approach' to the environment, with a Countryside Stewardship Scheme (CSS). The ancient and semi-natural woodlands tumble down the Till Valley to the river, which is itself a Site of Special Scientific Interest (SSSI) and has recently been classified as a Special Area Of Conservation (SAC), Europe's highest grading.

So what are these different varieties that Carroll's have available in their present catalogue?

Arran Victory 1918

A late, main crop potato, named to celebrate the end of the First World War. It was bred in the Isle of Arran by Donald McKelvie and is the oldest Arran still available. It's a vivid, blueish purple outside with deep eyes and snowy, white, fine-textured flesh with loads of flavour. Makes fantastic mash that crisps well on things like shepherd's pie. Good roaster, fine chips, tends to fall apart when boiled.

Dunbar Rover 1936

A second early, very rare, with oval tubers, white skin, deep eyes and snow-white flesh. It has a good, strong flavour and a fine, floury texture, making it exceptional for baking, frying and mashing. Bred by Charles T. Spence of Dunbar, Carroll's call them 'a Celtic fringe favourite'.

Pink Fir Apple 1850

This main crop, salad potato was imported into Britain and kept going for decades solely by enthusiasts who loved its flavour. It has a pink skin and is famously knobbly and difficult to peel. The flesh is pinky-yellow and has a fantastic, nutty flavour and a firm, waxy texture. They should be cooked whole, boiled or in stews, and can also be sliced or diced in classic salad fashion.

La Ratte (Asparges) 1872

Some people might say that this is a sensible Fir Apple with a lot less knobbles. The flavour and cooking qualities are very similar, although its stems are shorter and its flowers prettier. This main crop is a classic of French cuisine, with an almost chestnut flavour, although there are those who dare whisper, nay loudly remark, that this potato may have started life as the Danish Asparges. You could start a duel like that!

Roseval 1950

This is the classic, French, red-skinned potato, an early main crop with firm, yellowish flesh that sometimes has a pink blush when it is boiled. It's very good to sauté and in salads.

Yukon Gold 1980

A great name and just about the darndest yellow potato around. This one is a modern potato from Canada, a second early crop that was a product of the breeding programme at Guelph University. Known as a specialist baking potato, it's also very good for frying and makes a light, almost sweet mash with a buttery flavour.

Red King Edward 1855

This is a rare, pale red version of King Edward, with a higher dry matter and a good flavour. The flesh is white and when boiled the skin's red colour with white flushes is palely retained.

Fortyfold 1836

This is probably the second oldest variety in the collection. It dates from somewhere around 1800 and was one of the varieties that Wellington's troops and Nelson's sailors came back to grow in their gardens and allotments. The tubers are round with purple, white-streaked skin, but this varies greatly from all purple to all white. The flesh is white, the eyes quite deep. The size is notoriously variable, with a majority being small. The flavour is good, with a nutty quality not found in modern varieties.

These eight varieties, along with British Queen and Red Duke of York, form Carroll's current catalogue. They are also growing, in association with Speciality Potatoes, trial areas of Shetland Black, as well as Salad Blue and Highland Burgundy Red, which can be seen in the photographs.

The strong blue patterns in the vascular ring of the Shetland Black could offer some great opportunities for creative cookery. The Highland Burgundy dates back to at least 1936, when it was used to add appropriate colour to a meal at the Savoy in honour of the Duke of Burgundy. The Salad Blue is blue, very blue, both outside and inside. The blue pigment is anthyocyanin, which is an antioxidant. Boiling this potato dilutes the colour, but any other cooking method retains the blue in full. Popular with Manchester City fans.

And lastly we come to

Mr Little's Yetholm Gypsy.

This has 'a vivid blue outer layer overlying a layer rather like the skin of a King Edward. As the tuber expands, breaks are formed at random in the blue to show some of the white and red underneath'. Voilà! The only red, white and blue tuber that's known to man. It is said to have been the pride of the so-named local gentleman in Yetholm and was handed down through families. The story is told that when a collector came to seek it, there was none to be found, until a search of the midden for cast-offs revealed one single specimen, from which the line is now descended.

Tiptoe Farm has recently been accredited with the LEAF marque and they have a LEAF track number (25027) to track the potatoes back to their roots.

The heritage potato business seems to be entering a new phase. Anthony Carroll is the first to admit that he's been on a very fast learning curve. Not that he claims to know all the answers now, but he thinks he does know what some of the questions might be! This is a period of some consolidation and careful response to customer demand for different varieties at certain times of the year. Attention to such marketing details is necessary, because the lead-in time to a product like Heritage Potatoes is months, maybe years. You can't just switch on a machine and make a few more. There will be further expansion of the business as more people are getting to know Carroll's Heritage Potatoes, through direct marketing on the internet, weekly visits to farmers' markets and via email.

But one things stands out; Anthony Carroll is still getting enormous enjoyment out of producing what he does. And he wants other people to enjoy his produce too. His dream is that one day, potatoes will not be an afterthought on a menu, but will feature as part of the latest culinary concoction in *cordon bleu* restaurants. He also dreams that connoisseurs will be requesting them. Can you imagine it?

'And for the potato, sir?'

'Well, I'm spoilt for choice waiter, but I think I'll have the 1918 Arran Victory roasted, please.'

'A very good choice if I may say so sir. They're from Tiptoe y'know. A very good choice indeed!'

Potatoes

The words humble and potato are too often thrown together. And therein lies the problem. Because it is such a staple of our diet, potatoes are overlooked and undervalued. Chefs, sadly, are some of the biggest culprits. It's viewed as an also-ran, something to fill up the plate. Yet potatoes are masterpieces of invention. There are dozens of different varieties, each with its own characteristics. A good chipper is not necessarily a good masher. It is certainly not a good boiler and definitely won't work in a salad.

The next problem is that everybody likes potatoes. One of the first lessons I teach my apprentices is that mashed potato should be treated like a luxury product. Everybody's mum makes the best mash, so everybody is an expert. Watch someone eating mashed potato and it will be treated to as shrewd an appraisal as an oenophile sampling vintage claret. When a customer says, 'Wow, I didn't know mashed potato could taste like this', you know you've cracked it.

So, start with the right potato for the job, and then treat it with respect.

I learnt my first potato lesson early. When I was growing up, potatoes were either new or old. Most people had a potato patch in their gardens, so we were governed by the seasons. As a result, we never ate chips in summer. If we did persuade Mum to make them, they tasted awful. You can't make a good chip out of a waxy, new potato.

These days, anything small is labelled a new potato. But a true new potato is a 'first or second early', i.e. the first crop of the spring season. If you can't rub the skin away with the thumb, it's not a new potato. For me, the king of new potatoes is the Jersey Royal. Introduced in 1878, it is a second early, kidney-shaped with thin, creamy yellow skin and flesh, and a firm, moist texture. It's the best of all in

terms of flavour. Boil briefly with a sprig of mint and eat with loads of butter. They are great cold, they sauté well and make good rösti.

The Jersey Royal is absolutely seasonal, only available from the end of February to mid-May, and only seems to grow successfully on the island. Maybe it's the salt in the air or the salty earth that surrounds the growing tubers, but it has the most incredibly intense, buttery flavour. Attempts to grow it here have failed miserably. You shouldn't mess about with Jerseys; simply scrub, and add to boiling, salted water with a sprig of mint.

Having said that, it does make the most fantastic rösti (a fried, grated potato cake that I first encountered whilst working in Switzerland). The trick to keeping the outside crisp and the insides meltingly soft is to cook them slowly, and run a generous piece of butter around the rim of the frying pan half-way through the cooking. If you can't get Jersey Royals, any small, waxy potato, such as La Ratte, will work well.

La Ratte is also a good salad potato, but the best is the Pink Fir Apple. Wonderfully rich and nutty, the Pink Fir Apple is a pig to peel – almost as bad as a Jerusalem artichoke – because of its knobbly, awkward shape.

56

Tips

Potato buying and storage:

Look for smooth, taut skins and avoid anything that is bruised or beginning to sprout. If you can, buy in a regular, uniform size. It makes for an even cooking time and better presentation. Buy frequently rather than in bulk. Store in a dark, cool – not cold – place. Try to avoid keeping potatoes in the fridge. If a potato is stored at less than 8°c, it partially freezes. When it thaws, it will start to sweat, turning some of the starch into sugar. This will give an oversweet mash or, if you try to fry it, the outside will quickly darken while the inside will still be raw.

Cooking:

When boiling old potatoes, place them in a large saucepan and cover with cold, salted water. Don't start them in hot water, which will make them mushy.

Place new potatoes into boiling, unsalted water; if you cook them in salted water they have a tendency to disintegrate. It's better to salt them just before they are cooked.

The perfect mash:

Cut the peeled potatoes into uniform chunks, no smaller than 1½ inches. Place them in a pan of water, bring to the boil and skim off any impurities before salting (15g to 1ltr). Lower the heat to simmer for 10 minutes. This gentle, initial cooking fixes the starch and prevents them from collapsing. Drain immediately when cooked and leave them in the pan over a low heat with the lid on. Periodically, lift the lid to wipe away the condensation. Once the condensation has disappeared, mash quickly over the heat. Add your choice of enrichment – milk, cream, butter (or all three), or olive oil – and fold in quickly, but don't beat.

You could get away with scrubbing them, but do make an effort. Potatoes with their skins on, to my mind, demonstrate laziness. Always dress salad potatoes while still warm, unless you're going for the traditional English potato salad with mayonnaise and chives – great with cold meats – when you should wait until they've cooled. The Germans do a terrific, beefed-up version in which sliced, warm potatoes are tossed in a mixture of onions, thin slivers of bacon, mustard, vinegar and oil, mixed with a bit of beef stock.

When it comes to chips, you enter a world bristling with opinions. Sliced thin or thick? Cooked soggy or crisp? Cut random or uniform? Squared off or left natural? Or are the best ones those little thin stragglers, crisp and crunchy, that sit around the edge? Personally, I'm a thin chip man. Whichever chip school you belong to, there are three unbreakable rules: always use beef dripping, never fill the basket more than half full (too many chips bring down the fat temperature and they will poach rather than fry), and give them a good sprinkling of Maldon sea salt. The Belgian Bintje potato is recognized as the best chipper but, as with roasting, you can, to a degree, get away with most varieties of large, floury, main crop potatoes.

For mashing, you also need a potato that is dry and starchy. You're aiming for lightness; waxy potatoes tend to be more

dense and make nasty, elastic mash. Yukon Gold is perfect. Not only does it have a lovely hint of sweetness, but also, as its name suggests, a buttery colour that lifts it above the ordinary.

Making good mashed potato is not difficult, but it pays to be diligent and not to take any short cuts. Ensure that the potatoes are precisely cooked; if they are undercooked your mash will be lumpy, if overcooked the potatoes will disintegrate and absorb water. One easily rectifiable mistake people make is to mash the potato at too low a temperature. It needs to be above 70°c, otherwise the starch content becomes gluey and you'll end up with a blob of grey chewing gum. So don't let the potatoes hang around. But don't, please, be tempted to use a food processor; it agitates the starch and you get more chewing gum. A masher, vegetable mill or a couple of forks are fine.

Potatoes are one of the foods I would encourage people to experiment with. The possibilities are endless; *La Répertoire de la Cuisine* lists 118 different potato dishes with grandiose names like Pommes Pont Neuf or Pommes Chatouillard. There was a time, when I was a young chef, when I could recite most of them off the cuff. Great for showing off, but what no one knew was that I could only cook about three or four of them.

MASHED POTATOES

(Serves 6)

*"Mashed potatoes are a luxury product, treat them with respect" is a rant regularly heard around the kitchens of our restaurants.
I get frustrated to hell by young chefs who don't give potatoes the respect that they deserve. They seem to feel that mash is something that
anyone can make without any care or attention whatsoever. Needless to say that is well wide of the mark. When made with care, with the
correct potatoes and the correct technique, mashed potatoes can rank alongside foie gras, truffles and caviar as a great culinary luxury.*

*Since Joel Robuchon reinvented mashed potato and made it hip in the late eighties, all sorts of varieties of flavoured mash have
appeared on restaurant menus. Not my thing at all, I'm afraid. I think that a lot of these were invented by lazy chefs
who made their lives easy by making one pot of mash for a service and dividing it up into six, adding a different flavour to each.
They then went out and had their names embroidered on their jackets and told everyone how creative they were!*

*Traditional flavours work well, cabbage and onions in bubble and squeak; the Irish versions are great, champ and colcannon.
I like to add goat's cheese to serve with lamb or beef, and even sautéed black pudding to serve with pork.
Saffron, a little garlic and a nip of chilli is fabulous with sea bass or red mullet and I quite like really good olive oil
drizzled into coarsely crushed potatoes to serve with cod or lamb.*

1kg	floury potatoes
(Arran Victory, Dunbar Rover or Yukon Gold),
peeled and cut into 1" dice
	coarse sea salt
120ml	double cream
150g	unsalted butter
	nutmeg

Cover the **potatoes** with cold, salted water. Bring to the boil,
turn down the heat and simmer very, very gently for 10
minutes. Warm the **butter** and **cream** together without
boiling. Increase the heat a little and simmer till tender.
Drain in a colander, return to the pan and steam-dry.
Pass quickly through a fine food mill.

Fold in the cream and butter mixture without overworking.

Check the seasoning and add a pinch of **nutmeg**.
Adjust the texture with more cream and butter if necessary.

NB It is vital that the potatoes remain very hot during
the mashing process.

WARM POTATO SALAD

(Serves 4)

I love to eat this salad when very fresh. Leave it lying around for two hours and it will taste tired and stale.
It makes a fantastic accompaniment to boiled ham, or even better, smoked pork sausages (Morteux, Saucisson Lyonnaise
or any of the Polish varieties, which may be more readily available). I quite like it alongside smoked fish, too, kippers or smoked mackerel.
It's really important to use firm, waxy potatoes. Serve the salad lukewarm for the best flavour.

1kg	small salad potatoes (Pink Fir Apple or La Ratte), washed but not peeled
50g	smoked streaky bacon
1	onion, peeled and finely diced
500g	good beef or ham stock (made with a stock cube is fine)
4tbsp	sunflower seed oil
3tbsp	white wine vinegar
	salt and milled pepper
2	radishes
1	small bunch chives

Cook the **potatoes** in salted water for 20 minutes or so until tender. Drain and plunge briefly into cold water to arrest the cooking. Drain and peel the potatoes whilst still warm and cut into slices 4mm thick. Transfer to a bowl and cover tightly with cling film to keep warm.

Cut the **bacon** into fine dice and fry in a dry, non-stick frying pan until it releases its fat. Add the **diced onions** and continue cooking slowly until the onions are soft and transparent, but without colour. Spoon the onions and bacon over the potatoes.

Heat the stock and mix with the **oil, vinegar, salt** and **pepper**. Pour over the potatoes and mix through very gently. Cut the **radishes** into fine slices and snip the **chives**. Add these carefully to the salad and check the seasoning. Serve immediately.

JOEL ROBUCHON'S MASHED POTATOES

(Serves 6)

1kg	potatoes (La Ratte or Belle de Fontenay)
20–30ml	full fat milk
250g	cold, unsalted butter, cut into small pieces
	sea salt to taste

Scrub the **potatoes**, but do not peel. Place in a large pot and add enough cold water to cover them by 2 inches.

Add coarse **sea salt** at a ratio of 10g salt per 1ltr water.

Simmer gently for 20–30mins until tender. Drain as soon as they are cooked.

When cool enough to handle, peel them and cut into pieces. Pass through the finest grid of a vegetable mill into a thick-bottomed saucepan. Place over a low heat and stir the potatoes vigorously for 4–5 minutes to dry them out. Heat the **milk**. Begin adding the **butter** a few pieces at a time, stirring vigorously between each addition. Continue until all of the butter is incorporated. Slowly add the hot milk in a thin stream, stirring vigorously. Pass the purée through a fine drum sieve. Return to the pan over a low heat and whisk briefly until light and fluffy.

POTATO CREAM SOUP WITH LEEKS

(Serves 8)

It doesn't seem to matter how creative I try to be with soup, the old favourite of leek and potato is inevitably the best seller.
Use Yukon Gold for the best flavour, they have a great affinity with leeks. You can jazz this soup up in a hundred and one ways;
I've listed a few versions below.

200g	floury potatoes
600ml	double chicken stock
200g	leeks, washed and trimmed
1	large bunch flat leaf parsley
130g	butter
	salt and milled pepper
2 pinches	caster sugar
	freshly grated nutmeg
250ml	whipping cream
1 slice	white bread, crusts removed
3tbsp	clarified butter

Cut the **bread** into 3mm dice, scatter on a plate and leave in a warm place to dry out for 30 minutes. Fry in a non-stick frying pan in **clarified butter** until golden brown, drain and keep warm. Wash, peel and slice the **potatoes** 1cm thick. Cover with the **chicken stock** and simmer gently.

Wash the **leeks** and cut into fine rings, pick and chop the **parsley** finely. Drain the potatoes, retaining the stock, pass them through a vegetable mill and whisk into the stock. Sweat the leeks gently in 30g **butter** without colouring. Season with **salt, pepper** and **sugar**.

Reheat the soup and add the **cream**. Do not allow to boil.

Add the remaining 100g **butter** and process in a liquidizer. Pour into another saucepan, check the seasoning and adjust if necessary. Stir in the leeks and parsley, add a pinch of **nutmeg**.

Divide between the hot soup bowls and sprinkle with the croutons.

Variations

1. Add a tablespoon of whipped cream to lighten the soup.

2. Steam some small mussels, remove from their shells and add to the soup along with their juice.

3. Cook 4 slices of dried ceps along with the potatoes.

4. For a heartier soup, add slices of cooked potato along with the leeks.

5. Substitute tarragon, chervil or basil for the parsley.

6. Add 16 shucked oysters and their juice when liquidizing the soup. Finish with a generous pinch of chopped chives.

HOT POT POTATOES

(Serves 4 as an accompaniment to roast lamb)

*This recipe comes from my great friend Paul Heathcote. Paul deconstructed traditional Lancashire hot pot
at his restaurant in Longridge and served the potatoes alongside a roast rack of lamb. Not only does it taste great,
but is visually stunning too. Make sure you have a very sharp, serrated knife, otherwise it will be a challenge to cut.
It can be made successfully a day in advance, cut into portions and reheated in a low oven.*

100g	soft butter
1kg	potatoes
2	carrots
250g	clarified butter
1	onion, sliced
1	thyme sprig
1	rosemary sprig

Preheat the oven to **180°c**. Heavily butter a round, 1ltr ovenproof dish, 2" deep, using the soft butter. Peel the **potatoes**, slice very thinly, sprinkle with a pinch of **salt** and leave in a colander to drain for 5 minutes. Meanwhile peel the **onion** and **carrots** and slice thinly. Strip the leaves from the **thyme** and **rosemary** sprigs and chop finely.

Drain the potatoes and pat dry on a clean cloth, Select some of the most attractive slices and arrange them in a single layer in the bottom of the dish. Using some of the larger slices, cover the sides of the mould also, overlapping as you go. When the bottom and sides are covered, begin arranging more potatoes on the base. Create 3 layers and add a sprinkling of carrot and onion and a pinch of chopped herbs. Add 3 tablespoons of **clarified butter**, and season with **salt and peppe**r. Create another 3 layers of sliced potatoes, then more carrots, onions, herbs, butter etc. Continue building in this way until the mould is full to the brim and all of the ingredients are used up.

Cover the mould with a sheet of buttered aluminium foil. Place on a tray in the centre of an oven at **180°c** and bake for 1 - 1½ hours, or until a small knife slices easily through to the centre. Remove from the oven and allow to rest for at least 5 minutes, before turning out and cutting into generous wedges with a very sharp knife.

GOAT'S CHEESE MASHED POTATOES

(Serves 6)

1kg	floury potatoes (Arran Victory, Dunbar Rover or Yukon Gold)
120–180g	milk
1tsp	thyme leaves, chopped
125g	unsalted butter
	salt and white pepper
160g	goat's cheese

Cook and steam-dry the potatoes as in the recipe above. Heat the *milk* with the *thyme*, remove from the heat and cover with a lid. Allow to infuse for 15 minues then reheat with the *butter*. Force the potatoes through a food mill and mash, together with the butter and boiling milk. Add the goat's cheese and mix until well blended.

CHIPS

(Serves 4)

Any chip cut more than ½" thick needs to be cooked twice, firstly at a low temperature, to cook the potatoes through gently, and then re-fried at a much higher temperature in order to colour and crisp them. Extra thick or 'fat' chips are actually better when first blanched in boiling water, before being crisped at a high temperature. Thinner varieties can be fried in one go at 185°c.

800g	large floury potatoes
	beef dripping for frying
1tbsp	fine sea salt
1tbsp	flaked sea salt

Peel the **potatoes** and cut them lengthways into chips, no thicker than ½". Rinse in a bowl under a running cold tap until the water is clear, but do not soak. Drain and leave to dry before frying.

Heat the fat in a deep fryer to **150°c** and add the **potatoes**. *(Don't fill the basket more than half full or you risk over-cooling the fat.)* Fry for 5–6 minutes, stirring occasionally, before checking the chips for doneness by squeezing between thumb and forefinger. They should be soft right through. Lift the basket and set aside.

Increase the temperature of the fat to **190°c** and replace the chips, frying for 2–3 minutes until golden and crisp. Remove from the fryer, shake dry and then tip onto a tray lined with absorbent paper before transferring to a bowl. Mix the two **salts** together and season the chips. Serve immediately.

Willie & Daphne Robson
Chainbridge Honey Farm

Honey

"We move them to the spring sites, onto crops like oilseed rape, but you'd still have to take care they had some shelter. A good supply of early spring pollen is essential for the development of the colony. Then we put the shallow boxes onto the hive and they start and produce honey. In summer they would be put onto field beans, borage, summer rape, maybe rosebay willow-herb; and with set-aside these days, fields of wild flowers."

W

e're off to Berwick today, to the very banks of the River Tweed, where stands the Union Chain Bridge, from which the Robson's honey farm takes its name. The foundation stone for the towers was laid in August 1819 and the bridge completed in 1820, when it would have been the longest suspension bridge in the world. It cost the enormous sum of £7,700 to build, against estimated costs of £20,000 for a masonry bridge. At the opening, its designer, Captain Samuel Brown RN, demonstrated his confidence in his creation by storming across in a curricle – a light, fast, two-wheeled, two-horse carriage. He was then slowly followed over by 12 loaded carts. After this display of chutzpah, 700 reassured spectators surged across – all paying their toll at the booth on the English side.

It has to be said that they were probably right to wait for Captain Brown's 'test flight', as early nineteenth-century bridges did have a bad habit of falling down. There is a local legend that the bridge blew down inside six months of being opened and was rebuilt, but there's no historical corroboration of that; it was probably a rumour started by other toll companies, whose business was threatened by the new bridge. Rather than having a short life, the Union Chain Bridge is, in 2004, the oldest suspension bridge in Britain still open to traffic.

It stands in a glorious spot in the Tweed valley, with good walks on either side of the river. To get to the honey farm we're going to take a walk up the road to the visitor centre and the shop, where all of the Chainbridge products can be purchased. I have no idea how a honey farm works, and

suspect a steep learning curve beckons, so when I'm ushered into the presence of Mr William (Willie) Robson, and he's cutting combs, I'm gobsmacked and can't think of where to start.

I've seen a little comb honey in my time, but never so much of it in one place that it's taking three people just to cut and package it into half-pound blocks. Comb honey is taken from the hive with the wax comb still in it. It's worth twice as much as ordinary honey and is twice as difficult to produce, because the colony of bees has to expend energy building the combs anew each year, rather that just filling the same lot up again.

Chainbridge Honey is the largest producer of comb honey in the country, and their 1700 hives probably constitute

the largest number owned by a single producer. As Willie Robson puts it; "We Robson family have been involved in producing honey for a canny time now. My great uncle had 60 'skeps' (basketwoven hives) in the early years of the twentieth century, which was an impressive number for them days. My father, Selby Robson, now he'd been a well-known beekeeping advisor in the Borders before he founded this business, Chainbridge, in 1948. I started with him in '62, and my wife Daphne joined in '73, and we've both a son and a daughter in the business... although we have to send a vehicle round on Monday morning to find Stephen". Mr Robson regards me in apparent seriousness, and then breaks into a wide grin "Aye, go on, you can put that in".

During my visit, his pride in the achievements and hard work of his family becomes very apparent. Likewise his family's pride in the single-minded, hard slog that Father put into

the business in its early years. "Dad once put 200,000 miles on the Volvo going round this country, cold-selling honey", emphasized Stephen when we met later.

So, Mr Willie Robson and family, how do you and your bees produce all this honey, not to mention beeswax and propolis as well? What kind of bees are they?

"Local bees," states Mr Robson, "brown bees; the best. The system we use is called 'migratory beekeeping'. We move all the hives several times a year. We keep them in sheltered sites during the winter, walled gardens and such like. They feed on heather honey that's been stored for the winter, but if for some reason a hive gets bit short, then as a fallback we feed them on 'baker's fondant'. That's just sugar, of course, but it comes in a handy slab that's easy to introduce into the hive."

And when winter's finished?

"We move them to the spring sites, onto crops like oilseed rape, but you'd still have to take care they had some shelter. A good supply of early spring pollen is essential for the development of the colony. Then we put the shallow boxes onto the hive and they start and produce honey. In summer they would be put onto field beans, borage, summer rape, maybe rosebay willow-herb; and with set-aside these days, fields of wild flowers".

Early summer's the time the beekeeper really has to work. As well as removing the honey-filled supers (frames) and replacing them with empty ones, the hives have to be checked for health, and the bees for ailments such as foul brood or the varroa mite. Production levels are checked, too.

"Some hives can become honey-bound. You might find that you've got an old queen. You've got to keep an eye out, too, for signs of swarming. Hives have got to be healthy, for soon they'll be moving onto the heather and it can still be quite cold and difficult for the bees, but you want them producing because the heather honey, with its strong flavour, is what is most sought after and fetches the best price."

So as the year progresses, Chainbridge move their hives on to the heather site. At the moment they use three sites: Lauderdale and the Lammermuirs, Hepburn Moor and Debden Moor at Rothbury. Now they're in the hands of nature. The heather season can be affected very badly by the weather. It could be 'dusting nicely' (producing pollen), and then a spell of heavy rain could put a stop to it and that might be the end of things for that year. Recent years have seen exceptionally good seasons, if somewhat dry. 2003 saw only nine inches of rain on the moors all year. The heather is resilient and can normally stand up to such dry conditions, but Willie Robson remembers when the heather was nearly droughted out in 1976.

When the heather season is over, what happens next depends very much on the weather. An Indian summer can see the honey-making season extended a little, but soon it will be time to move the hives back to the sheltered winter sites, and the whole process starts all over again.

At this stage of our conversation, Mr Robson has finished cutting comb and he and he his daughter Frances begin to gather the offcuts, ready to be machine-spun to extract the wax and honey separately. As they're busy for a while, I'm given a cup of tea and packed off to look at the displays in the visitor centre and the full range of items on sale in the shop.

(A slightly surreal moment occurs while I am browsing in the shop. A very elderly gentleman appears, as if from nowhere, and asks me to move from where I am standing, because I am affecting the clock. This is a surprise, because I look around me and can't see any clock, and he has disappeared again. Only later do I discover that the clock is in the next room; I was standing on a floorboard that runs through both rooms and underneath it!)

Chainbridge plays host to visitors all year round, and people can spend quite a time in the various rooms, engrossed in the many displays. I find the actual working of the hive fascinating and spend quite a while on that, but I'm surprised at the wealth of other material also available, such the history of beekeeping, and the displays describing the efforts of first-world beekeepers to help those in the third

world. On a lighter note, you must see the photographs of the 'bee beards'. There's one chap with thousands of them hanging round his chin. It looks amazing, but please do NOT try this one at home.

In the shop you can see the full range of products. There's the comb honey we encountered earlier, jars of Chainbridge Quality Honey, both heather honey and flower honey. There's honey mustard, crunchy honey mustard and crunchy honey mustard dressing.

We're not just talking honey, though; the wax is used in beeswax and carnauba polish for shoe leather and furniture. There's a cosmetics range too. Previously, wax would have been sold into the wholesale trade, but now Chainbridge use it themselves and turn it into various hand and face creams.

They also use the propolis – a natural antiseptic produced by the bees – to make healing ointments and tinctures.

And then there are the candles. Mr Robson took me to see the candle-making studio, and though I missed the candle-maker, I couldn't miss the results of his day's labour. Candles in all kinds of shapes and sizes. Hundreds of them. "About five hundred pounds' worth made in a day here," surveys Mr Robson. "My wife Daphne taught herself to make pure wax candles, and then she passed on everything she's learnt."

"Have you seen the vehicles yet?" asks Willie Robson, and as I haven't, he sends me outside to take a look. Around the side of the honey farm, a spacious new exhibition building has taken shape. In and around it is the Chainbridge Collection of Historic Commercial Vehicles, tractors and military vehicles. Big'uns they are, the sort of thing with which you could drag a tank out of a ditch. They've all either been restored on site or are in the process of being restored, and I'd like to bet there's going to be one or two 'historic commercial' and tractor enthusiasts who are going to develop a sudden interest in honey!

This is where I bump into Stephen Robson and the guys working on a Scammell. We talk motors and I get as good a diagnosis as I've had for a while of the overheating problems of my 1960s Saab 96. Stephen returns to the subject of honey, and explains to me how the company has become vertically integrated. They're not only breeding the bees to make the honey, but buying the trees to make the hives, building the hives, producing the honey and marketing it through both wholesale and retail.

Chainbridge Honey can be found in over three hundred, quality food outlets; no supermarkets. Look for the very simple and effective Chainbridge labels – a very good piece of design and marketing. You can also buy direct and online.

Chainbridge is perfectly situated for what they do, in the middle of one of the richest and most diverse areas of farmland in Britain, but it's not all plain sailing. Stephen also reiterated just how much hard work and skill goes into honey farming, and how much of that his father has taught him. They sometimes work on as many as a hundred hives in a day. You definitely have to know what you're doing on that scale, or you would have thousands of very angry bees intent on giving you more than a beard!

As I prepare to leave, Mr Robson sends me on my way with not only a very welcome sample of their wares, but also a reminder that it has taken two lifetimes to build up this business. He's very proud, too, that not a penny of subsidy has gone into the enterprise, which employs fourteen people, seven full-time and seven part-time. All the development at Chainbridge has been paid for by the profits from sales of honey. You have to be doing something right with your bees when you can say that.

I thought I'd end with a bee-related quotation, like 'the bees knees' or some such *bon mot*, but then I thought maybe not. There's a good quote from Marcus Aurelius: 'That which is not good for the beehive cannot be good for the bees', but that doesn't quite fit. Nor does Cassius Clay or Arthur Askey. So I'll leave you with a quote from the top of a honey jar: 'Robson's Superior Quality'.

Honey

The beauty, but also the difficulty, of honey is that its flavour varies. You might buy the same heather honey from the same producer in two successive years and find they taste vastly different. But that's the measure of a totally natural product. The rainfall, the temperature, the number of bees, their little mood swings, all these things will affect the final product.

The other characteristic that is often overlooked in honey is its power. It is twenty per cent sweeter than sugar, which means you can use far less for the same level of sweetness. Before the arrival of cane sugar and sugar beet in the seventeenth century, honey was the primary source of sweetening. However, the dissolution of the monasteries in the 1530s caused a huge honey shortage, because monks were the country's primary beekeepers. As sugar proved cheaper, neutral in flavour and easier to use, honey has never regained its popularity. Yet I find honey is a hugely versatile flavouring – in savoury as well as sweet dishes – and one that, unusually, retains its individuality rather than having it diluted by other ingredients.

Its other useful property is that it's an invert sugar. This is a scientific way of saying that it's a liquid sweetener. Hence it doesn't crystallize easily and is great for adding to cakes to delay them from drying out.

There are two principal types of honey. Polyfloral, as its name suggests, is a honey made from a natural blend of different flowers. Light and delicate in flavour, it is typically used in salad dressings or to roast fruits. Monofloral honey is produced from a single flower source, such as heather, lavender or acacia, and has very distinctive flavours. Lavender and acacia honeys, for example, are light and aromatic, while others, such as heather and chestnut, are much stronger and darker. These honeys are better suited to adding sweetness to robust or spicy dishes.

Whichever honey is used, the golden rule is to use it with care. Precisely because it's a natural product, its strength and complexity will vary. You can always add more, but you can never take away. It's also messy. I always place the opened jar in the microwave on defrost for a minute or so. The warmed honey is not only easier to measure out, but much easier to combine with other ingredients.

Honey is fantastic for poaching fruits and works particularly well for pears. Caramelize the honey with butter and spices, such as cinnamon, vanilla and star anise. This gives the pears a wonderfully exotic, butterscotch flavour. For the same reason, honey works well in Asian dishes. Combined with ginger, soy sauce, garlic and chilli in marinades for duck, pork or spare ribs, say, it adds a distinctive sweetness that perfectly balances the sharp spices.

It is this ability to stand up to other powerful ingredients that makes it such a clever and economical secret weapon to keep in the store cupboard. Add it to fruits poached in red wine and it brings a real tingle. Add it to gingerbread and it gives a complexity you won't get from sugar. Honey ice-cream has a rich (but not cloying) sweetness, with the added benefit that the honey helps keep it smooth and soft. And a little bit of honey in a pizza dough not only gives a great crunch and caramelized flavour, but makes the dough easier to work.

One of the best dishes I've tasted recently was in a restaurant in Pisa, beside the toppling tower. A plate of *stracciatelli de bufala* – the stringy by-products of Mozzarella cheese – was accompanied by a slice of *panforte*, and drizzled with chestnut honey. The darkly powerful honey stood up to the chocolatey cake, at the same time emphasizing, rather than overpowering, the delicate, milky-soft cheese. An amazing combination, and one I would never have dreamed of trying.

Tips

All jars of honey will eventually thicken.
Those with a high glucose level – oilseed rape honey, for example – will set
very quickly, whereas those containing a
higher level of fructose will stay liquid
longer. If liquid honey begins to
crystallize it is not such a bad sign; it
indicates that the honey has been
extracted simply and not heated to high
temperatures. To reabsorb the crystals,
place the opened jar in a microwave on
defrost.

Honey-glazed carrots:

Peel and quarter the carrots into long
sticks. Fry them gently in butter for a
minute or two. Add a tablespoon of
honey, a splash of vinegar and a glug of
white wine. Transfer to the oven and
roast for twenty minutes or so until
tender and beginning to caramelize
along the edges. Any root vegetable can
be done in the same way.

Great with:

brandy, carrots, chestnuts, chocolate,
cinnamon, duck, ginger, lemon, mustard,
orange, pears, pork, soy sauce, sprouts,
Greek yoghurt.

74

FILLET OF TURBOT WITH CRUNCHY HONEY MUSTARD, BEER SAUCE AND ONIONS

(Serves 4)

Turbot is terribly expensive, but I'd be loath to recommend an alternative to it for this dish.
Cod could work flavour-wise, but the texture would be all wrong. Perhaps if a cod fillet were sprinkled lightly with coarse sea salt and left for 3–4 hours to extract some of its moisture, maybe…

This recipe is not as complicated as it looks. It can be prepared in stages and finished at the last minute; if you make the stock and fry the onions well in advance, the cooking and finishing are a piece of cake. It may seem an odd combination, fish, onions and beer, and I suppose it is really. Turbot is a very bold fish, though, and can stand up to almost anything you care to throw at it. I always seem to end up pairing turbot with either onions or mustard.

The beer is fairly bitter, of course, but the addition of the caramelized honey and the honey mustard more than compensate. Deep frying the onions in this way seems to heighten their savouriness. And don't forget the salt; deep-fried food needs salt! If you've got the time, take the trouble to braise some Savoy cabbage to go with it.

1 tbsp	soft butter
1 tsp	vegetable oil
10	chicken wings, each chopped into 3 pieces
4	shallots, roughly chopped
½	celery stick
½	carrot
1	bay leaf
1 sprig	parsley
4	juniper berries, crushed
6	white peppercorns, cracked
1 tbsp	honey
1 tbsp	white wine vinegar
200ml	light beer or lager
200ml	fish stock or water
1 pinch	coarse sea salt

To finish

	a little soft butter
4 x 170g	turbot fillets
100ml	light beer
1 tbsp	whipping cream
40g	cold, unsalted butter, cut into 1cm dice
½	lemon
1 tbsp	crunchy honey mustard

Onions

2	Spanish onions, peeled
	plain flour
	salt
2 ltrs	oil for deep-fat frying

First make the onions. Heat the *oil* in a deep-fat fryer to *160°c*. Slice the *onions* into rings as thinly as possible (a sharp mandoline is the best tool for this job). Dry them on a clean cloth, separate the slices into individual rings then toss them in *flour*. Transfer to a sieve and shake off the excess flour. Tip into a deep-fat fryer and keep moving whilst they cook. When they are light golden, remove with a slotted spoon and drain on absorbent kitchen paper. Season generously with salt and set aside.

Preheat the oven to *150°c*. In a large, thick-bottomed sauté pan, melt the *butter* with the *vegetable oil*. Add the *chopped chicken wings* after the foam subsides, and cook for 2–3 minutes, stirring constantly. Add the *shallots, celery* and *carrot*. Cook over a medium heat until the vegetables have softened and coloured a little (only a little; we do not want a lot of colour at this stage). Drain off any excess fat released from the chicken wings and add the *honey*. Cook until just beginning to caramelize before adding the *vinegar*. Boil until completely evaporated, then add the *beer, fish stock* and a pinch of *sea salt*. If you have any trimmings from the turbot, or any other white fish, you could add them too at this stage. Bring to the boil, skim off any impurities that rise to the surface and add the *bay leaf, parsley* and *peppercorns*. Simmer for 35 minutes before straining through a fine sieve. Reserve.

Butter a shallow baking dish, large enough to hold the turbot comfortably, with the *soft butter*. Season lightly with *salt and pepper*. Place the *turbot fillets* on top and season the fish also. Add the remaining *100ml beer* and *stock*.

Cover with a butter paper, or a piece of buttered foil, and place in the oven. Cook for 8–10 minutes depending on the thickness of the fish. (If you are unsure as to when the fish is cooked, you could use an instant-read digital thermometer. At *45°c* your fish will be perfect.)

Remove from the oven and transfer the fish to a plate. Cover loosely with foil to keep warm. Tip the cooking juice into a saucepan and boil rapidly to reduce to about an espresso cupful. Add the whipping cream, followed by the cold, diced butter, and swirl around continually until fully incorporated (do not allow the sauce to boil once the butter is added). Stir in the mustard and chives. Check the seasoning and adjust if necessary, adding a little squeeze of *lemon juice* to 'lift' the flavours.

Using a fish slice, transfer the fish to warm plates, spoon the sauce over and pile crispy onions on top. Some boiled potatoes and Savoy cabbage braised with a few juniper berries would make the ideal accompaniment.

HEATHER HONEY ICE CREAM

(Serves 6)

This is a great ice cream to make at home, as you don't need an ice cream machine, and, because of the richness of the honey, there is no need for egg yolks. Serve in winter alongside an apple tart made from Cox's Orange Pippins.

180g	heather honey
600ml	whipping cream, well chilled
2	vanilla pods

Split the **vanilla pods** lengthways and scrape out the seeds.

Place in a small saucepan with the pods, **honey** and 80ml of the **cream**. Warm over a medium heat, stirring to dissolve the honey. Cook for 3–4 minutes, then remove from the heat and cover with a lid to infuse for 1 hour. Remove the pods from the mixture and discard.

Whip the chilled cream until quite firm, but not dry. Scoop all of the honey mixture from the pan with a rubber spatula and fold it gently into the whipped cream. Spoon into a 750g loaf tin, lined with cling film. (Or, if you wish, you could use 6 individual moulds.)

Cover and freeze for several hours.

HONEY AND SPICE LOAF

I love gingerbread in any shape or form, and that includes gingersnaps and gingernuts too. Just dunk a gingersnap into a cup of tea to experience how a little spice can wake up your palette and lift your mood; one of the great flavour experiences! You don't always need foie gras and truffles.

More spicy and not as sweet as traditional gingerbread, moister than the French pain d'épice and more delicate than German lebküchen, this version is a versatile, best-of-three-worlds hybrid. Eat it spread with a thick layer of unsalted butter, or broken into pieces and stirred into vanilla ice cream.

At Café 21 we sometimes dry it, crumble it and use it to flavour a sauce for venison. My friend Alain Coutourier uses it to great effect in his signature dish of pan-fried zander, which has crumbled honey and spice bread in the beurre blanc sauce, at his Michelin-starred restaurant, La Roche le Roy, in Tours, France.

225g	plain flour
55g	rye flour
2tsp	baking powder
1tbsp	ground cinnamon
½tsp	ground ginger
	pinch of salt
2	eggs
225g	mild honey
1 scant tsp	ground aniseed
	a little butter and flour to prepare the mould

Preheat the oven to **180°c**. Butter and flour a 1litre terrine mould or loaf tin. Sift **both the flours, salt, baking powder** and **spices** into a bowl. Gently warm the **honey** and beat the **eggs**. Make a well in the centre and add the eggs and warmed honey. Gradually draw the dry ingredients into the liquids to make a smooth batter. Pour into the prepared mould and bake for 40 minutes in the centre of the oven, or until an inserted skewer comes out clean. Remove from the oven, allow to cool for 5 minutes and turn out onto a wire rack to cool.

HEATHER HONEY MADELEINES

(Makes 24 small madeleines)

A madeleine is a small, buttery sponge that is eaten like a biscuit, often with coffee. These feather-light cakes are baked in special madeleine moulds, which have 12 small, shell-shaped indentations. They are inevitably at their best eaten fresh from the oven, whilst still warm on the inside but with a thin, crispy exterior. They can, though, be kept successfully for a couple of days in an airtight container; the honey slows down the normal staling process, keeping them moist for longer.

75g	unsalted butter
2	large eggs (or break 3 medium eggs into a bowl, beat with a fork and weigh out 110g beaten egg)
60g	caster sugar
1tbsp	dark brown sugar
2tbsp	heather honey
90g	plain flour
1tsp	baking powder

For the Moulds

2tbsp	softened butter
1tbsp	flour

Prepare the *beurre noisette* by heating the **butter** in a large saucepan over a medium heat. At first it will foam, then clear and then begin to colour light brown and give off a nutty aroma. At this stage, tip the molten butter immediately through a fine sieve into a cold bowl to arrest the cooking.

In the bowl of an electric mixer, whisk together the **eggs, sugars** and the **honey** until foamy and pale (about 3–4 minutes). Sift the *flour, baking powder* and **salt** over the mixture and fold in, using a rubber spatula. Fold in the *beurre noisette*. Transfer to a clean bowl, cover with cling film and refrigerate for 2–3 hours.

Prepare the madeleine moulds and preheat the oven to **200°c.** Brush the moulds with an even layer of soft butter. Dust with flour and shake off the excess. Set the moulds aside until needed.

Spoon the batter into the moulds, half-filling them. Bake in the hot oven for 5 minutes until fully risen and golden brown. Remove from the oven and turn the madeleines out of the moulds immediately. Transfer to a wire rack to cool.

HONEY-ROAST PEARS
WITH SPICES

(Serves 4)

This dish fulfils all the criteria for a great dessert. It has everything: fresh fruit, sweet, spicy flavours, great aromas, hot and cold temperature contrasts, it's easy to digest and quick and cheap to produce. I just wish more restaurants would serve this sort of thing, rather than overworked, overpriced towers of flavourless tripe.

6	round dessert pears, ripe but firm
500g	caster sugar
60g	flower honey
60g	unsalted butter
200ml	double cream
	juice from 1 lemon
2	cinnamon sticks
2	star anise
3	cloves
1 coffee sp	black peppercorns

Put the **sugar** and **1ltr of cold water** into a large, stainless steel pan. Add the **lemon juice**, stir until the sugar is dissolved and then bring to boiling point. Peel the **pears**, leaving the stalk intact, and place carefully into the syrup. Cover the pears and syrup with a clean, damp tea towel, to keep the pears submerged, and poach gently for 8–10 minutes.

Remove the pan from the heat and allow the pears to cool in their cooking syrup. Preheat the oven to **190°c.** Crush the **spices** and **peppercorns** coarsely and tip into a sieve. Shake lightly to remove any dust.

In a 22cm non-stick frying pan, heat the **butter** and **honey**.

Add the coarsely crushed spices to the frying pan along with the drained pears. Cook gently over a medium heat, rolling the pears around to coat them with butter and honey on all sides. Transfer the pan to the oven. Roast for 5 or 6 minutes, until the pears are golden and tender, regularly basting the pears with the spiced honey and butter mixture.

Remove the frying pan from the oven and lift the pears carefully from the hot caramel, transferring them to warm dessert plates. Add the **double cream** to the caramel and return to the heat. (Be careful, as the pan handle will still be very hot.) Simmer for 2–3 minutes.

Spoon the caramel sauce over the pears and serve very hot with good quality, vanilla ice cream.

HONEY ROAST
SPARE RIBS

(Serves 4 hungry chefs)

11.30am is time for staff lunch at Café 21; all of the staff sit down together for thirty minutes every day. The food is simple, quick and generally very tasty. These ribs are a favourite from the staff lunch repertoire. Eat them with your hands if you like, but be prepared with plenty of napkins for your sticky fingers.

Start a day in advance:

2½kg	pork spare ribs, in 4 pieces

Marinade

1	small garlic clove, crushed
2tbsp	heather honey
1tbsp	smoked paprika
1	small pinch dried chilli flakes
2tbsp	balsamic vinegar
3tbsp	soy sauce

Warm the **honey** and **mix with all of the other ingredients for the marinade** in a large bowl. Add the **spare ribs** and mix around to coat them well. Cover and refrigerate overnight.

Next day, preheat the oven to **200°c.** Place the ribs on a roasting tray and roast for 18–20 minutes until crispy.

Serve with steamed rice, flavoured with ginger and chopped coriander, and a simple salad of dressed iceberg lettuce.

BRAISED RHUBARB WITH GREEK YOGHURT AND HONEY

(Serves 4)

This springtime dessert has a hint of the Middle East, with yoghurt, orange flower water, pistachio nuts and cinnamon.
The tuile mixture makes more than you need for this recipe, but it keeps quite well for a few days in an airtight container.
Try sandwiching them together with some whipped cream flavoured with orange flower water.

250g	tender young rhubarb
110g	granulated sugar
500ml	water
125ml	grenadine syrup
120g	Greek yoghurt
4tbsp	mild honey
1tsp	orange flower water
20	pistachio nuts, peeled and coarsely chopped

Spice tuiles

95g	icing sugar, sifted
45g	flour
½tsp	ground cinnamon
	pinch of nutmeg
	pinch of ground star anise
2	egg whites
60g	melted butter

Bring the **water, sugar** and **grenadine** to a boil in a stainless steel saucepan. Cut the **rhubarb** into slim 2" lengths. Throw them into the boiling liquid, lower the heat and simmer for 1–2 minutes until tender. Remove the pan from the heat and allow the rhubarb to cool in the syrup. Refrigerate, still in the syrup.

Warm the honey very gently (you can do this in a microwave on defrost setting). Stir in the orange flower water.

To make the tuiles, preheat the oven to **200°c**. Combine the **dry ingredients** and whisk in the **egg whites** followed by the melted butter. Cover with cling film and refrigerate.

Spread very thinly, with a palette knife, onto a non stick baking mat or silicone paper and bake at **200°c** until golden and crisp – about 4 minutes. Remove, allow to cool and store in an airtight tin.

Assembly

Drain the rhubarb and place a mound, off centre, on each dessert plate. Arrange a large spoonful of **yoghurt** alongside. Drizzle the whole with **honey** and scatter the **pistachio nuts**. Place a spice *tuile* in between the rhubarb and the honey.

Chris & Helen Sutherland
Ross Farm

Oysters

“ Lindisfarne Castle stands on its hill, the Whin Sill, wreathed in the mist like a fairy tale illustration, or a *Lord of the Rings* Hollywood fantasy…

St

Cuthbert used to spend time on Holy Island, immersed up to his neck in the cold waters of the North Sea. Unfortunately, at this moment I am about to emulate him, for my wellington boots are stuck fast, deep in the Lindisfarne mud. Both feet remain well apart, planted firmly where they landed on the last of my sliding, slipping, staggering stumbles amongst the mussels and seaweed along this mudbank, far from the shore and far below high tide.

So I totter, legs akimbo, trying desperately to keep my balance and not fall into the seawater channel to my left. It's not going to work. My top half is moving, whether I like it or not! So I make a break for it, wrenching my wellies free, and lurch about like Boris Karloff for a few paces before regaining firmer ground and equilibrium. There's a metal trestle in front of me with its feet in the water. I take a hold and try to get my breath back. There are more of the trestles all around me, all covered with plastic mesh sacks, full of oysters. Lindisfarne Oysters.

"Everything alright?" asks Chris Sutherland, who returns from tending to his oysters on the far trestles, already half submerged by the incoming tide. And then I look around and realize that everything is alright. Indeed, things are much better than alright. Everything is truly wonderful.

It is a beautiful day, a spring morning, early, so we could catch the low tide when the sacks of growing oysters are exposed. Later it will be sunny, very sunny, but at the moment there is a sea mist. Lindisfarne Castle stands on

its hill, the Whin Sill, wreathed in the mist like a fairytale illustration, or a *Lord-of-the-Rings* Hollywood fantasy. Built in 1549–50, the castle never did see much action; no border battles or great sieges to weave a ballad around. A local Jacobite occupied it in the 1715 rising, but there was no glorious charge and sally over the walls. Oh no. He came to dinner with the Governor the night before and, as he was leaving, he said he'd forgotten his watch and nipped back inside and occupied the place for a wee while. I'm not sure how the stand-off concluded, but I wouldn't have put it past the chap to tell the besiegers he was popping out for some milk and a paper.

The last garrison left in 1819, and then, nearly one hundred years later in 1902, Edward Hudson, the owner of *Country Life* magazine, had Sir Edwin Luytens convert it into a private residence with a garden designed by Gertrude Jekyll.

In 1944 the National Trust acquired Lindisfarne Castle and today it is open to the public.

Chris opens a sack, takes out a few oysters and bags them in clear plastic, so they can be sent off for testing when we get back. All part of the meticulous and continuous environmental monitoring. He then begins to select several sacks for 'picking'. I return to my rêverie as gulls, ducks and many more birds that I cannot recognize wheel and soar. A heron leaves its sentry post and beats its way upward. Lindisfarne, home of saints and gospels.

In 635, Oswald, King of Northumbria, granted land for a monastery and charged Aidan, the first Bishop of Lindisfarne, with the task of converting his Anglo-Saxon kingdom to Christianity. The Northumbrians were a tribe of violent heathens and it can't have been an easy job.

Lindisfarne, home of saints and gospels...

They're a tough lot still, and the flapped 'r' sound of the Holy Islanders' Northumbrian dialect harks back to their Saxon forefathers. They have a particular look, silent but strong, that can't be missed. They made tough herring fishermen and herring lasses… a large-scale trade that's long gone, though there's a few cobles still fishing off the island, and upturned boats can still be seen on shore, now used as sheds.

Aidan and Oswald succeeded in turning the islanders' prayers heavenwards, as a seventeenth-century skipper noted them dropping to their knees to pray for a ship in trouble in a storm off their shores. It wasn't until they cursed at its escape from their rocks that he realized they were praying for it to be sent in!

Aidan died in 651AD, an event which is said to have been foretold to Cuthbert, a shepherd boy from the Borders, in a vision. This led him to the religious life, and from a monastery in Tweeddale he rose to become St Aidans's

fifth successor as Bishop of Lindisfarne. His reputation for acts of healing and miracle-working spread far and wide, and pilgrims flocked to Holy Island. Cuthbert died in 687 and was buried according to his wishes. On the island, eleven years later, the monks discovered his body to be in an incorrupt state, and were convinced that this signified Cuthbert's sanctity. Pilgrims flocked to the island in even greater numbers; the old pathway by which they crossed over from the mainland is stilled marked by a line of withies. (You can see it from the new causeway built in the 1950s, but don't stop your car and stare too long or you'll find yourself sitting in the little crow's nest platform awaiting rescue. People do it every year.)

In the ninth century the Vikings turned up, laying waste the religious sites of Lindisfarne. The monks fled the island with St Cuthbert's body and went on a wander throughout the north of England, until, in 995, they finally laid him to rest in Durham, where he remains. A Norman priory was built

c. 1093, ten years after the site was refounded, by the first Bishop of Durham. The dramatic remains of this be seen today, hard by the visitor centre. There you can see the most modern displays of the history of Northumberland, and even turn the pages of a facsimile of the Lindisfarne Gospels.

Chris Sutherland breaks in on the romance: "Better get a move on". Indeed we had, for the tide is well turned now and it's a fair trip back to dry land on the quad bike and trailer. We load up a dozen sacks of oysters and then I climb up and perch in the trailer too. Then we're off, trundling across the sands with a fair old breeze in our faces. I'm sorely tempted to hang my tongue out and do my impersonation of a Border Collie, but I don't want to confuse the sheep; not after this morning, when Chris and I made our way out through the dune pastures and they thought it was their feed delivery. One quad bike looks much like another to a sheep.

As we reach the high water mark, I look back at the island before we disappear back into the dunes. It is an amazing sight. Obviously filmmaker Roman Polanski thought so too, for he made his cult film *Cul de Sac* here. Today, in the firelight of a winter pub, Holy Islanders still tell stories of the weird ways and goings on of the actors and film people. It has to be said that in the firelight of a Soho pub, old actor-Johnies also tell stories of the weird ways of the Islanders!

I take a last look at the romantic sight of the two tall, slender pyramids standing on the shoreline of Ross Sands, with a small house between them. The two columns are actually a navigational leading line, to aid mariners to enter Lindisfarne Harbour. The boats that used them were mainly owned by colliers, bringing in coal to be landed at the staithes and trundled on a track out to the lime kilns below the castle. The treated lime would then have been trundled back, loaded onto boats and shipped away to be spread on the fields of England. Lindisfarne would have been a pretty

smelly industrial backwater in the late 18th and early 19th centuries. Channel 4's Time Team confirmed that when they came looking for a mediaeval manor house, and found an armoury and commissariat from the Napoleonic era.

We've bounced through the dunes now and Chris pulls into Ross Farm, the Sutherland family's 900-acre arable and beef establishment, and HQ of Lindisfarne Oysters. They have converted some of the buildings into well-appointed holiday cottages (oysters laid on, for that special weekend!). The holiday cottages, the oysters and the farm walks (for both children and adults, led by Chris's wife, Helen), give an indication of how seriously the Sutherlands have taken diversification.

The quad bike and trailer stop, and the oysters are unloaded and given a power wash. Once clean, the markings and colours on the shell can be seen more clearly. Then these Pacific beauties (also known as rock oysters or gigas) take a trip to the washing machine designed by Chris's father, John Sutherland, the man who founded the Lindisfarne Oysters

business in 1989. He won't say much about the design, but he does confess to an old potato riddle donating itself to form the prototype. From there the oysters are moved to a series of storage tanks, where they undergo a period of purification, as a cascade of artificial seawater flows through them for 42 hours. The water, which is temperature-regulated and monitored for the correct salinity level, is also irradiated with UV light to kill off any impurities.

After purification they are washed for a second time and are ready for sale, accompanied by their own health mark to say that they are 'purified, live, bivalve molluscs', with a dispatch centre approval number. The work put in over the years to meeting all of the industry's requirements, and paying attention to the details, fills a very large and bulging box file!

Although Chris, who has a BSc in Agriculture from Newcastle University, does have some native oysters growing out there on the trestles, he explained the advantage of the Pacific variety:

"We use them – well, they're the most commonly farmed oyster – because they are quicker growing to maturity than the native oysters, and they're not seasonal. You don't have to worry about 'oysters and r in the month', because the waters in our part of the world are too cold for the Pacifics to breed. The native oysters 'self spat' and go into their reproductive cycle, and so can't be used."

I ask, "And where do you get your Pacific oysters from in the first place, Chris?" And then wonder if that's a very daft question to which the answer is "the Pacific". Thankfully, it isn't

"We buy our oysters as seed oysters from Guernsey, they're as big as about a thumb nail and go into the smallest mesh sacks to start with. As they grow we split them into separate sacks with larger mesh. They live out there in the bags, strapped onto the trestles. They're ideal stock, really, we don't have to feed them, spray them or take them to the vet; they depend on solely natural resources in the sea for their food."

I told Chris I thought it still looked like fairly hard work out on the flats, and he smiled the smile of a man who has been farming in Northumberland all his life; but he did confess "Yes, it has been harder work than I first imagined when I took over from my father. The sacks are quite heavy and you've not much of a firm footing for lifting anything. You have to move them and turn the bags to give all the oysters a chance, keep moving them into bigger mesh and resealing the end of the sacks with what we call a 'jonk', a plastic strap which weaves in and out of the mesh. Sometimes a trestle gets knocked over by the sea and has to be hauled back into place. When we're picking oysters we have to haul a little barge thing out there and use that as a worktable, so to speak. It can be a bit bleak out there too."

Have they ever found any pearls? Helen Sutherland answers that one. "I take some oysters to farmers' markets, and one week a woman came back to me and showed what she had found the week before. It was definitely pearl-coloured, but it was the shape of a squashed chocolate raisin and you really wouldn't have wanted a necklace of them."

But why oysters? Why here? Whose idea was it?

This is where Chris hands me over to his retired father, John Sutherland, a member of The Shellfish Association of Great Britain. "Why?" His eyes sparkle. "Curiosity. A Challenge. Fun. I thought I'd like to have a go." But then he gets serious. "My wife and I spend some time in France, she used to cook professionally and we enjoy their food and their attitude to food. I think we in Northumberland ought to be more interested in the quality of what we eat and in producing quality."

What started him off?

"In 1989 I was walking on the shoreline and I noticed oyster shells at low tide. Now we know from records in the late fourteenth century that the monks had grown oysters, and that in 1881 Thomas Bewey was listed as Keeper of the Oysters on Lindisfarne for the Chillingham Estate. The islander Ralph Wilson also knows that his grandfather was the last Oyster Keeper before the estate was broken up. So I thought, if they could farm oysters, then why can't we farm them now?"

And John Sutherland found out everything he could about oysters; from local people, from books and from other oyster farmers. It also left him with some hard detailed work, dealing with all the relevant authorities. He also laughingly tells me that it led to "meeting some very interesting people in dirty, mucky estuaries". And so he persevered and the Sutherlands at Lindisfarne are now the only oyster farm on the north-east coast; indeed, the only one between Norfolk and Scotland.

John Sutherland then gives me a little tip. He thinks that the Lindisfarne oysters are growing about one-and-a-half times slower than those in the East Anglian creeks, and he believes that's what makes them taste better. That's what their customers are saying. They say that if you build a better mousetrap in a forest then people will beat a path to your door. Well, if you grow a good oyster on an island you can bet an increasing number of people are going to beat a path down this particular Northumbrian *Cul de Sac* too!

Oysters

Legend has it that English serfs rebelled against their lords and masters over the quantity of oysters they were forced to eat. A deal was struck and it was agreed that they would only have to eat them twice a week.

The details may be apocryphal, but it nicely illustrates the point that our native oyster beds were once considerably more numerous than they are today.

Of the few places in Britain that now harvest native oysters, without doubt the finest come from Whitstable and Colchester. Unfortunately, they are insanely expensive. Luckily, Pacific oysters – or rock oysters – were introduced to Britain in the seventies. Deeper, more gnarled and oval in shape than natives, they are not only cheaper, but are available all year round.

I was a late developer. I didn't meet my first oyster until I was eighteen. It was on my first trip abroad – well, Jersey felt very exotic to a north-eastern lad; when I stepped out of the plane onto the tarmac, I expected tropical temperatures and coral sands. I'd secured a job as a commis chef in the Mermaid Hotel, which is sadly no more. The word oyster for me conjured up luxury cars, champagne in silver coolers and women who would lead you astray. So when I ate my first oyster and could only taste seawater and iodine I wasn't too impressed. It was only some time later that I realized, it's not just the taste but the texture, the slipperiness, the icy thrill as it slides down your throat, the dribbles down the chin, the clatter of shell against ice as you share a tottering plateful with friends. Throw all those ingredients together and it's sensational. Like olives and anchovies, oysters seem to be a strangely adult thing.

Oysters should only be bought live. Buy from a merchant whom you trust, who knows exactly what he is selling and when and where the oysters were harvested. The oysters should be tightly shut with their shells intact, not cracked or crushed. They shouldn't be too heavy for their size, which may indicate that they are full of silt, nor feel hollow. Don't worry about a little mud on the outside, as it is advisable to wash just before opening anyway. The fresher an oyster, the better its flavour. Once harvested, oysters live in and on the seawater in their shells, which necessarily changes flavour as it deteriorates. From a hygiene point of view, it is probably less important how long an oyster has been stored than how well. Even a brief period of raised temperature can encourage the reproduction of bacteria, which can kill the oyster and result in a bad experience for the diner. Store them on a tray, upside-down, i.e. flat shell uppermost. They're inquisitive creatures and if they lift their lids, that all-important juice could dribble out. Keep in the coldest part of the fridge (around 3–7°c), away from light, and cover them with a damp cloth.

Ideally, oysters should be opened just before they are brought to the table. Difficult, I agree, if you've got two dozen shells to split open at a dinner party. In that case, open them no more than two hours in advance, replace the top shell, pile them tightly in a dish, cover with a cloth and place in the fridge. Before serving, remember to check that there are no loose bits of shell floating around.

Opening oysters sounds complicated, but is quite logical. An oyster knife with a protective guard is essential. Use no substitutes. Years ago, when working in a fish restaurant in Newcastle, I used an oyster knife which had lost its guard. I ended up with the arrowhead tip of the knife buried half an inch in my palm and spent the rest of the evening in casualty. I still sport the scar.

Purists declare that oysters should be served, virginal, on a bed of crushed ice. I would argue that they benefit from a squeeze of lemon and a dash of Tabasco or a sprinkling of

Tips

Oysters are great raw with:
caviar, chillies, ginger, lemon, red wine vinegar, shallots,
soy sauce, Tabasco sauce

and cooked with:
bacon, beurre blanc, black pepper, champagne,
cheese sauce, chives, cucumber, curry (strangely enough),
leeks, lemon, parsley, spinach, white wine, watercress.

shallot vinegar. The acidity makes them more digestible.
The bigger debate is over whether to chew or swallow.
I don't see the point of swallowing them whole, it seems
such a terrible waste. The taste is as much the feeling, as
the chilled flesh hits your warm insides. Incidentally,
they are surprisingly filling. Six per person, as a starter,
is ample.

Native oysters are too special to cook, but I find that Pacifics
respond well to a number of treatments. Cooking them
intensifies the flavour, although they lose that raw surprise.
They taste great poached in champagne, battered and deep
fried – hot and crisp outside, ice-cream cold inside, a real
flavour hit – or breadcrumbed and fried. Be ruthlessly quick.
We are talking, literally, seconds. You want them just
stiffened. Take your eye off them and you'll end up with a
rubber ball, and a superball at that. At our restaurants,
we sometimes use them in a fish soup. They're dropped
in at the last minute, more or less as we are taking the
plates to the table.

Oysters are surprisingly good in leek and potato soup.
As the cooked ingredients are being liquidized, drop in
several oysters – without the shells, of course – and throw
in generous quantities of chives. Three to four oysters to
a litre of soup are about right. Another odd combination

I came across was in Arcachon, on the west coast of France.
Here it is the custom to swallow an oyster, take a bite of
hot pork sausage and then a glug of white Bordeaux.
Weird but nice, once you get your head around it.

Apart from over-cooking, the biggest mistake you can
make with oysters is to eat them whilst drinking spirits.
Let's just say, it can have a disastrous effect on the stomach.
Champagne is the time-honoured liquid accompaniment,
but I'd rather drink something clean and lean. A simple
green Chablis or Muscadet, crisp and fresh, is perfect.

One of my greatest oyster experiences was in Brittany
in 1977. I was working at that aforementioned hotel in
Jersey and had taken the weekend off with a couple of
mates to watch the Le Mans 24-hour race. (Won by Jackie
Ickx and Derek Bell in a works Porsche 936, with Ickx
setting the fastest lap through the night in the rain!)
With several hours to kill before catching the hydrofoil back,
we drove from St Malo to Cancale. It was early June,
warm, but pouring with rain. We found a café with a
boardwalk overlooking the oyster beds. We ate oysters
followed by mussels followed by oysters. Then started all
over again. We drank far too much. Yes, oysters are costly.
But, if you're in the right place, with the right people,
in the right mood, you've just got to do it.

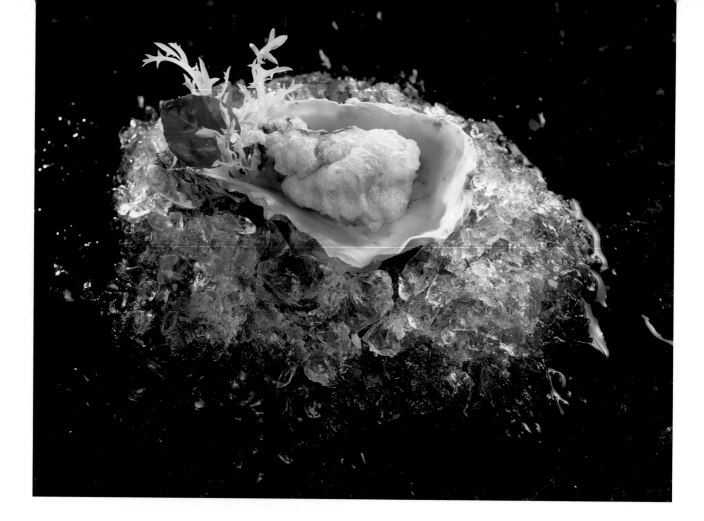

OYSTER FRITTERS WITH SOUR CREAM SAUCE

(Serves 4)

Batter

200ml	iced water
125ml	dry white wine
16	Lindisfarne Oysters
250g	flour
250g	cornflour
1tsp	vegetable oil
	salt & cayenne pepper

Sour cream sauce

150g	sour cream
4tbsp	natural yoghurt
	salt, lemon juice, cayenne pepper
2tbsp	finely cut chives

Garnish

a little	curly endive
a little	lambs' lettuce
	crushed ice

Open the *oysters* carefully and remove from the shells. Drain on a piece of clean muslin over a small bowl, collecting all of the juice.

For the *batter*, mix everything together and keep really cold over ice.

Mix the *sour cream* and *yoghurt* with a whisk, add cayenne pepper and lemon juice to taste. Stir in some of the reserved oyster juice and then check if the sauce needs salt.

Assembly

Preheat a deep-fat fryer to *180°c*. Arrange the reserved *oyster shells* (4 per person) on crushed ice. Place a tablespoon of sour cream sauce into each. Skewer each oyster with a cocktail stick. Dip one at a time into the batter and transfer carefully to the hot fat. Keep moving around in the fat for 2 minutes until crisp. Lift out with a slotted spoon and drain on kitchen paper.

Remove the cocktail sticks and place an oyster in each shell. Garnish with a few small salad leaves dressed in a little vinaigrette.

OYSTER SASHIMI

(Serves 4)

The Japanese-style dressing gives the oysters a savouriness which, ironically, seems to make the raw shellfish more appealing to a western pallet.

16	Lindisfarne Oysters
	coarse sea salt
	chopped chives

Dressing

2tbsp	lemon juice
60ml	rice wine vinegar
3tbsp	Kikkoman light soy sauce
1tbsp	Mirin*
	zest from ½ lemon
½tsp	grated ginger
½tsp	grated garlic
60ml	olive oil
2tsp	sesame oil

Open the **oysters** and place in a clean bowl, straining the juice onto them through muslin. Scrub the shells and dry thoroughly.

Bring the **lemon juice, vinegar, soy, mirin, lemon zest, ginger** and **garlic** to a quick boil. Remove from the heat and allow to cool and infuse. Strain through a fine sieve, mix with **olive oil** and **sesame oil**. Refrigerate.

Assembly

Scatter a bed of **coarse sea salt** on 4 cold plates. Place an oyster in each shell. Spoon over a little sauce and sprinkle generously with chives.

*Mirin is a Japanese sweetened rice wine, used in sauces, marinades etc, readily available in Asian delis.

OYSTERS ROCKEFELLER

(Serves 6)

This is an American classic. I think it originated in New Orleans, probably at Antoine's or Gallatoires. If you are in New York City, try it at Grand Central Station Oyster Bar, which is more like Oyster Grand Central, with 54 varieties on offer.

6tbsp	unsalted butter
3tbsp	chopped, flat leaf parsley
1 dash	Tabasco
36	oysters
1 handful	spinach
2 slices	white bread, crusts removed
½tsp	Pernod

Open the **oysters** and remove them from the bottom shell, reserving any juice. Strain the juice through a piece of clean muslin into a medium saucepan. Place in the oysters and heat very gently for 2 minutes to slightly poach and stiffen the oysters. Remove from the heat.

Chop the **spinach** with a large knife. Process the **bread** to make crumbs. Heat the **butter** in a non-stick frying pan until it sizzles. Throw in the breadcrumbs and stir until the crumbs brown slightly before adding the spinach, **Tabasco** and **Pernod**. Remove from the heat and season with salt and black pepper.

Sit the oyster shells on a bed of **rock salt** and place a poached oyster in each. Divide the crumbs between each shell and place under a hot grill until browned.

OYSTERS ON ICE

As many oysters as your party can eat

Plenty of ice

Lemons

Tabasco

Brown bread, preferably rye

Butter

Shallot vinegar

240ml	Cabernet Sauvignon vinegar (Forum is the best brand), or other good quality red wine vinegar
2	shallots, very finely chopped
1tbsp	coarsely milled black peppercorns
½tsp	fine sea salt

Whisk all of the *vinegar ingredients* together and keep at room temperature.

Spread some crushed ice on a large, round plate. Blanch some fresh *seaweed* in boiling water for 1 minute and then plunge into cold water. The blanching brings out a fantastic, vivid green from the seaweed. Strew the seaweed over the ice.

Rinse away any mud from the *oysters* under a cold tap; any stubborn particles can be removed by scrubbing with a nailbrush. Hold the rounded part of the oyster in a damp tea towel, with the left hand (right hand if left-handed). Look for the spot where the shells are hinged, which is normally very obvious. Holding the oyster knife with the right hand, probe at the joint, gently working the flat blade into the slit. Apply pressure and wiggle the blade around until you feel the shells pop and come apart. Carefully twist the knife to lift open the 'lid' or upper shell. Gently slide the knife along the inside of the upper shell to cut the muscle, which is attaching the oyster to the lid. Discard the upper (flat) shell and smell the oyster, discard it if it smells unpleasant. Now slide your knife under the oyster meat, close to the deep shell, and free that side of the muscle. Inspect the oyster for any fragments of broken shell or tiny pieces of mud.

Bed the oysters in the ice, so that they sit nice and level and none of the precious juice is lost. Serve with *lemon wedges, Tabasco, brown bread, butter* and chilled *Muscadet*. Serve the shallot vinegar alongside in a small dish or ramekin.

OYSTER SHOOTER

(Serves 2)

Great for cocktail parties or garden parties, where you don't want to mess about with shells.
Just serve everyone a glass each and let them get on with it.

6	small oysters
2–3 drops	Tabasco sauce
1 tbsp	tomato ketchup
a few drops	Worcestershire sauce
6 drops	lemon juice

Shuck the **oysters** & discard the shells. Place 3 oysters into each shot glass. Whisk the other ingredients together and spoon over. Serve very cold

Neil Robson
L. Robson & Sons

Crabs, Lobsters
& Kippers

It's a bit of a misleading statement to talk of Northumbrian fishermen. They came from such small communities that they didn't think of themselves in those terms. They were 'Craster men', 'Newton men', or 'Seahouses folk', or they 'belonged Boulmer, or Amble, or Beadlin', as Beadnell used to be known.

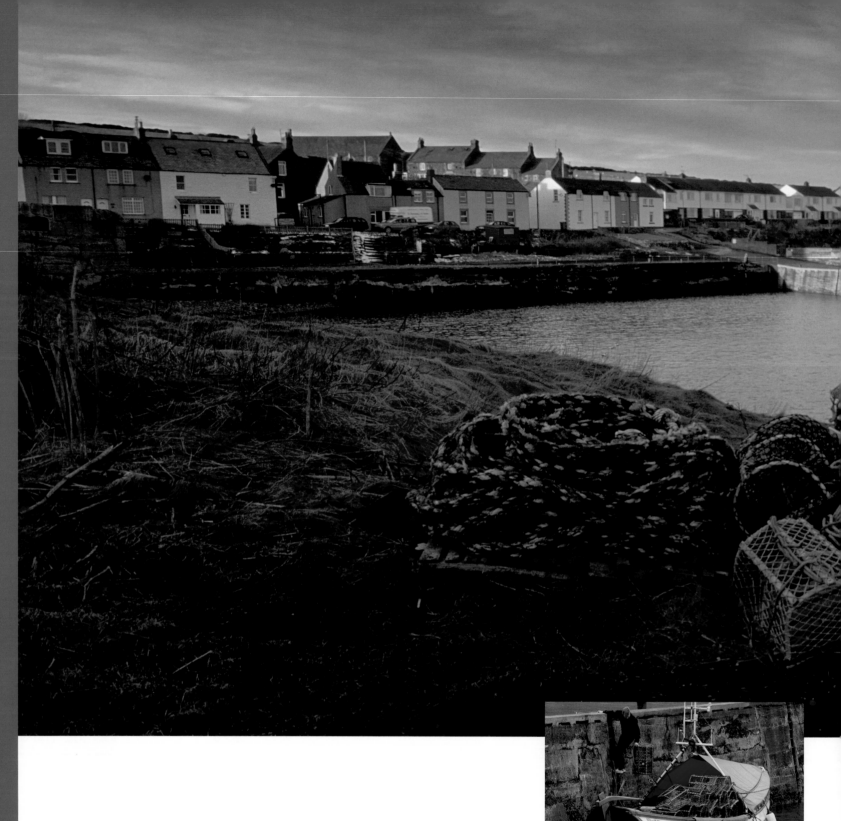

The village of Craster lies on the 'heritage coast' of Northumberland, now designated an 'Area of Outstanding Natural Beauty'. It is beautiful, but Northumbrians would like to point out that it always was, before anybody designated anything. Indeed, there is some feeling locally that folk should kindly keep their designations to themselves.

Standing about a mile-and-a-half's walk outside the village is one of the most romantic ruins in the world, Dunstanburgh Castle. Thomas, Earl of Lancaster, nephew of King Edward 11, began building it in 1314. It looks picturesque now, standing out there on its promontory, but it was built for practicality; out of the way, easily defended. Ironically, Thomas himself proved less defensible and was executed in 1322, for rebelling against the King, by which time the castle was largely complete. Later, 1380–84, John of Gaunt, fourth son of Edward 111 and Lieutenant of the Scottish Marches, extended the castle and it became a Lancastrian stronghold during the Wars of the Roses, until technology caught up with it in the sixteenth century and cannon turned it into a romantic ruin.

Back in the village we find Craster harbour. On a plaque on the north wall is a rather poignant inscription: 'Constructed in memory of Capt. John Charles Pulleine Craster, 46th Punjabis, who fell in action during the Tibetan Expedition 1904. He took a deep interest in the provision of a harbour at Craster and his brother and sister chose this way of perpetuating his memory'. Today it's high tide and there are a couple of boats waiting to take line-fishermen out for a day's sport. There are a also couple of traditional Northumbrian cobles, with their crews attending to the lobster pots piled high on the quays. In days gone by, during the season, as the herring moved down the east coast, the harbour would have been packed full of boats landing them, and full too of the 'herring lasses' who followed the fleet.

100

students. It kept them in their place and meant they didn't leave their beds unmade or leave dead animals lying around. You were only allowed to aim directly at them if they had both a beard and corduroy trousers.

Here, the fisherfolk and their rivalries meant clogged shins at football matches and glowered mutterings of 'Keep away from wor lasses' at village dances. Mind you, a fisherman had to make sure he could get himself a good wife… who else was going to bait miles of long line with a hundred weight of mussels, all opened with a bent tea spoon. And if you were launching the boat from the beach, in the days before engines, she'd do most of the work. To be fair, the men needed all their strength at sea, to row away from the surf line.

Wearing men's seaboots to keep them from the mess accumulating at their feet, and with their fingers tied up to protect them, their knifes would have flashed like lightning as they worked in teams to gut and pack the herrings. They were a tough and independent lot, many of them Scots from the far north who would never work on a Sunday.

It's a bit of a misleading statement to talk of Northumbrian fishermen. They came from such small communities that they didn't think of themselves in those terms. They were 'Craster men', 'Newton men', or 'Seahouses folk', or they 'belonged Boulmer, or Amble, or Beadlin', as Beadnell used to be known.

There were often fierce rivalries between Northumbrian fishing villages, which probably started at sea as they vied for a shoal or for a fishing ground. Wherever they started, they continued ashore. You could get a brick chucked at you for being on the wrong side of a road or stream. It was accepted as the norm then. I'm not surprised. In Sheffield in the 1950s, we bairns were still allowed to throw stones at art

There was one thing in which all the fishermen were united. They were a superstitious bunch, particularly when it came to – well, to 'the articles'; y'know, 'the ministers'. Alright, 'guffies'. Oh, for heaven's sake, the unmentionable animal in the sty with the curly tail. Terrible bad luck the things were.

They never actually said the word. That superstition still holds today in some places. I know one inland pub where the darts team, whenever they play the lads from the coastal village, still hang up a butcher's calendar for 1976, always open at April: Gloucester Old Spot. It doesn't work; the landlubbers always lose.

These seafaring folk didn't see many strangers, and didn't much care for the ones they did, so it's a bit ironic that the main industry in the area today is tourism. It has to be said that there was one massive exception to the strangers thing. The Northumbrian fishermen manned the lifeboats, and for any stranger in danger at sea they would risk their lives. And still do.

To the landlubber, the sea is a flat surface on which boats sit; a two-dimensional world. Those of us who venture out to sea with our modern echo-sounders and radar know different. We can see the bottom changing on our instrument displays. The amazing thing is that the old Northumbrian fisherman could do the same, without instruments. To them, their part of the sea would have been very much a living, three-dimensional world. They knew both the contours of the sea-bed, and the condition of the ground on the bottom. Inshore they would have used transits and landmarks known only to themselves. You had it drummed into you as a lad; there were no maps or diagrams. All the knowledge was in the older men's heads and they passed it on, usually from father to son. The herring fishing was done by the keelboats, and although some men bought themselves larger, Scottish-type vessels, the main inshore – the small, wooden fishing boat which mainly carried the pots out – was and is the coble.

In some parts of the east coast, further south, you might hear similar boats being called 'cobbles', but in Northumberland they're cobles, and with the Northumbrian accent it sounds more like 'kerble'. Those with some knowledge of Germanic languages will recognize this sound as an accented 'o' (an umlaut in German). This isn't surprising, as the koeble is thought to be of either Viking or Saxon origin. They do have lines redolent of the Viking long boat, but don't have a pointed canoe stern. Rather, they sweep back to a steep-angled flat one. They were relatively flat bottomed, which made them easy to launch from the beaches. Until the 1920s, when engines were introduced, they had only sails.

Cobles were always built by eye and from memory. If your builder had his eye in, you'd end up with a good, strong and handy boat. If he got it wrong, say by building it a couple of feet too long, or with the side planking wrongly angled, you'd be left with a clumsy pig (now I've gone and said it) of a thing, impossible to manoeuvre in tight places inshore. Men liked to keep a close eye on the building of their cobles, although I'm told that some of the 'master chaps' didn't permit it, preferring to keep their coble-building secrets to themselves. You had to take them on trust.

In the nineteenth century, crabs were often fished using an iron hoop with a net across. Your crab crawled into the hoop to get at the bit of bait in the centre, and bingo, you whipped up the hoop with your catch. After this, people moved on to using pots. On Holy Island they're known as creels, which seems to have been corrupted to 'creeves' at Boulmer and Seahouses. Somewhat confusingly, they were referred to as 'nets' further south, around Craster and the picturesque Newton-by-the-Sea (which other villages called 'Stinky', a nomenclature which may come as a surprise to the upmarket visitors of today). The pots would have been made out of natural materials, willow sticks for the hoops, sisal and rope for the netting. Plastic and polyurethane took over in the 1980s.

It seems to have been the accepted norm to shoot a line of crab pots out at sea, just where the hard ground ends and the muddy bottom starts. It would have been hard work, because the pots would have to be hand-hauled back to the surface. One at a time was hauled into the boat, emptied, re-baited and then shot back in, the man beside you having the next pot ready for you to deal with right away. Some men could empty and re-bait about fifty in a quarter of an hour. You had to watch the tide; get your timing wrong and the nets and ropes were swept under the boat, which made it even harder work. After engines were introduced, this could be even worse, as the ropes could catch around the propeller, leaving you with no drive and at the mercy of the wind.

Crabs are caught in the spring and early summer, until they start to cast their shells in June. Then it's August or September before they're ready to be landed again. According to official figures, of the 26,000 tonnes of crabs landed by the UK fleet in 2002, 36% were landed in the North Sea . Many of the velvet crabs, brown crabs and lobsters landed on the north-east coast are exported to France, Spain and Portugal. So you can take a Lisbon tram up the hill, past the Cathedral, and wander through the alleyways in the Alfama, till you come to a Mozambican

restaurant with a magnificent view over Baixa, the 'modern' city centre that was rebuilt after the earthquake of 1755. And if you sample their exotic crab and plantain stew, there's a good chance that the former ingredient was once a Geordie.

We've all seen lobster pots, piled up on the quay, when we've been on a visit to the seaside; the ones with a trap, a one-way system, and extra space, sometimes called a parlour. Surprisingly, this kind of pot is a relatively modern invention, only coming into usage in these parts in the 1950s. Some of the lobsters caught in Northumberland go on another journey, this time to Ireland, where they are used for breeding.

Fishing for crabs and lobsters was, and in some cases still is, just one part of the Northumberland fisherman's season. In summer they would have concentrated on herring, in winter they caught white fish with a long line, and then, of course, there was the salmon. Crab and lobster fishing took up the spring and part of the autumn. The fishermen concentrated on whatever was in season that would 'fetch a living', such as it was. There were times when the pots produced nothing. Then there were times when crabs and lobsters were found in good numbers, but the prices were too low. Prices are relatively high these days, but the numbers are down.

In the days before refrigerated, fast transport, the glut of herring would either have had to be salted in the barrel or smoked to preserve them. The fish caught off Craster were thought to be in a particular condition that made them suitable for smoking. They hadn't spawned yet and were plumper, still retaining more of their oils. The vast shoals of herring are no longer moving down our coasts, although I did once recently see a small shoal off Craster, being driven together by a pod of dolphins, which were feeding off them like crazy.

Craster is busy with tourists today, and in the harbour there are plenty of youngsters, both boys and girls, jumping off the wall into the sea. They have all obviously been here before and know the chill of the North Sea well, because they are all wearing wetsuits. One young man has climbed on top of the concrete platform at the end of the south harbour wall and is jumping from some considerable height, severely aggravating the men trying to fish.

That concrete construction tells something of a story, for Craster was once, in fact, a thriving port, and on that concrete tower was part of the crane system for loading the boats. An overhead bucket-way brought stone from the Whinstone Quarry, which closed in 1939 and is now a nature

reserve and car park. It's said that most of London's kerbstones passed through here. I mention this because, whilst there is the romance of a quaint fishing village here, underpinning Craster is a streak of practicality to which we will return, as we find out about more about Craster Kippers and L. Robson and Sons Ltd.

Human beings have been smoking food for an awful long time. A man called John Woodger is usually credited with the invention of the kipper, but I can't help feeling that there ought to be some truth in the story that kippers were discovered through an accidental fire in a herring-salting hut. 'By! That smells nice!' thinks someone, 'I wonder if we can do that deliberately!'

Lots of visitors are milling around the smokery and queuing in the shop. A languid couple go to enter the yard, then turn up their noses.

'Very smoky. What is it?' says she.

'Oh, it's just a fish shop' drawls he, and they retire, having perpetrated one of the biggest errors of category I've heard anybody commit in a long while.

This is not 'just a fish shop!' I want to holler. This is L. Robson and Sons, one of the best, if not the best traditional smokers of fish in the country. Four generations this business has been in the family, since 1865.

'Would you like some kippers?' says he.

'No,' says she, 'they're just as nice in Waitrose.'

Well, honestly! Where do you think Waitrose buy them?

The couple leave, but the better informed move forward in the queue to make their purchases, and I make myself known and am ushered into the office to meet Mr Neil Robson, who is, as mentioned, the fourth generation of the family to be involved in the business. The third generation, it has to be said, is still going strong, whizzing about expertly on a fork-lift truck, readying tomorrow's batch of fish for the start of the process. It's that sort of 'hands-on' family business.

Neil Robson tells me that there were another three smokehouses in the village until the beginning of the twentieth century. They depended purely on the herring landed at Craster, which meant a short season and a bit of a gamble on the size of the catch. The smokehouses were rented on an annual basis, and if you didn't make any money in your season, then maybe someone else would have a go next year…"a bit like having a market stall". The other smokeries fell by the wayside. Only Robsons persevered and became a permanent feature of Craster.

As with all the people I've spoken to for this book, it's at this juncture that I lean forward and ask the definitive question.

"So, what is a kipper?" Mr Robson fixes me with a look and I can see him marvel at my piscine ignorance.

"A kipper," he tells me, "is a herring that has been split and smoked".

In previous years, women would have done the splitting by hand, about ten to fifteen of them, but since the late 1950s that part of the process has been done by machine. It whips them round rapidly and, blades flashing, relieves them of their innards. The gills are then removed by hand, which also gives an opportunity to check that the fish have indeed been properly cleaned. The waste products from the cleaning process are not thrown into the sea, but collected by a company who specialize in the processing and use of such material.

The next stage is the salting. The brine tanks are made of stainless steel, and so are the 'tenter-sticks' on which the fish are hooked, ready to be hung in the smoke rooms. (Yes, that's where 'to be on tenterhooks' comes from.) Wood was the traditional material for both tanks and sticks, but over the past few years, hygiene regulations have seen it phased out. I ask Mr Robson if this was the stumbling block that had brought them into a well-publicized conflict with the EEC in the early nineties. He plays things down very matter-of-factly. "The papers got it out of proportion. The EEC gave us five years to upgrade and it's nothing that wouldn't have happened anyway. Our Environmental Health would have forced the change anyway."

What happens next to the herring?

What doesn't happen is more important. In some larger commercial smokeries, this is when the fish will be dyed and preservatives added. But that does not happen here. The brine-soaked fish are taken on their tenter-sticks and hung up in the smoke rooms, where they will be smoked for 14–16 hours. Neil Robson continues: "There will have to be four different firings until the first lot are ready. It isn't a case of lighting a fire and standing back until it's all done. The fire is lit and goes out four times. We use oak sawdust, which is getting harder to find."

"Why is that?" I ask, the journalist in me hoping that I can lay before you, the reader, news of a threat brought to the kipper industry by the ending of a symbiotic relationship with some time-honoured craft. "Is that the end of some ancient process causing that?" I ask.

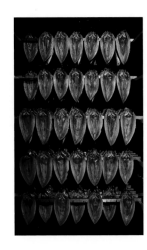

106

"Yes," confirms Neil Robson, "It's the end of the ancient process of cutting down oak trees".

Oh well. Back to the smoke rooms. They do have a certain atmosphere, a 'wizard's cave' sort of place. Although Mr Robson plays this down, this is where the smoke-wizard's art takes over. It's not a case of just flicking the switch on some massive electric kiln and waiting until a bell rings, saying 'time's up, they're all ready'. No, this is where the experience and the knowledge take over and where the traditional process is labour intensive. Not all of the kippers will be ready at the same time, so the fires will have to be watched and tended. An eye will have to be kept for changes in the weather. The process can be affected by conditions outside becoming hotter or damper. The direction and strength of the wind greatly affects the fires, and you have to be ready to alter the setting of the shutters in the smokehouse roof if a haar – the north coast sea-mist – rolls in.

The fires should smoulder slowly. Too much heat and the fish will cook. The smoking process causes a layer to form on the outside of the fish called a pellicle, which means that heat can't penetrate inside and start cooking it. One of the main advantages of the traditional way of smoking is that much more of the moisture content is retained, whereas the large-scale process tends to dry the kipper out. One of the main reasons I've heard people give as to why they don't like kippers is that they are 'too dry'. I've felt that myself about some of the examples I've been served for breakfast. What I've realized, following my visit to Robson's, is that they don't have to be like that. Indeed, they are not supposed to be like that.

How do you tell when the kippers are done?

"Firmness of flesh, the colour and a sheen of oil. Here, have a look, " says Mr Robson, showing me some examples of Craster Kippers that had just come out of the smoking process. It genuinely is an eye-opener. They have a red-gold hue, with, as he says, a wonderful sheen of oil on them; omega oils, that we're now told are so good for us.

It's at this point that I remember something Terry Laybourne once said to me. "Put real quality in front of people and I defy them not be able to tell the difference." Here was absolute proof of that remark. Those dyed, dried things that look like sole-replacement kits for shoes, you'll find none of those here and if you've any sense you won't find any on your plate either.

Thousands of people already know this; Robsons sell a million kippers a year, both to large outlets such as Waitrose, delis such as the Corbridge Larder and to farm shops. An awful lot of people are beating a path to Craster to buy direct. "It just used to be the school summer holidays, but now, on a dry winter's day, the place is full of visitors and we can be very busy". There is still a great deal of mail-order business for dried fish that is exempt from the EEC ban on mailing food. Indeed, this side of things has increased now that you can order from the website. Delivery is guaranteed within two days.

Kippers are sent out from Craster all over the world. One long-standing customer sends his present tags to Robsons at Christmas for them to put on his Christmas boxes. The cost of postage can be a bit of a heart-stopper, like the famous order to Down Under, where the postage cost £47, four times the price of the kippers.

L. Robson and Son smoke salmon as well. It is farmed, but sourced from a small firm in the Shetlands with a very good record in husbandry. Rather than being dry-salted, the salmon are soaked in brine at Robsons, for better flavour

and texture, and smoked for 48 hours. Although demand and output does rocket near Christmas, they turn over a fair amount all year. They smoke some cod and halibut too, and even a small amount of bacon for a local producer.

Robsons do also handle lobsters. They're landed locally and are kept swimming in tanks until it's time for them to be handed over to a specialist shellfish merchant. Some will find themselves on the plates of connoisseurs in France and Spain.

As Neil Robson and I stand in the yard, looking into the what can be only described as a small factory, with it's dedicated team hard at work in their modern working-with-food gear, I ask him if there are any awards that he would like mentioning. "No," he says, "we don't go in for that sort of thing". This makes me think back to Craster's hidden practicality, and I realize that the quest for quality in a traditional product means not being taken in by show. Beware the marketing ploy of 'Ye Traditionale Wares'. Conversely, be prepared not to imitate my somewhat exaggerated couple from earlier, and make the mistake of thinking that a quality product has to be produced with a degree of self-important fanfare and show.

Cecil Sharpe said that when he was travelling around, collecting English folk songs, you could always tell the real traditional musicians from the revivalists, because they never smiled. They didn't go on at great length about what they had done for generations. They just did it, and very well indeed.

"We take that little bit more care," say the Robsons, "and everyone here takes great pride in what they're doing. Then we let the product speak for itself."

Crabs, Lobsters & Kippers

In the 'seventies, when I was learning my trade around hotel and restaurant kitchens in Europe, English food was the source of much banter and ribaldry amongst the foreign chefs. The two things that left them speechless – quite hard for a chef – were pickled eggs and kippers. *Why?* was the question they were struggling to ask.

Pickled eggs I will leave to one side. But kippers, I feel, are an unfairly maligned food. They are uniquely British; indeed, invented by a Northumbrian, John Woodger, who, in the 1840s, was looking for a way to preserve herring in a similar fashion to the Scottish method of cold-smoking salmon. This was in the great herring bonanza era, when fleets of fishing boats would follow the 'silver darlings' down the east coast from Peterhead to Lowestoft. Well, we paid the price for that. Over-fishing lead to quotas in the 1970s, and now most of our herring are imported from Iceland. Along with the loss of our herring fleets, we seem to have lost our taste for kippers, relegating them to breakfast 'treats' when having a weekend away in a country house hotel.

A pity. Kippers, when matched with waxy new potatoes, and perhaps a little beetroot and soured cream, are a terrific taste sensation. And, as an oily fish, they are the heart's best friends: full of friendly fatty acids and very good for breaking down cholesterol.

The aroma, I concede, is a big deterrent to cooking kippers at home. Certainly it's a smell that seemed to fill my grandmother's house. But that was in the days when, despite the fact it was a terraced house, all the eating, talking and living was done in one room.

There's a simple way to counteract it: the jugged kipper. Put the kippers in a Pyrex jug, pour over boiling water and leave for five minutes before draining. Effectively, it poaches the kippers. At the same time, it removes the aroma, a degree of oil and certainly makes them easier to digest – although, to my mind, they also lose an element of tang and bite.

I've tried a multitude of tricks with kippers: kipper oil (a sort of smoked fish oil to use for dressing strong salads); kipper cream sauce to serve with salmon; fancy potted kippers. It was all, I admit, a bit self-conscious, but one of the good things to come out of it was kippers marinated in a vinaigrette of oil, vinegar, lemon, coriander seeds and lots of black pepper. It gave the fish a deliciously moist and slippery, smoked- salmon texture, and worked well as a light lunch served with new potatoes and thin slices of raw onion.

Kipper pâté, traditionally made with puréed potatoes, malt whisky and mace, is worth pursuing. But we find a fresher, more contemporary version goes down well with our lunchtime business crowd. Don't be mean with the toast. It needs a healthy pile of good, brown, thin slices.

But kippers are such a singular taste. There's nothing to beat a plate of grilled kippers. Try and buy them whole, i.e. with the bone in and the head on. Modern smoking has a tendency to dry out the fish, which is exacerbated if you grill them as a fillet, and means you lose that nice balance between the moist flesh and the firm crust. Cooking is dead easy. Simply put under the grill for 3 - 4 minutes. Lift out the bone, add a knob of butter – after, rather than before, grilling; there's enough oil in the fish to help them cook – and serve with waxy new potatoes and something fresh and clean-tasting, like a simple salad, beetroot and soured cream or sliced, raw, red onions.

The same rules apply with jugged kipper. For only a little extra effort, you can make terrific potted kippers. Drain the kipper, place in a bowl with a good knob of butter, and crush with a fork. Spread over toast and be generous with the black pepper. What to drink with kippers? Oddly enough, I once had a very successful supper in a London wine bar of kippers, hot new potatoes and a glass of black velvet…

MARINATED KIPPERS

(Serves 4)

Marinating the kippers in oil transforms them into something much more delicate – almost sophisticated.
The technique is a French bistro standard, which is normally used for fresh herrings. I've adapted it a little to balance with the strong,
smoky flavour of the kippers. If you can find some La Ratte or Pink Fir Apple potatoes, just scrub and boil them and serve warm,
alongside the marinated kippers. This is terrific lunch food.

300g	kipper fillets
1	red onion, peeled and sliced into fine rings
2	shallots, peeled and sliced into fine rings
2	small carrots, peeled and sliced into fine rings
4	small, fresh bay leaves
1	thyme sprig
8	juniper berries
12	coriander seeds
12	black peppercorns
10	Sichuan peppercorns
150ml	extra virgin olive oil
150ml	sunflower oil
	zest from 1 lemon, cut into fine strips, blanched for 1 minute in boiling water and refreshed in iced water
	juice from 2 lemons
	sea salt flakes and milled black pepper
	potato salad
	fresh herbs (dill and flat-leaf parsley)

Scatter a layer of **sliced vegetables** in the base of a porcelain dish and place the **kipper fillets** on top. Scatter the remaining ingredients over the kippers then pour in the **oil**. Cover tightly with cling film and refrigerate for 3 days.

Remove the fillets from the marinade and drain well. Pat dry with kitchen paper, then slice fillets thinly with a sharp, flexible knife. Arrange the slices attractively onto salad plates and scatter some of the vegetables from the marinade over. Season with **sea salt** and **milled black pepper**. Drizzle with a little of the oil and garnish with some **fresh herbs**.

Serve a small pile of **potato salad** alongside.

Spicy crab soup with spring rolls

(Serves 4)

2	large crabs
3	tomatoes, chopped
½	onion, peeled and chopped
1	carrot, peeled and chopped
1	small leek, washed, trimmed and chopped
2 stalks	lemon grass
1tbsp	chopped garlic
½tbsp	curry powder
250ml	white wine
2ltrs	fish stock
1 handful	uncooked rice
	vegetable oil

Spring rolls

2	spring onions
1	garlic clove
8	won ton wrappers

Garnish

½	cucumber
1	celery stick
½	leek
1	small carrot
2tbsp	rice wine vinegar
1½tbsp	toasted sesame oil
½ bunch	coriander leaves

Preheat the oven to **200°c**. Cut the **garnish vegetables** into thin strips.

Heat a roasting tray and roast the **crabs** in **vegetable oil** for 5 minutes. Add the **chopped tomatoes, onion, carrot** and **leek, garlic, lemon grass** and **curry powder** and roast for another 5 minutes. Remove the tray from the oven and add a little **white wine** to loosen any sediment. Transfer the contents of the tray to a large pan and add the remaining **wine** and **fish stock**. Bring to the boil and simmer for 20 minutes.

Remove the crabs with a perforated spoon, add the **rice** and continue to simmer for another 30 minutes or so. Strain through a fine sieve into another pan. Retain the vegetables, purée them in a liquidizer and add to the soup. Simmer for a short while longer to concentrate the flavours.

Crack the crab claws with a wooden mallet and remove the flesh to a bowl. Discard the shell. Chop the **spring onion** and the **garlic**, mix with the crabmeat and season with **salt and pepper**.

Prepare the spring rolls by filling each **wonton wrapper** with a teaspoon of crab mixture, rolling tightly and sealing with a little water. Deep-fry the rolls at **180°c** until crisp. Keep warm.

Quickly sauté the vegetable strips in a non-stick frying pan with a little sesame oil. Season. Divide between 4 soup bowls. Reheat the soup and whisk in the **rice vinegar**. Check the seasoning.

Ladle the soup into the bowls, drizzle with the remaining sesame oil and scatter with the **coriander leaves**. Serve the spring rolls alongside.

GRILLED CRASTER KIPPER, HOT NEW POTATOES AND BLACK VELVET

(Serves 4)

4	whole plump kippers
50g or more	unsalted butter
1	lemon
	milled black pepper
400g small	new potatoes (Pink Fir Apples or La Ratte), scrubbed
1tbsp	chopped chives
	sea salt flakes

Black Velvet

600ml	chilled Guinness
600ml	chilled champagne

Preheat the grill. Cook the **potatoes** in boiling, salted water. Cut the heads cleanly from the **kippers** with a large, sharp knife. Place them on the grill tray and cook under the hot grill until the bones can be removed easily.

Drain the potatoes and toss with the **chives** and a knob of butter.

Transfer to warm plates with the hot potatoes alongside. Place a slice of good butter onto the kippers and serve piping hot, together with a glass of cold **black velvet**.

Pour the **Guinness** between 4 chilled, half-pint schooners. Top up carefully with **champagne** and serve immediately

ROAST TOMATO SALAD WITH LOBSTER

(Serves 4)

4	large, ripe, round tomatoes
1	live lobster (1lb)
12	asparagus spears
100g	fine French beans, topped and tailed
	heart from 1 curly endive
4	very thin slices dry-cured, streaky bacon, grilled until crisp
	shavings of Parmesan
	extra virgin olive oil
	aged balsamic vinegar
	sea salt and milled black pepper

Rub the **tomatoes** with **olive oil** and place in the oven to roast at **200°c** for 20minutes. Remove and allow to cool to room temperature. Bring a large pan of salted water to the boil, plunge in the **lobsters**, cover and simmer for 4 minutes. Remove the lobster from the water and allow to cool.

In another pan of boiling, salted water, cook the **French beans** and then the **asparagus**. Refresh in iced water. Slip the skins from the **tomatoes** and place 1 tomato on each plate with a little **curly endive**. Cut the lobster into bite-sized pieces. *(Remove the claw-meat from the shells, but cut through the joints in the tail in order to leave the flesh attached to the shell.)* Place a pile alongside the tomato.

Dress the beans and asparagus with olive oil and **balsamic vinegar**, and season. Place a pile of beans and asparagus onto plates in a pyramid. Drizzle extra virgin olive oil and balsamic vinegar over and season well. Crumble the **streaky bacon** over the **endive** and finish with some **shaved Parmesan**.

Roast beetroot salad with jugged kippers

(Serves 4)

4	plump kipper fillets
100ml	olive oil
2	sliced shallots
	milled black pepper
4	large raw beetroot
4	handfuls small, peppery salad leaves (mustard leaves, red chard watercress, rocket, flat leaf parsley, mizuna), washed and spun dry
1	small bunch chives, cut into 1" sticks
1tsp	Dijon mustard
1tsp	crunchy honey mustard
120ml	extra virgin olive oil
1tbsp	sherry vinegar
	salt and pepper
½tsp	honey

Place the **kipper fillets** in a large, pyrex jug. Boil a kettle full of water and pour over the kippers. Leave for 5 minutes and then drain. Transfer to a porcelain dish in a single layer and pour over the **olive oil, shallots** and **pepper**. Leave to marinate overnight.

Wrap each **beetroot** in foil and bake for about 45 minutes to 1 hour, at **160°c** until tender. Remove from the oven and allow to cool enough to handle. Peel with a small knife, then cut each into eight wedges. Place in a bowl, season with **salt and pepper** and drizzle with **extra virgin olive oil**. Leave to marinate.

Whisk together the **mustards, vinegar, olive oil, salt, pepper** and **honey**. Toss the salad leaves together in a bowl, drizzle with **extra virgin olive oil** and season with **salt and pepper**. Arrange on four plates with the beetroot. Remove the kipper fillets from their marinade, cut neatly at an angle and place on the salad. Spoon the dressing over and around.

Potted kippers

(Serves 8)

100g	soft, unsalted butter
4tbsp	natural yoghurt
2tbsp	olive oil
2	egg yolks
450g	kipper fillets
4tbsp	chives, chopped
	juice from ½ lemon
	salt and pepper
50g	melted butter, cooled

Jug the **kipper fillets** by placing them in a pyrex bowl and covering with boiling water. Leave for 5 minutes before draining and allowing to cool. Mix the **egg yolk, lemon juice** and **yoghurt** in a liquidizer.

Slowly add the **olive oil** and **butter**, a little at a time. Remove to a bowl and stir in the **chives**.

Flake the flesh from the fish and add to the bowl with the chives and butter mixture. Stir, season with **salt** and lots of **milled black pepper**. Check the seasoning and spoon into 3" ramekins, filling to within ½" of the top. Seal each one with a tablespoon of **melted butter** and refrigerate.

Remove from the moulds and serve with some crisp salad leaves and lots of hot toast.

Mark Robertson
*Northumberland Cheese
Company*

Artisan Cheese

"I thought, well I've got the sheep, so why not give it a go? So we milked, and low and behold, turned it into a lump of concrete!

Back to the drawing board. Skills, knowledge, information and experience all needed to be acquired ASAP."

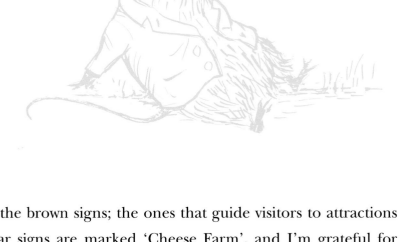

Today we're following the brown signs; the ones that guide visitors to attractions and places of note. These particular signs are marked 'Cheese Farm', and I'm grateful for their presence as we turn off from main road to side road to country lane to single track, and finally into the farmyard of Make Me Rich Farm, the present HQ of Mark Robertson's Northumberland Cheese Company.

But don't let me give you the idea that we're 'out-by', somewhere up in the hills and miles away in the back of beyond. This is the front of beyond, as we're but a few miles from the A1 and not many minutes from Newcastle International Airport; so not far from Newcastle's suburbs of Ponteland and Darras Hall. It looks as though a few denizens of those fair places have followed the brown signs too, and with good reason, for the Northumberland Cheese complex, with its tea room and shop, is now a popular stop for people combining a run out into the country with a chance to pick up some of their favourite cheese.

That name, Make Me Rich Farm. A lot of people, including me, have made the mistake of thinking that this is an ironic joke of Mark's. It isn't. This has been the name of this particular farm on the Ridley estate since at least 1700, long before the Northumberland Cheese Company came here. The name was generated by the quality of the land, for the farm sits on a patch of loam twenty feet deep, whilst the farms on either side are on yellow boulder clay. There is another similarly named farm in Northumberland, hard by Capheaton, which again owes its name to the quality of the land.

Although the present location of Northumberland Cheese Company isn't 'out-by', it used to be, for Mark Robertson started making cheese, in the early 1980s, at Soppit Farm in Redesdale, above Elsdon. (Not too far away from Monkridge Hill, Steve Ramshaw's farm, featured in the first chapter.) Originally, his family were from Scotland. Mark, a keen and very young flier (flying licence at sixteen and a half), was destined for the Fleet Air Arm until he found himself ruled out with a perforated eardrum.

So he turned to farming. Mark recalls, "I'd realized twenty years ago that the future of hill-farming wasn't exactly looking rosy, and was casting about for other ideas when I came across an article in a journal called the Business Opportunity Digest. The article featured a woman called Olivia Mills and she was milking sheep and making cheese."

You can tell by the way he remembers details and names that this was a momentous moment for Mark. He continues, "I thought, well I've got the sheep, so why not give it a go? So we milked, and lo and behold, turned it into a lump of concrete!"

Back to the drawing board. Skills, knowledge, information and experience all needed to be acquired ASAP. Mark's wife at the time was Dutch and so it seemed a good idea to visit her homeland and have a look at the way farmers in Holland were making cheese. Mark's reaction was, "If they can do it, so can I." He bought some Dutch equipment (everything in those days had to come from Holland), including an hundred-and-fifty-litre cheese vat, and came back and started milking sheep; by hand at first, although they soon moved on to platform-milking by machine. Mark also bought specialist milking sheep, Frieslands, and over the years moved on from that first lump of concrete to producing the Redesdale cheese that got him noticed as a cheesemaker of some repute. He did also milk some cows and used their milk to make Coquetdale and a Northumberland Gouda.

"Things weren't easy back then," says Mark with a shake of the head. "I was out on a limb in more ways than one, up in Northumberland with a new cheese. Trying to sell it was a nightmare. Making cheese on the farm, from sheep, was seen as a new thing, which is a bit odd because people in the past had obviously been doing it for a considerable time…

but customers had short memories. I was out there on my own. People had to be convinced and educated. There just weren't the knowledgeable customers. Now there's been a complete transformation. Nowadays people know about products such as my cheese, which is fine, but also these days people expect even higher standards and there's an awful lot of competition."

So there was Mark in the '80s, milking his sheep and inventing cheeses. He'd go off on busman's holidays and visit French cheese-making areas and find out how they did things. Mark remembers "my wife and I being on one French farm, waiting all morning for something to happen, like two little acolytes in a cheese-making temple. At 11.15 something did happen… a tray of coffee appeared for the high priest who then put in an appearance and solemnly pronounced it time for the curds to start their journey."

After watching the way the French used their texturing machines, Mark came back and had one of his own machines made, all the time working hard to improve his cheese, experimenting and making small changes. Mark is keen on texture and works hard on getting it right. The 'feel' is a great part of the attraction; he's really keen on getting his hands into the vat. "I find working the curds quiet therapeutic, actually," he smiles "and I'm sorry that concentrating on other aspects of the business keep me out of the cheese vat. Mind you, the cheese-making team are very happy that I'm not interfering."

Just getting people to stock his wares was a difficult task for Mark in the early days, and he acknowledges a debt to a man called Patrick Rance who ran the well-known Wells Store in Streatley, Berkshire. Mark feels that Rance single-handedly encouraged small scale, artisan cheesemakers in the 1970s and '80s by stocking and selling their wares. Mark knew

he'd got a good product, now the trick was to find some customers and get people talking about it. As time went on, more and more people began to take Mark's cheeses nationwide, although Mark is also keen to remember those local customers such as Corbridge Larder, Fenwicks, Linden Hall and the George Hotel.

Mark continued doing things right and keeping ahead of the game. People were beating a path to his Redesdale farm, eager to part with their money. So the cheesemaking was going well until 1993, when, as he puts it, his personal life took a drastic turn for the worse and hit the buffers, which ultimately meant that Soppitt Farm had to be sold. In 1996 Lord Ridley offered the now-divorced Mark the tenancy of the present farm and he started again. It wasn't easy. In fact it was a struggle, and it required taking out some loans, which thankfully have all been repaid now that the company is re-established and profitable, turning over half a million pounds under the Northumberland Cheese Company label, with which we now are familiar.

A French female graduate, who worked for Mark for a time in marketing, prompted this move from the Redesdale name. She felt that, outside the immediate area, few people would be certain where Redesdale actually was. (Most people probably associate 'dale' with North Yorkshire.) She was right; the name change has given the company a much stronger identity.

Despite all the obstacles, Mark started to graft his way back up. I've spoken to several people who know Mark well and who have great respect for the way in which he worked to get back on his feet again.

Mark's struggle to rebuild his business was not helped by the "nightmare" purchase of a pasteurizing machine that contaminated the process. It turned out to have a hidden design fault, which allowed raw milk to seep into the pasteurized. The location of the fault (a valve overcome by the head of pressure in the milk tank) took a great deal of time, effort and money to sort out. As did getting the manufacturers to take financial responsibility for the effects of the fault. It's long gone now, though.

The abolition of the Milk Marketing Board didn't help Mark either. Instead of dealing with a public monopoly which, as a small purchaser, he'd seen as largely benevolent, Mark found himself dealing with a private monopoly which he describes as "bloody vicious". Milk went up 30% in price overnight.

"Back then (immediately after privatization) the milk company saw me as a relatively small purchaser, as a pain in the neck, but things have changed. Via one of the companies, I'm able to pick and choose quality milk from single sources such as the Blagdon Herd and Wheelbirks Herd, whose Jersey milk goes into the Chevington Cheese. The goat's milk comes from a single source too. Nowadays I'm seen as quite an important customer, able to pass on a premium back to the supplier".

Mark feels that the way his life and cheese-making have evolved so far, as a small-scale producer, he couldn't both milk his own animals and make cheese; there just wasn't the time, and he'd been stretching resources well past the limit already. But in the future, who knows?

Current regulations don't allow Mark to make unpasteurized cheese from bought-in milk, so he has to pasteurize on site. The problems he had with that pasteurizing machine have led Mark to turn his back on the modern, standard method of flow pasteurization, and depend instead on a simpler, old-fashioned system of batch pasteurization. It is, as it sounds, a system where the whole batch of milk in the cheese vat is pasteurized, by being heated slowly to just over 60°c. This system has proved more thorough, but is also kinder on the milk than bashing it up to 72°c in a few seconds. Mark is certain that the consistency of the cheese in improved by the batch method, as it doesn't break down the protein in the milk.

So, when the milk has been pasteurized, what happens next?

"Well," jokes Mark, "I'm in the business of managing bugs… so we set them to work". Starter cultures are added to the milk and the bacteria become active, sending the milk on a journey towards destination cheese.

This is where technical change has, for once, favoured the small dairy, as formerly only the big places would have had the space and the finance to grow and manage the cultures. It's a very delicate job, as the cultures can be attacked by other organisms, including something called 'phage', a cheesemaker's nightmare.

From the 1980s onward the process of DVI, Direct Vat Inoculation, has made life much easier. This means that cultures can be bought freeze-dried and introduced directly into the milk in the vat. Mark would very much like to impress on people the idea that not all bacteria are bad and that many of them work for us. Indeed, some of them are essential for our survival.

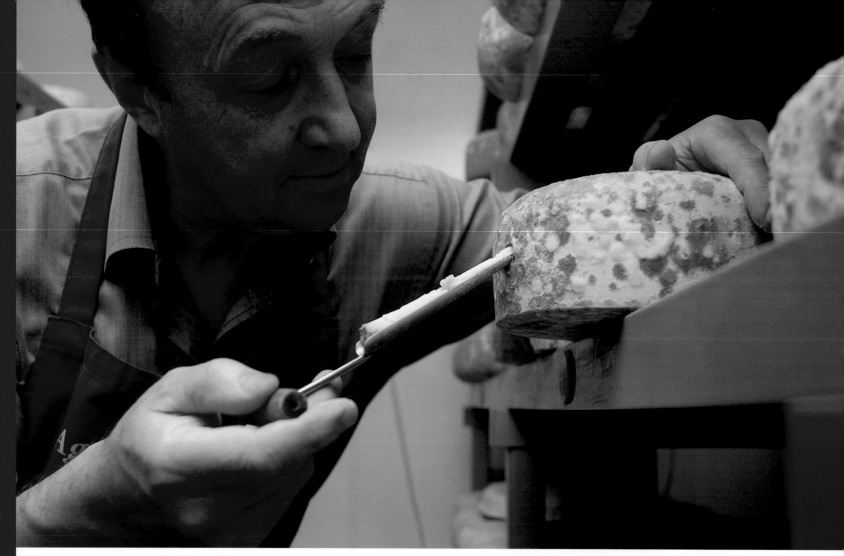

The starters work for Mark by creating acidity. Then the rennet is added to coagulate the milk, which produces the curds and whey. An important point to mention here is that the rennet used at Northumberland Cheese Company is non-animal rennet, so the cheese is suitable for vegetarians. Next, the curd is cut carefully and then, as the curds firm, the whey is separated off. The curds are then put into moulds, which are pressed. Mark does possess some beautiful, wooden, traditional presses, but also has some up-to-the-minute stainless steel versions, which hold more cheeses and are easier to use and manoeuvre.

After the cheeses have been pressed, then comes a crucial bit: the brine bath. "This is the stamp of individuality," states Mark proudly. " This is what alters the cheese and makes it our own". I ask what is in the brine baths and am told "salt". Which is fair enough, but I was wondering if I could get a little more specificity? "They're a world unto their own, are brine baths," is as much as Mark is prepared to divulge.

From the brine baths the cheeses go into store, where they start to dry; except for certain cheeses, which are kept in

damp conditions so that mould can begin to form on the cheese surfaces. The cheeses are carefully monitored, turned and moved, and the temperature and humidity of the stores are carefully controlled.

The whole process is painstaking, both in the long and short term. Cheese-making is affected by so many organic factors. Even the weather can affect the milk or the developing cheese. A careful eye has to be kept on the process at all times. Hygiene standards are very strict and there are lots of checks and verifications carried out with great regularity. Records are kept meticulously as batches progress through the process, with temperatures and other criteria recorded for future reference.

So, at the end of the process, what kind of cheeses do we have?

Mostly variations on the 'washed curd' recipes, and of a continental, smooth-textured cheese, rather than the traditional, English, crumbly, open-textured type. There's Original Northumberland Cheese, which is loosely based on a Gouda-style recipe. Mark describes this as having a "creamy and smooth, compact texture, with a mild initial taste followed by a lasting, full-flavoured aftertaste". In addition to Original, there's Nettled, and Smoked. Nettled has the said ingredient added to the cheese vat, so that the flavour spreads throughout the whole cheese. Smoked is slowly oak-smoked for up to four days at cool temperatures, so as not to affect the texture of the cheese. Smoked won the gold medal at the 1996 London International Cheese Competition and a first prize at the 2003 Bakewell Show, where Nettled took a second prize, too.

There's also Coquetdale. a French-style, semi-hard cheese. Maturing it in damp conditions, mentioned above, causes natural cellar mould on the outside, which partially softens the cheese when ripe. It won first prize at the Bakewell Cheese Show in 1993 and was described by the judges as ' a wonderfully creamy, clean cheese... a very fine cheese of good character... rich and buttery... a triumph of independent thinking!'

They liked it, then. A cheese 'of good character'; well, you just can't have a cheese hanging around racecourses in an old mac and a trilby now, can you? Seriously, Coquetdale deserves its prize and won a whole host of other awards too.

Next we'd better mention New Chevington. This is a semi-soft, mould-ripened cheese made with rich Jersey milk from Wheelbirks. It was first made well over a century ago, but then, after the death of the original cheesemaker, production ceased and the cheese vanished into obscurity. It has taken some patient detective work from Mark Robertson to track down a description of the original recipe in the Northumberland Records Office.

Now, with one or two variations necessary to comply with modern standards of cheese-making, Chevington is available again. Mark describes this one as "a cheese of delightful contradictions". At the British Cheese Awards at Blenheim in 2003, Chevington won a gold, which is very impressive indeed.

Then there's the Northumberland sheep's cheese, Redesdale, a pale cheese with a delicate taste when young, but which packs a punch at three months. Mark is absolutely clear that Redesdale is "sweet and pure with no hint of sheepiness". This one was on the prize-winner's podium too, at the 2003 Great Yorkshire Show, where it took a First. We must also mention the Northumberland goat cheese, of which there are two varieties, Elsdon and Brinkburn. Both have the same core characteristics: full, rich yet light, without excessive goaty tang. Brinkburn was developed from the Elsdon and is slightly drier, smoother and sharper. Mark believes the Elsdon is excellent for cooking. The Brinkburn won Silver Prize at the International Food Exhibition in 1999 for best new cheese, and took a silver at the 2003 British Cheese Awards. The details of all these cheeses and the many awards they have won can be inspected on Northumberland Cheese Company's website.

Finally, Mark wanted me to make sure that his dedicated team of cheese-makers got a mention for all their hard work, and for putting up with him. They're a very hands-on bunch, easily visible through a large, glass viewing panel in the wall of the cheese-making room as they get stuck in.

So follow those brown signs, take a look at what they're up to, and then pop upstairs for a cuppa... oh, and some cheese!

Cheese

Tips

Serving cheese:

Never serve cheese straight from the fridge. Leave at least an hour for the unwrapped cheese to have time to breathe and come up to room temperature. To get a balanced spread of textures and flavours, allow five different cheeses. A mature, hard cheese, a goat's cheese, a blue cheese, a soft cheese and a washed-rind cheese. Try and include a sheep's cheese, perhaps as the blue cheese. Serve with crisp, dry biscuits, sticks of celery and sweetish fruit, such as grapes or pears.

Sunday tea at our house was always homemade stotties with 'a slice of Dutch'. For years, the shiny, soapy, red-rind Edam was the only cheese I ever ate. Occasionally, for a treat, I might be given something even soapier, a bright orange brick called, rather pompously, Empire Cheddar. When I was a little older, I got hooked on Kraft Dairylea spread. If I'm honest, I'm still partial to a bit of Dairylea spread on toast at breakfast.

It wasn't until I worked in Europe – first in Switzerland, then France – that I discovered cheese came in all shapes, sizes and textures, and that it wasn't restricted to Sabbath-day eating. I discovered fondues, soufflés, quiches, sauces, pastries, even cheese for breakfast and cheese for pudding. Of course, when I returned to England, I was even more dismissive of British cheeses; clearly cheese was something that could only be made 'on the continent'.

A couple of days after we opened 21 Queen Street, in 1988, I had a visit from a chap called Charlie Wilson, from whom I bought various supplies. He presented me with a Bonchester cheese, a Camembert-type cheese made from unpasteurized Jersey milk on a farm in the Scottish borders. I laughed. To me, Camembert and Scotland went together like – well, like chalk and cheese. In a huff, he dumped it on the bench and marched out. That night, I took it home and tried it. I was staggered at the quality.

And so began a new interest in British cheeses. Happily, it coincided with a renaissance in British cheese-making, for which two people are largely to be thanked: Patrick Rance of the Wells Stores in Berkshire, a terrific authority on cheeses, Randolf Hodgson of Neal's Yard Dairy in Covent Garden and Juliet Harbut of Jeroboam's in London. For years, we have bought from Neal's Yard. I never phone and tell them what I want. Instead, I ask what's best.

They have a love affair with all their cheeses, nurturing, wooing, caring, so that nothing leaves the dairy in less than perfect condition.

When buying cheese, ask for a taste. A good cheesemonger, who cares about cheese, shouldn't object. Make sure it has been matured correctly. During maturation, the bacteria are getting to work, giving the cheese its depth and complexity of flavour. This is a process that can't be hurried. Any cheese that is pre-cut and vacuum-packed, by definition, has not been allowed to mature naturally. Avoid any cheese with a white 'bloom'; this means it has been sweating. Soft cheeses should be shiny in appearance and 'give' when gently prodded. A soft cheese that is chalky is under ripe, and hasn't a hope in hell of ripening once cut.

Anything that has been added – apricots, cranberries, herbs – is pure gimmick and should be avoided. My one exception to that rule is truffle-infused brie, which is split, flooded with fresh truffles and sandwiched back together again. Eaten with a glass of Cahors or good claret, this is heady but serious stuff.

The perennial debate is when to eat cheese. The English, traditionally, eat it after pudding; the French before. I side with the French on this one. The mouth is too full of sweet flavours if pudding is eaten first. Having said that, a bit of sweetness can do magical things to cheese. Blue cheese with pear, for instance, or mature cheddar with grapes – although I can't get away with the Yorkshire fad for eating apple pie with Wensleydale. One of the most extraordinary combinations was served to me recently in an Australian restaurant in London. (Unlikely, I know, but bear with me.) Exmoor Blue cheese was drizzled with truffle-infused honey, a handful of toasted walnuts slipped on the side. I practically scooped the glaze off the plate.

When it comes to cooking with cheese, the general rule is to choose a mature rather than a young cheese. As the cheese is going to be added to other ingredients, its own flavour is necessarily diluted, so you need something powerful. You also need a reasonably high fat content so that it will melt easily and smoothly. A soufflé, for example, needs good, mature cheddar to give bite and acidity to all that butter and cream.

Having said all that, I'm now going to contradict myself. Gruyère is often the cheese of choice for cooking, particularly in a quiche, and Mozzarella is traditionally used in pizzas, as well as making a fantastic accompaniment to tomatoes. Both cheeses are relatively bland. The lesson? Experiment and see what you like.

And then there's goat's cheese. Never has the humble goat been so fashionable. Its chalky-white cheese pops up on menus from the grandest dining rooms to the scruffiest motorway service station. I first came across hot goat's cheese in France in the early '80s. It was served, just melted, in a salad. I realized that, when cooked, it takes on a wholly different flavour and texture, losing its dryness and 'goatiness', becoming sweeter and milder. It's great breadcrumbed and deep-fried, crumbled in a salad or used in a soufflé. We put a spin on the traditional burger by serving lamb, spiced with cumin and coriander, and served with a wedge of goat's cheese on top. Beware the goat's cheese that is too young. Too high a moisture content and it can taste soapy and bland.

Cheese is one of life's great comfort foods. In many ways, it is at its best when very little is done to it. A wedge of blue cheese eaten with a sweet Williams pear and a glass of sauternes is simple but perfect.

Mark Robertson *Northumberland Cheese Company*

Artisan Cheese

NORTHUMBERLAND CHEESE, LEEK AND MUSTARD SOUFFLE

(8 soufflés)

50g	soft butter
50g	dried breadcrumbs
450ml	full fat milk
½	onion
1	bay leaf
1	clove
75g	butter
75g	flour
1tbsp	English mustard powder
175g	leeks, cut into 1cm dice, washed and drained
25g	butter
250g	grated Northumberland cheese
6	egg yolks
2tbsp	chopped chives
6	egg whites
1 tiny pinch	salt

Heavily butter eight 3" ramekins and dust out with breadcrumbs. Chill.

Stud the **onion** with the **clove** and **bay leaf**. Add to the **milk** and bring to the boil. Remove from the heat, cover with a lid and allow to infuse.

Melt the **butter** in a small, thick-bottomed saucepan. Stir in the **flour** and allow to cook over a gentle heat for 15 minutes to make a roux. Stir in the **English mustard powder**. Strain and reheat the milk. Add to the roux, one ladle at a time, stirring continually with a spatula and allowing the sauce to boil between each addition. When all of the milk is incorporated, reduce the heat to low and allow to cook gently for 15–20 minutes, stirring regularly.

Place the **leeks** in a small saucepan with the butter and 2 tablespoons of water. Season with **salt and pepper**, cover with a lid and cook gently over a medium heat. Drain in a colander when tender. Stir into the sauce.

Remove the sauce from the heat and stir in the **cheese** and **egg yolks**. Cover with cling film to keep warm.

Preheat the oven to **135°c**. Boil a kettle of water. Whisk the **egg whites** until they begin to thicken, add the **salt** and continue whisking until quite firm (beware of 'graining' and drying out). Beat ⅓ of the whites into the sauce with a wire whisk. Fold in the remainder carefully.

Divide the mixture between the soufflé moulds and place the moulds into a deep roasting tray. Pour boiling water around them, transfer to the oven and bake for 25 minutes.

Remove the soufflés from oven and allow to cool for 2–3 minutes.

Increase the oven temperature to **190°c**. Turn out the soufflés into individual ovenproof dishes and pour over 200ml **double cream**, dividing it between the four. Return to the hot oven for 8 minutes, or until golden brown and double in size.

Serve immediately with a salad of crisp leaves in walnut oil dressing.

THREE CHEESE RAVIOLI

(Serves 4)

You can simplify this recipe if you wish by using Won Ton wrappers, readily available in Asian supermarkets, rather than making your own pasta dough. Simply place a little filling on each wrapper, brush the edges with water and fold over to seal. Poach in boiling, salted water for 1 minute.

110g	Brinkburn goat's cheese, grated
55g	New Chevington cheese, crumbled
55g	Redesdale cheese, grated
1	small baked potato, pulp removed and mashed
2	eggs
2tbsp	chopped chervil
2tbsp	chopped chives
	salt and milled white pepper
350g	pasta dough
1	egg, beaten
a little	semolina

Sauce

250ml	chicken stock
110g	soft butter
3tbsp	grated Redesdale cheese
1tbsp	chopped chervil
1tbsp	chopped sage
1tbsp	chopped marjoram

Combine the **cheese, potato** and **eggs** in a bowl. Beat well with a wooden spoon and add the herbs. Season with **salt and pepper** and set aside to chill in the refrigerator. Cut the **pasta dough** in half and work with half the dough at a time, keeping the other half covered with cling film.

Lightly dust your work surface with a little flour. Using a pasta machine, roll out the dough thinly into a strip about 125mm wide x 700mm long. Brush the pasta with a little **beaten egg**. Divide the filling into teaspoon-sized portions and place them on the dough about 50mm apart. Roll out the second piece of pasta dough and lay over the first, pressing down well to seal around the filling. Cut out each ravioli with a 30mm fluted pastry cutter. Set aside on a tray, lightly dusted with **semolina**.

Bring a large pan of salted water to a full boil. Throw in the raviolis and allow to come back to the boil. Allow to simmer for 1 minute before removing with a slotted spoon and refreshing in iced water. Drain well and store refrigerated, covered with cling film until needed.

To make the sauce, bring the **chicken stock** to the boil with freshly milled pepper. Whisk in the **butter** and allow to simmer for a few minutes. Remove from the heat and keep warm. Just before serving, stir the **Redesdale** into the sauce, add the raviolis and chopped **herbs**. Cook together for 3–4 minutes and divide between 4 large bowls. Offer additional grated parmesan and milled black pepper.

WARM TOMATO AND GOAT'S CHEESE TART

(Serves 4)

225g	puff pastry
1	egg
2tbsp	milk
12	large, ripe, plum tomatoes
8	garlic cloves
1	sprig thyme
2tbsp	extra virgin olive oil
1tbsp	unsalted butter
200g	sliced onions
3	thyme sprigs (leaves only)
115g	soft goat's cheese
2tbsp	double cream
2tbsp	pesto
2tbsp	chopped chives
1tsp	puréed garlic

Salad

1	small head curly endive
8	black olives, halved
8	cherry tomatoes, halved
1tbsp	chervil leaves
4	chive stalks in ½" lengths
8	basil leaves
16	fine French beans, cooked
65ml	extra virgin olive oil
½tbsp	lemon juice
2tbsp	pesto, thinned with olive oil
	sea salt and milled black pepper

Preheat the oven to *80°c*. Plunge the **tomatoes** into a large pan of boiling water, count to 5, remove immediately and plunge into iced water. Remove the tomato skins, cut the tomatoes in half and gently squeeze out the seeds. Arrange, cut-side down, on a stainless steel baking tray, sprinkle very lightly with **coarse sea salt**, scatter with the **thyme sprigs** and **whole, unpeeled garlic cloves**. Drizzle over a little **olive oil** and place in the oven until semi-dried (4–6 hours).

Raise the oven temperature to *200°c*. Roll out the pastry onto a floured board to a thickness of 2mm and cut with a 100mm pastry cutter into 4 discs. Refrigerate for 20 minutes. Beat the **egg** together with the **milk** and brush the pastry with this. Prick the pastry all over with a fork and bake until golden (10–12 minutes).

Sweat the **onions** and **thyme leaves** in butter, season and cook until lightly caramelized. Set aside. Mix together the **goat's cheese, cream, pesto, chives** and **garlic**. Season with **salt and pepper**.

Brush four 100ml non-stick tart tins with **olive oil**. Arrange the semi-dried tomatoes so that both the base and sides of the moulds are completely covered. Warm through in a low oven. Warm the caramelized onions also.

Place a scoop of **goat's cheese** into each mould, spoon a portion of onions on top, place a puff pastry disc on top of both and press down gently. Invert each tart onto the centre of a salad plate.

Toss the **salad ingredients** together in a small bowl. Remove the mould and arrange a bouquet of salad on top of each tart. Drizzle a little thinned **pesto** around.

WELSH RAREBIT

(Serves 4 as a light snack)

Welsh Rarebit and Welsh Rabbit are both English terms for a dish of melted cheese and beer on toast, presumably so-called as an insult to the once impoverished Welsh, who were said to eat it instead of the rabbit meat which they lacked.

50g	butter
50g	flour
210ml	milk
75ml	beer
25g	English mustard
340g	mature Cheddar-type cheese, grated
	salt and pepper
4 slices	Ciabatta, toasted
3–4 drops	Worcestershire sauce
	chopped chives
	cracked black pepper

Pre-heat the grill to its highest setting. Melt the ***butter*** in a small saucepan and stir in the ***flour***. Cook slowly over a low heat for 5 minutes. Heat the ***milk*** to boiling point and add, one ladle at a time, stirring until smooth between each addition. Add the ***beer, mustard*** and ***Worcestershire sauce***. Add the ***cheese*** and cook gently for 3–4 minutes until melted. Do not boil. Season with ***salt and pepper***.

Spread the mixture onto the ***ciabatta*** and brown under the grill. Sprinkle with the ***chopped chives*** and ***cracked pepper***.

Farmers' market salad

(Serves 6)

This is a 'no rules' salad; visit the market, buy what is good and sling it all together.
This version is designed around spring ingredients; it would be a very different salad in winter where it would include
celeriac and leeks, sliced very finely and deep-fried for extra texture.

300g	seasonal salad leaves (Cos, oakleaf, endive, lambs lettuce, watercress, rocket, dandelions etc)
1	fennel bulb, very thinly sliced
100g	radishes, very thinly sliced
225g	asparagus
110g	green beans
	salt and milled black pepper
60ml	honey and lemon dressing
110g	Redesdale cheese
1	avocado pear
1	lemon, halved
1	roasted beetroot, peeled and cut into fine matchsticks
	rind from 1 lemon, removed with a potato peeler, cut into very fine strips and blanched for 1 minute in boiling water then refreshed in iced water
3 slices	white country bread, crusts removed and turned into breadcrumbs
50g	clarified butter

First make the dressing. Combine the **honey, lemon juice** and **mustard** in a bowl. Season with a little **salt and pepper**. Whisk in the **sunflower oil** slowly, followed by the lemon oil.

Heat the **clarified butter** in a large, non-stick frying pan. As it begins to sizzle, throw in the **breadcrumbs** and stir continuously over a medium heat. Continue cooking until crumbs are golden brown and crisp. Tip immediately into a colander to drain, then transfer to a plate lined with kitchen paper, season.

Trim and wash all of the **salad leaves** then mix in a bowl with the **fennel** and **radishes**. Peel the **asparagus** and cook in boiling, salted water for 4–5 minutes before refreshing in iced water. Drain.

Cook the **beans** in boiling, salted water also and refresh. Drain. Add the vegetables to the salad leaves and toss gently with the dressing. Cut the **cheese** into fine slivers. Peel and halve the **avocado**, slice as thinly as possible, squeeze the lemon juice over.

Divide the lettuces and vegetables between six bowls. Top with several slivers of **Redesdale**, 2 slices of **avocado** and a small bundle of **beetroot**. Sprinkle with the fried breadcrumbs and **lemon zest**.

Honey and Lemon Dressing

3tbsp	Dijon mustard
50ml	lemon Juice
1tsp	honey
150ml	sunflower oil
2tbsp	lemon-flavoured extra virgin olive oil
	salt and pepper to taste

Anne, Hugh,
Archie & Lizzy Gray
Ravensworth Grange Farm

Pork

"Dead Opposite The Angel"

That's how Hugh Gray now describes the location of their family farm, Ravensworth Grange. In the past you might have said 'near Ravensworth Castle' or 'near Kibblesworth Pit', but Lord Ravensworth's Victorian pile fell into ruin and was knocked down in the 1930s and the pit went in 1974. So nowadays, saying that the farm is facing Anthony Gormley's sculpture *The Angel of the North,* on the opposite side of the

134

To get to Ravensworth Grange from Newcastle, we head south on the A1, gratefully exiting the tailback of traffic at the Lamesley turn, not far from the bustling Metro Centre and Team Valley trading estate. We find ourselves, somewhat surprisingly, moving straight out into countryside, where we quickly encounter the ancient church of St Andrew, Lamesley, its tower and graveyard complete with be-mossed and canted eighteenth-century gravestones. We turn at the church to head up the western side of the valley, passing the thriving Ravensworth Arms. In contrast, we also pass through the forlorn ex-pit village of Kibblesworth, where half a winding wheel is set up on the village green as a memorial to bygone mining days. There's a distinct lack of thrive.

We head out of the village, and although you know that the A1, the trading estate and the rail marshalling yards are only a little way behind, up here you could be back a hundred years. Avoiding horses, you wend a narrow way down leafy lanes, past high hedges and Victorian cottages. Cresting the hill you get a view across the High Pennines, and south towards the famous Beamish Open Air Museum only a few miles away. We can also see the Ravensworth opencast mining site. Extraction has stopped now and the site is in the process of being filled in and landscaped.

Nearby we take a track, and this leads us to Ravensworth Grange Farm, where, outside the buildings ranged on the hillside, Hugh Gray is waiting with a welcome. Several sheep dogs also wait with their own welcome. An older dog eyes me with the malevolent stare that spaghetti western locals reserve for strangers in town. Like them, he doesn't stir from his patch and doesn't give much away. Another dog, Sweep, is young, boisterous and welcoming.

Hugh takes me inside, and I'm just sitting down to a cup of tea as Ann Gray returns from picking up son Archie from

school, accompanied by three-year-old-daughter Izzy. Before I can get onto the subject of pigs, Archie commands my attention to tell of his all-consuming passion for birds, particularly chickens. His father is building him a hen house and Archie already has his breeding programme mapped out. Archie is six. He draws me a picture as Izzy gets stuck into the biscuits.

Family life is obviously very important to Ann and Hugh Gray. They firmly believe that family farms are an important part of our heritage and culture, and worth saving. So retaining Ravensworth as a family farm is the driving force behind their diversification into high quality, rare breed pork production, and their strategy of selling directly to the public.

The family farm… that's why all their names are featured above.

As Ann says, "Family farms cannot compete directly with agribusiness, which can spread its costs across many acres. You have to do something different. I could have gone into teaching, or continued being an agricultural consultant, but that wouldn't have left us with a working family farm, so we went in for something different. Middle Whites"

Notice that word that brings that certain look into Terry Laybourne's eyes when he talks about produce. 'Different'.

Keeping it in the family

So we know the Grays want to keep the farm in the family, but how did it get there in the first place? Well, Hugh's great grandfather took the tenancy in 1888… except he didn't. His wife did. She was the widow of a corn merchant, and whilst Hugh's great-grandfather was away 'looking at farms', she made the decision for him and took the worst clod of coal and stone in the district, because she liked the name.

They'd decided to move from growing wheat at Birtley, because the opening up of the Canadian prairies meant that the price of wheat had plummeted. The move to Ravensworth in 1888 wasn't quite 'out of the frying pan', but very nearly, for they soon realized that whenever they ploughed a furrow there was always a dark line of coal showing across the field!

In the next generation, Hugh's grandfather didn't farm here. Great Uncle John Willie did. Great Aunties Lizzie and Mary lived here too. Great Uncle suffered from appendicitis, and Hugh's father (one of nine and the youngest boy) went up to Ravensworth to help out. Not that he was given much choice, but he didn't see it as being sidelined so much as his big break, a chance to strike out on his own. He was happy here and never left.

The farm was part of the Ravensworth estate and was later sold to the mine-owners, Bowes and Partners.

Just before nationalization they sold it to Hugh's father
as a sitting tenant.

Ann's family didn't actually farm back in West Yorkshire,
in *Last of the Summer Wine* country, but they were well
involved in rural life. What brought her to Ravensworth?
She came here as an agricultural student on attachment
from Harpur Adams College, and she married the farmer.
Now where have we heard that before? Oh yes. Ruth Archer!

Part of the large farmhouse at Ravensworth provides a
home for Hugh's sister, but in Hugh and Ann's part of
the dwelling, evidence can be seen of earlier occupation.
A thick, outside wall now runs through the middle of the
house. We know this because recently, when a damp-proof
course was added, plaster was scraped off the walls revealing
that the stones behind still had moss on them from their
sojourn outside. There is also a giant of a fireplace in the
kitchen, not a range, but a massive open fire with a
Cleopatra's Needle for a lintel. Upstairs, too, there's more
evidence of days gone by: initials carved into the window
sills, which are thought to be those of the hired lads who
would have mucked in together up there. There are also
dents in the door, made, it's thought, by Auntie banging
on it to wake up the said lads first thing in the morning.

So the Grays have been at Ravensworth for over a hundred
years, although Hugh and Ann joked that they like to tell

people they've just arrived… and that's why things are so untidy! The farm is about 200 acres at the moment. In addition to the pigs there are sheep, and Hugh grows his own barley for feed. There will also be some Aberdeen Angus cattle soon, as Ravensworth branches out into beef production, but for now let's concentrate on their pigs.

Middle Whites and serendipity

Middle Whites are a rare breed, with about three hundred and five breeding females in the UK. They originated by crossing Large Whites and Small Whites in Keighley, West Yorkshire, in the 1850s. They're white with prick ears and have a short, wide head, with a face that looks as though someone's clouted them with a shovel. In polite pig circles this is known as 'dished'. Early to mature and quick to grow, they have a reputation for succulent, sweet-tasting pork. They're very popular with the Emperor of Japan, where a shrine has been dedicated in their honour. Not a lot of people know that!

They are a specialist pork breed, not a bacon pig, although you can, like Ann Gray, produce bacon from them. The rashers just won't be very big. They're docile and easy to keep and are usually good mothers. They're economical, turning feed into pork very efficiently, which made them a popular pig between the wars: the pig at the bottom of

the garden or the allotment would have most likely been a Middle White. They lost some ground after the Second World War, as the push for large quantities of cheap food, standardization and the rise of the Danish bacon pig affected their popularity, but in the 1990s they started to regain it when meat quality, rather than quantity, became important.

Having decided to stay 'down on the farm' and do something different, what made the Grays plump for Middle White pigs? This is where fate stepped in, as Hugh explains: "About ten years ago I was working part-time on a city farm for the Council, and they had rare breeds, including a Middle White sow in pig. The piglets were brought up to weight and then offered to the staff as pork. I said, 'Yes. I'll have one, but I want mine live.' And that's how it came about. Then a woman in Devon offered the city farm a Middle White boar, but they didn't want it, so again, I said I'd have it. The city farm had bought a Tamworth Boar, which I had to go and collect, so I arranged to pick up the Middle White as well. The Council's transport department, they loved us at the city farm, I can tell you!" laughs Hugh, remembering the looks on faces when he filled in 'purpose of journey' as he requisitioned a van.

He continues his tale: "We set off, met the other people halfway and did a transfer at a motorway service station.

Which was an interesting experience, swapping pigs between vehicles in a car park! So there I am heading back to the north east with two boars in the back. They were alright whilst we were moving, but every time I stopped at a traffic light they chased each other around the van. That's how that first Middle White boar came here and we ended up with a pair of Middle Whites."

That was in the early days. Now, Ravensworth moves its pigs, on the one journey they are forced to take, in more comfort than that first Middle White hitch-hiker.

When Hugh and Ann had kept Middle Whites for a while and tasted the meat, the penny dropped that these pigs exactly fitted the bill as that 'something different' in which they'd been looking to specialize. But they also knew that the price of Middle Whites meant selling directly to the public, and soon Ann was turning up at the farmers' markets in Newcastle and Whitley Bay, where now they're doing very nicely, thank you.

At the moment Hugh and Anne have six sows and two boars. Why two? Because that means they can have two lines without interbreeding. Actually, they have three boars, because they have a lodger. A young boar was prevented from leaving when foot-and-mouth broke out. By the time the all clear came, he was too mature to send to slaughter, because the hormonal changes produce a very noticeable taint in the meat. At the moment he's eating and growing and Hugh is very fond of him, but he's looking for a good home, because he's eating and growing and…

Ideally the Grays ought to be able to produce nearly a hundred pigs a year, but despite good breeding stock and the best of husbandry, nature never lets things go ideally to plan, so actually it's a few less. Still, very good for a small family farm.

The Grays' pigs are fed on a mixture of home grown barley and bought-in soya as the source of protein. No growth promoters are used and no antibiotics. As a registered feed mixer, Ravensworth Grange is subject to random checks by Trading Standards officers, who have the feed analysed. The randomness of their visits can be a little difficult. One lot of inspectors turned up just after feeding time and demanded to look at the feed. "It's in there", said Hugh, pointing to the pigs. Ravensworth have passed all these feed checks with clean bills of health.

The development of pigs to a weight where they can be sent off for slaughter is not time-scaled, like a commercial farm. They leave when they are ready. When I asked Hugh how he knew, he gave me a look; the same look he had given me when I asked how he decided which gilts to keep for breeding. Instantly, I knew where I'd seen that look before: in the eyes of old stockmen of previous generations. I have written several plays about life on the land in the early twentieth century, and interviewed lots of old farm workers in their eighties. If I asked them a similar question, they would give me this look and say, "Well, you just knew these things", or "you had an eye for it". What they meant was that

140

it was experience, intuition and stockmanship. The same applies to Hugh. He has an eye for it. Interestingly, he told me that after the break for foot-and-mouth, he made a mistake in keeping a pig back a bit, and he realized that he would have to get his eye back in.

We're not, however, talking guesswork here. No, we are talking about judging things exactly right, without the need for a lot of weighing and measuring. I think we should point out that both Hugh and Ann have degrees in agriculture, and, if pressed, will be able to tell you the exact percentage of lean content and 'probe depth' of fat that their pigs have produced.

Sows at Ravensworth are farrowed inside with access to heat. The piglets leave their mother at eight to ten weeks old, which is somewhat later than the commercial herd time of three weeks. They're allowed to trundle along outside, in and around the arks. They are not fed a high density diet,

family groups are not mixed, and Ann and Hugh do not find it necessary to dock tails or cut teeth. If the animals are not stressed then they don't need it. In winter they're housed inside, as Middle Whites really do not like being outside when it's cold. (No-one from Keighley does.)

When Hugh decides they're ready, they're sold at about six months. They are taken away for slaughter locally, 'first up the line', with as much care as Hugh can oversee. Then it's back to be dealt with by the resident butcher in the cutting room, which is a recent addition to the farm. From there Ravensworth Middle White Pork goes out for sale.

The farmers' market

As briefly mentioned, Ann retails most of her specialist pork at the local farmers' markets, taking leg joints, loin joints, chops, diced pork for casserole, stir-fry strips and dry-cured bacon. She also makes her own sausages to various recipes: Traditional, Cumberland, Pork and Leek, and Garlic. For anyone with a gluten intolerance, Ann will produce gluten-free sausages. Now they have a reputation, more and more people are coming to the farm to buy direct. This will increase when the farm buildings currently being renovated come into use as a sales outlet.

On my visit to Ravensworth, it was obvious to me that we were looking at good stock which was well fed. The pigs looked happy outside on the sunny day I visited, but they're well cared for inside when necessary. Hugh and Ann are folk of generous spirit and are not keen to criticize their fellows, but, at the risk of embarrassing them, I'll venture that they are definitely a cut above the average pig producer, and are succeeding at their family-farm-saving goal of producing something different and special.

Pork

I don't know anyone who doesn't salivate at the smell of
sizzling bacon. Even vegetarians will admit to a wave of
nostalgia for a bacon sandwich. A piece of bacon seems to
sum up, in a very ordinary way, what a well presented piece
of meat should be: succulent yet crisp, simple yet satisfying.

But there is far more to pork than bacon, or the popular
roast joints, very good though those all are. Unfortunately –
possibly because of its tendency to dryness and blandness,
possibly because of bad memories of school dinners – pork
has always been rather underrated, overshadowed by the
more regal beef or the sweeter lamb. This is a pity; it is a
hugely versatile meat.

My eyes were first opened to the potential of pork when
I worked in Germany in the seventies. Cuts such as
pork knuckle – a poor man's dish in Britain – were served,
crunchy, moist and juicy, in classy, five-star hotels.
Back in the UK, however, I couldn't find a comparable
quality of product. The appetite, both in fashionable
restaurants and, indeed, of the public, was for leaner
meat. It looked nicer and was, supposedly, healthier.
Pigs were reared to have very little fat covering. However,
although a fat-free joint may look attractive on the
butcher's slab, for me to be able to deliver a succulent,
moist piece of pork, I want, and need, fat.

All this changed, thank goodness, with the growth of interest in rare breeds. Breeds such as the Middle White pigs which we buy for our kitchens are reared as nature intended, with a natural, and fairly high, fat content. To a chef, it's a joy. When cooked, the fat lifts and separates into feather-light layers, just like puff pastry.

One of the biggest attractions of pork is that there is very little wastage. In kitchen parlance, it's 'nose-to-tail' eating. I worked with an Italian chap called Franco Cetteloni, who owned The Fisherman's Lodge in Jesmond, Newcastle. Franco came from a village in the hills near Sienna. Every family in his village kept a pig and once a year the pig-slaughterer would come to kill the animals. The first product that was made was black pudding, as the blood needed to be used while still fresh. Then they ate dishes made with liver or kidney. Slowly, throughout the year, the family ate their way through the animal. The most desirable parts, certainly for a young boy, were the dried sausages, the *salumi* or *salssiccia*. But no one was allowed to touch these until the very end. After hearing this, I came away thinking I knew very little about cooking!

With a little bit of application, however, it's possible to use pork in almost the same creative way as those Italian families. I say almost. I've tried all sorts of clever, continental ways to air-dry the meat to make salamis and salted hams, but with not very clever results. The British air, I suspect, is too damp.

So here's what we do in our kitchens. The trotters, wonderfully fatty and gelatinous, we add to veal stock, or use to give succulence when braising drier meats such as venison. The belly we braise – sometimes marinating first in something spicy, like soy sauce with Chinese spices – and serve with lentils. We do the same with the spare ribs, which make a very quick and tasty staff lunch. Liver we pan-fry, kidney we grill.

The loin can either be cut into pork steaks, pan-roasted and then finished in the oven, or stuffed, rolled and roasted. (If the joint is particularly lean, soak overnight in a brine bath to counteract the dryness.) Pork loves a little sweetness, so experiment with stuffings made of apples, prunes or apricots. The shoulder we use as the basis for game and duck terrines.

A joint not normally used in this country is the neck, but when working in Germany I discovered that it is a fantastically moist, flavoursome piece of meat. I have the butcher take out the neck muscle, then give the meat some fairly serious seasoning, or salt it overnight, before cooking it very slowly in rendered pork fat. I promise you, the end result will surprise you. It has a lot more interest than roast loin.

TERRINE OF HAM KNUCKLE AND FOIE GRAS
SERVED WITH PEASE PUDDING

(Serves 12)

This terrine became the signature dish of 21 Queen Street and I think embodied everything that that restaurant was about; quality, simplicity and generosity, with just a note of humour. I made this for the first time to poke a little fun at some over-serious foodies, and it was intended as a once-only dish. I was still making it 12 years later, and every time I tried to take it from the menu there was a public outcry!

Foie gras

1	fresh foie gras, around 625g
1½tsp	salt
½tsp	sugar
½tsp	milled white pepper
1 pinch	mace
2tbsp	Armagnac
2tbsp	Madeira

Ham

4	ham knuckles, soaked overnight in lots of cold water
6	carrots
2	large onions
4	celery sticks
165g	leeks
1	bay leaf
2	cloves
8	black peppercorns
1	bunch thyme
5	garlic cloves
3½tbsp	vinegar

Pease pudding

350g	yellow split peas
1 tiny pinch	bicarbonate of soda
100ml	walnut oil
45ml	tarragon vinegar

Remove the *foie gras* from the fridge and allow to soften at room temperature for 30 minutes, still in it's vacuum bag. Separate the two lobes and make a lengthways cut down the inside of each lobe. With a small knife, remove any veins or stained areas. Turn over and remove the delicate outer skin from the liver. Place the pieces of liver side by side in a small dish. Season with the *salt, sugar and pepper*. Sprinkle over the *Armagnac* and *Madeira*, cover with cling film and r efrigerate overnight.

Soak the *split peas* overnight for the pease pudding.

Next day, allow the *foie gras* to come to room temperature again before rolling in a double thickness of cling film into a sausage shape, 12" long and about 2" in diameter. Heat a pan of water to *72°c* and poach the foie gras for 20 minutes. Keep checking that the temperature of the water doesn't creep above *72°*. Remove from the water and plunge into a tray of iced water to cool immediately. When cool but not cold, twist the ends of the cling film in order to tighten up the sausage shape. Chill.

Place the *ham* in a large pot and cover with plenty of cold water. Bring to the boil and skim off any impurities. Add *vegetables, herbs, spices* and *vinegar* to the pot. Simmer very gently for 4 hours. Cool.

While the ham is cooking, make the *pease pudding*. Rinse the soaked peas, place in a saucepan and cover by about ½" with fresh, cold water. Bring to the boil, skim and simmer very gently until the peas are tender. Season with *salt* and simmer a little longer until the peas start to collapse. Drain in a sieve and allow to cool. When cold, process until smooth in a food processor, adding *walnut oil* and *tarragon vinegar* a little at a time. Check seasoning and adjust if necessary.

When the *ham* is cooked, lift it out of the water with the *carrots* and discard everything else. Line a 1½ltr cast iron terrine with a triple thickness of cling film. When the ham is cool enough to handle, strip off the skin and set aside. Strip off the meat in large chunks and cut the *carrots* into ½" dice. Scrape and discard excess fat from the inside of the ham skin.

Line the base of the terrine with a layer of skin, then place in a *layer of ham pieces*, season and scatter some *diced carrots*. Add another layer of ham. Unwrap the foie gras and lay it down the centre of the terrine, cover with a layer of ham, season and scatter more carrots. Add one more layer using all of the remaining ham, then cover with the remaining skin. Cover with cling film, place a wooden board on top and press with a very heavy weight. Chill overnight with the weight still in place.

Next day, turn out the terrine, trim the sides neatly and cut into thick slices. Serve with a small bundle of *salad leaves* dressed in *walnut oil*, and a large portion of *pease pudding*, which should be at room temperature.

PORK GOULASH

(Serves 8)

I find the food of Eastern Europe very comforting if perhaps a little filling.
Make this in large quantities; it reheats really well. Perfect late night party food where lots of beer is involved!

60ml	vegetable oil
1125g	pork shoulder cut into 1½" dice
2	onions, sliced
2	garlic cloves, finely chopped
150g	streaky bacon cut into ½" lardons
1ltr	chicken stock
60g	sweet paprika
1tbsp	hot paprika
2	bay leaves
450g	sauerkraut
1tbsp	red wine vinegar
750g	potatoes, peeled and cut into 1" chunks
	sea salt
½tsp	caraway seeds, finely chopped
	sour cream to serve

Season the *pork* and fry in *half of the oil* until well browned on all sides. Lift out onto a plate and reserve. In another pan, sweat the *onions, garlic* and *lardons* in the remaining oil, without allowing them to brown. Add the *pork*, along with any juices which may have collected. Add the *paprika, bay leaves* and *chicken stock*. Bring to a boil and reduce the heat to a simmer. Cook very gently, uncovered, for 45 minutes, skimming any fat as it comes to the surface. Stir in the *sauerkraut, vinegar* and *potatoes*. Continue cooking until the pork is tender (about 30 minutes).

Remove from the heat and check the seasoning. Add the *caraway seeds* and *more paprika* if needed. Serve piping hot, in large bowls, with a dollop of sour cream on top.

MARINATED PORK STEAK
WITH ROSEMARY AND GARLIC

(Serves 4)

We don't normally associate pork with rosemary. In Italy, however, it's a different story. Eat porchetta from one of the many il porchetaro vans in Tuscan villages and it will be packed with the stuff. It doesn't take a lot to become addicted. If you really enjoy big herby flavours you could add some sage and oregano, or even a pinch of dried fennel seeds.

6 x 225g	boneless pork loin steaks, 1" thick from a Middle White pig
	salt and milled black pepper
2tbsp	lard
2tbsp	butter
	needles from 4 rosemary sprigs
1	lemon
150ml	Noilly Prat
150ml	brown chicken stock
25g	unsalted butter, chilled

Marinade

3tbsp	lemon juice
3tbsp	olive oil
4	rosemary sprigs
1	garlic clove, crushed and puréed

Marinate the **pork** by seasoning the steaks with **salt and pepper**. Place in a deep stainless steel tray or china dish. Pour over the **oil** and **lemon juice**. Strip the needles from the **rosemary** and add along with the **crushed garlic**. Turn the steaks 3 or 4 times to ensure that the rosemary and garlic is well distributed. Cover the tray with cling film and refrigerate for 12 hours, turning a couple of times during this period.

Remove the meat from the marinade and dry thoroughly on a clean cloth.

Heat a large cast iron frying pan over a high heat, add the **lard** and the **pork steaks**. Sear for 3 minutes before turning and searing for 3 minutes more. Remove from the pan to a plate.

Discard the fat from the pan and replace it with **2tbsp butter** and the **rosemary needles**. Turn down the heat and return the meat to the pan. Cover with a lid and cook slowly, basting regularly with the buttery pan juices, for 15 minutes or so. Remove the pork to a tray or serving dish to keep warm and squeeze the **lemon juice** over.

Skim the excess fat from the frying pan and deglaze with Noilly Prat. Boil to reduce by ⅔ then add the **chicken stock**. Boil again to reduce to a sauce consistency, then swirl in the **cold butter**.

Carve each steak into 4–5 slices and glaze with the sauce. Serve with good, buttery, mashed potatoes and some young vegetables.

PEPPER GLAZED PORK CHOPS WITH APPLE CHUTNEY

(Serves 4)

4	pork chops, 1" thick
5	garlic cloves, peeled and chopped
4	sage leaves, chopped
70ml	olive oil
	salt

Glaze

420ml	apple juice
55ml	honey
2tbsp	cracked black and white peppercorns
	zest of one orange

Chutney

8	cooking apples, peeled, cored and chopped
140g	raisins
330ml	cider vinegar
100g	white wine vinegar
100g	brown sugar
2	garlic cloves
½tsp	ground nutmeg
½tsp	cinnamon
2	cloves
	pinch of salt

Cooking the pork

2tbsp	olive oil
2tbsp	soft, unsalted butter

To make the marinade, cook the **garlic** and **sage** slowly in the **olive oil** until the garlic has softened, then cool. Place the **pork** in a deep dish and pour the cooled oil over. Cover with cling film and refrigerate for 4 hours.

Meanwhile, *make the glaze* by mixing the **honey** and the **apple juice** and simmering in a stainless steel saucepan over a medium heat until reduced by half. Stir in the **pepper** and **orange zest** and set aside.

To make the chutney, combine everything in a stainless steel pan and simmer until thickened. Set aside to cool.

To cook the pork, remove **pork chops** from the fridge 20 minutes beforehand. Lift out of the marinade, wipe clean with absorbent kitchen paper and season with **salt**. Heat a heavy, cast iron frying pan over a high heat. Add *2tbsp olive oil* and *2tbsp butter* and then the **pork chops**. Cook for 5 minutes without disturbing or turning the meat. Turn the chops and continue cooking for a further 3 minutes, basting with the fat from the pan as the pork cooks.

Lift out the pork chops and discard excess fat from the pan, return the pork to the pan and then spoon the pepper glaze over. Cook for a couple of minutes. The glaze will bubble up and create a sticky coating on the pork.

Transfer the chops to a cutting board and slice each into three before arranging onto hot plates. Add a tablespoon or two of **brown chicken stock** to the frying pan and quickly bring to a boil before spooning this mixture over the chops, Serve with a large spoonful of chutney, some deep-fried sage leaves and potato rŏsti.

ROAST MIDDLE WHITE PORK LOIN
WITH APPLE STUFFING

(Serves 8)

200g	day-old white bread rolls
250ml	milk
120g	diced onion
4	Granny Smith apples
120g	butter
2tbsps	freshly chopped sage leaves
	salt, pepper and nutmeg
1 pinch	sugar
2kg	Middle White pork loin with rind, boned, but retain the bones. Ask the butcher to score the rind for you.

Warm the *milk*, slice the *bread* thinly and pour the milk over. Melt *60g of the butter* and sweat the *onions* until soft and golden. Peel, core and chop the *apples* and add, with the *sage* leaves, to the onions. Cook for a further 2 minutes.

Heat the other *60g butter* in a small frying pan until nut brown. Add to the bread and milk, then add that to the onion and apple mixture. Season and mix lightly *(do not over mix)*.

Score the pork rind if your butcher has not already done so. Spread the stuffing down the centre of the loin, roll up and tie at regular intervals with kitchen string. Rub the skin liberally with sea salt and leave to stand for 1 hour.

Break up the bones and place in a roasting tray with the pork joint on top. Roast for *20 minutes @ 220°c*. Reduce the heat to *180°c* and continue cooking for *a further 45 minutes* or so until the core reaches *68°c*. (If you go beyond this temperature you run the risk of your pork being terribly dry.) Remove from the oven, lift from the roasting tray and allow to rest in a warm place before carving.

Meanwhile, pour away any excess fat from the roasting tray, leaving the bones behind, and add 4 cups of hot water. Bring to a boil and simmer for 5 minutes to produce a lovely, light, flavoursome gravy. Strain and set aside.

Remove the crackling and excess fat from the pork, cut it into nice slices, break the crackling into large pieces and serve together with the gravy and vegetables of your choice.

SPICY POTTED PORK

This is real gutsy, rustic food with bags of flavour. The sort of thing we love to order in provincial bistros or charcuteries when on holiday in France where it is called 'rillettes' but seem to neglect at home. Maybe it's got something to do with the fact that this type of product in the UK is generally factory made and delivered to restaurants in freezer vans!

2tbsp	sugar
1 lg pinch	ground cinnamon
1 lg pinch	ground allspice
1 lg pinch	ground ginger
1tsp	milled white pepper
1250g	pork shoulder, with a good covering of fat, cut into 2" cubes
110g	coarse sea salt
2 heads	garlic
2	cinnamon sticks
½tsp	juniper berries
4	cloves
4	star anise
1tsp	black peppercorns
2ltrs	duck fat or lard
75g	dried apricots, quartered
120ml	apricot brandy

Combine the *sugar, ground spices* and *white pepper*. Rub into the *pork* and transfer to a deep tray. Add the *sea salt, 1 peeled and crushed head of garlic, cinnamon sticks, juniper berries, cloves, star anise* and *black peppercorns*. Mix well to coat the meat with the salt and spices. Cover with cling film and refrigerate for 24 hours.

Melt the *duck fat* in a large casserole. Remove the meat from the cure, reserve the spices and tie them in a muslin bag with the *other head of garlic, cut in half horizontally*. Brush the excess salt from the pork and add the meat to the duck fat, together with the spice bag. Cover with a lid and cook in a gentle oven, *130°c*, for 3 hours or until the meat is very, very tender.

Soak the *dried apricots* in the *brandy*. Lift the meat from the duck fat and leave until cool enough to handle. Reserve *480ml duck fat* and set aside. Transfer the pork to a food processor and pulse until broken down into a purée. Add duck fat a little at a time, pulsing as you add. When all of the fat has been incorporated, remove the mixture to a bowl and stir in the soaked fruit. Check for seasoning and adjust if necessary.

Line a 1½ltr terrine or loaf tin with cling film and spoon in the mixture, smoothing the surface as you go. Bang the mould down firmly on the kitchen table to expel any air, and spoon over enough duck fat to cover the surface by 3mm. Refrigerate for several days to mature. Turn out of the mould and serve cut into 1" thick slices with pickles and lots of toasted country bread.

Jonathan & Dotty Benson
Lanchester Fruit

Asparagus

"All the doubting Thomases said
'What are you growing that weed for?
That'll never work.' But it did!"

We're making a journey south today, out of Northumberland but still in the ancient kingdom of Northumbria: we're visiting Brockwell Farm, near Lanchester, County Durham. Brockwell is home to Lanchester Fruit, where Jonathan and Dotty Benson are renowned for their excellent apple juices, soft fruits and for their English, green-variety asparagus.

152

Asparagus in County Durham?

Now we know for definite that some people don't have much of a clue about County Durham and its whereabouts. One contestant in a well-known TV quiz show forfeited half a million pounds because he didn't know that Durham County Cricket Club played their matches at Chester-le-Street. I'd like to bet that for a lot of people, their image of the county – if they have one, that is – is steelworks and coalmines. Well, they're gone now, and Durham is re-inventing itself as 'The Land of the Prince Bishops'. A place to be visited not only for its industrial heritage sites, such as Beamish Open Air Museum, but also for the rugged grandeur of its upland scenery; the North Pennines are now officially recognized as an Area of Outstanding Natural Beauty.

There's an awful lot of history in this neck of the woods. The Romans conquered the native Brigantes and ran part of Dere Street through Durham. Well, if you're building a straight road from York to the Firth of Forth you've not much option but to go through Durham. They threw up several forts along Dere Street, like the one here in Lanchester. After the Romans left, the Angles and the Saxons moved in, and by the end of the sixth century the area had become part of the Kingdom of Northumbria.

Durham plays a very important part in the story of early Christianity in Britain. It was the final resting place for the body of St Cuthbert (*d.* 687), after the monks fled with it from Lindisfarne in 875, driven out by Viking invasions. William the Conqueror built the commanding castle in 1072, and twenty-one years later the soaring Cathedral was begun (and was ready to receive the body of St. Cuthbert in 1104). Together they form a World Heritage Site.

Durham Cathedral was begun by William of St. Calais, one of William II's 'Baron Bishops'. Then came the time of the 'Prince Bishops' as their power escalated, and for several hundred years they were, in all but name, kings of the area between the Tees and the Tyne, and an effective buttress against the Scots. I'm sorry, Mr Gibson, but William Wallace didn't sack York. The Prince Bishop of Durham turned out his massive army and barred the way into England. Prince Bishops also levied their own taxes and minted their own coinage. Not surprisingly, Henry VIII looked at the situation, thought 'Do I not like this', and knocked it on the head. It was his favourite solution to most things.

In the seventeenth and early eighteenth centuries there was relative peace, and advances in agriculture brought some prosperity, which ushered in the arrival of county towns and comfortable country houses. Then came the Industrial Revolution, and the effects of mining and heavy industry kicked in quickly. County Durham became a major world industrial site, home to railway pioneers, engineers and shipbuilders. It was also home to some of the grimmest pit villages imaginable, and a short and dangerous life for many of those involved.

Now the heavy industry has gone and upland County Durham is going through more change, in which tourism and niche-market agriculture are both playing their part.

I'm driving down the spine of Durham in glorious sunshine, and amazing vistas of rolling countryside fall away on either side. I am given one brief reminder of the past by an ex-miner, crouched, 'shugged-up' against the wall of his terraced house. His flat cap and demeanour could be mid-twentieth century. Just for a second everything goes into black and white…then I leave his village and his world and once again I am out into upland splendour.

154

During the 1745 rebellion a very agitated officer from Lanchester turned up at Newcastle, saying that Bonnie Prince Charlie had arrived. The garrison was turned out in scenes of great turmoil and panic. Then another officer arrived, bearing the deflating news that the invaders were actually a herd of cows. Lanchester's quiet today, no invaders and no cows, so I pass through it to Brockwell Farm.

You know, for a little variety and drama, I'd like to be able to say I'm struggling on through tempest and hurricane, but the weather is utterly glorious. This means that, once again, I'm going to have my chat with folks sitting outside in the sunshine, having tea – and a very good cake indeed. I know it's hard work, but someone has to do it!

Jonathan and Dotty Benson came to the north east from Gloucestershire, although their roots are in Ireland. They've been in Durham over twenty years. Jonathan first came to the area as a farm manager, and then was offered a tenancy himself at Brockwell. After a while Jonathan was able to buy the place as sitting tenant.

He continues the story: "We started planting the fruit crops in '92, and then a few years later we came up with the idea of asparagus. People thought we were mad!"

Dotty (who isn't... she's definitely on the ball) Benson interrupts.

"All the doubting Thomases said 'What are you growing that weed for? That'll never work.' But it did!"

Jonathan goes on to explain. "Our timing was pretty good. People travelling abroad were ready to come home and try different food, things they'd encountered on holiday. And all the TV chef programmes meant that our kind of produce was being publicized. The farmers' markets were a boon to us too, as we were able to sell direct to the public."

But not without a lot of hard work, as Cito, green-variety asparagus – not to be confused with the continental white variety – is difficult to grow. "It likes sand and salt, as it's originally a coastal plant – a weed that people found was good to eat. It needs salty conditions that would kill most plants. The soil at Brockwell isn't sandy, but the drainage must be right, as the plant seems to thrive. It needs a lot of fertilizer, however. It also needs shelter, as it doesn't like getting cold and wet. Although we're far north here, the land at Brockwell is a sheltered, south-facing slope, which again seems to suit the crop. Because of the shorter days up here the crop does take longer to mature, but I think, because of that slow maturing, the flavour tends to be much more intense."

Getting started with asparagus in the first place wasn't easy work either, as Jonathan confirms. "You start with year-old crowns, which are not picked or cropped for three years,

which is one of the reasons that asparagus is expensive to buy. It needs to be well looked after. In the early years the plants have to be hand-weeded. You can weed them mechanically later and use chemical weedkillers in winter, but at the beginning it's all hand-weeding."

Dotty Benson: "Rabbits are a nuisance, as are slugs, but we have two families of hedgehogs who deal with the slugs, so no chemical control on those. Really slugs are only a problem if the weather's cold. When it's warm the plants just shoot up past them."

When it is time to cut the crop it has to be done by hand. Yes, each spear by hand. The process cannot be mechanized. When the spear has grown to about six inches, it's cut with a knife just below the surface of the soil. I came across the story once of a prize-winning asparagus picker who had only one arm. Apparently he had a technique similar to that needed for the children's game where you throw up stones and pick up some more whilst the others are still in mid air.

The crop has a short season, sometimes very short, but no matter how good the weather the picking must stop on June 21st. This is vital for the continuity of the crop. You have to let the fern grow, as it is effectively the reservoir for next year's growth. Jonathan: "It would be very easy to carry on cutting another week or ten days, but it would be a false, very short-term gain, as you'd seriously endanger next year's crop. But there you are, you've got your asparagus cut and you can get some steamed and have a wonderful excuse to eat plenty of butter!"

"You don't need an excuse," says Dotty, dryly.

He doesn't get a chance to argue, for at this point Jonathan gets a call from one of their staff, and bounds purposefully up the hill towards the buildings which house the apple juice presses. Something needs hands-on attention.

"He has worked terribly hard, built this up from nothing," says Dotty, watching him go. I believe her, because something is apparently keeping a man over sixty very fit indeed, and I'd like to bet it's not visits to a designer gym. "He pays the asparagus a lot of attention," continues Dotty, "cutting it no later than June 21st, making sure the weeds are kept at bay and that it's given fertilizer twice in the autumn, not just once. Jonathan went to France to see how they were growing it and he brought what he learned back here."

So what happens after cutting?

"Well then, next we have to sort and grade the crop. All by hand. We want a bunch to be all of similar thickness. The thinner spears are called 'sprue' and are very good for soups. When it's sorted we make up a bunch of a pound weight and put a rubber band around it, then it's off to the farmers' market or to the local greengrocer, where people are anxiously awaiting it. You can get asparagus all year round, but people still wait for the start of the English season. There is green asparagus being grown in Spain nowadays and it's not too bad, but it has been cut a while ago and been in a chilled wagon for two or three days. Not a patch on ours."

Dotty likes her asparagus: "No point in selling something if you don't like it. It's wonderful steamed but it's very nice roasted with lots of olive oil and sea-salt. You can add balsamic vinegar and grated Parmesan… Mmmm."

In addition to their asparagus, Lanchester Fruit grow six varieties of strawberries, as well as raspberries and autumn-fruiting raspberries, blackcurrants, redcurrants, gooseberries and beautiful, dark, dessert gooseberries. All are available as 'pick your own' at Lanchester, or from the many farmers' markets they visit throughout the year.

And then there's the apple juice; tens of thousands of bottles of farm-pressed, single variety, English Apple juice. I have to mention the apples, even in a chapter on asparagus.

Having said cheerio and thanks to Dotty Benson, I go to do likewise to her husband, who is busy in the apple-pressing sheds. As soon as I set foot on the threshold, an amazing aroma wafts over me. There are all kinds of shiny, artist's-model apples awaiting their journey through the press. Apples from Kent, apples from Yorkshire and from Hereford; Crispin, Sunset, Cox, Bramley, Worcester Pear Main (a very old apple), Warner's King and many more. The apples are never blended, so you always get only one variety to the bottle, although they do produce apple and rhubarb, apple and strawberry and a very tasty apple and elderflower (which is my particular favourite). They also do a non-alcoholic punch for Christmas.

Jonathan gives me a quick tour of the process; There's the 'cheese' and the barrels, that remind me of the old cider-makers I visited in Gloucester. However, unlike their set-up, there's a pasteurization step to the process at Brockwell, which prevents fermentation. Then the hundreds of bottles have their labels stuck on, ready for a trip to the farmers' market.

We leave the pressing-sheds and stand for a moment, surveying the scene across the valley. Jonathan points out the location of the Roman settlement on the opposite hillside, and the whereabouts of the conduits down which they piped their water supply for miles. He also points out the old mine shafts and entrances on the farm. I don't think many of the old miners would have believed you if you'd told them their route to the face would one day be festooned with acres of asparagus ferns waving in the breeze. Jonathan agrees, and we focus once again on the fields of asparagus spreading out below us. "Lovely stuff!" he sighs.

Asparagus

To others it's frustrating, but to me, the fact that English asparagus is only available for a few precious weeks each year adds to its attraction. It reminds us that seasons are there for a purpose. You should never find asparagus on a menu outside of its spring growing months. Seasons are there to be respected. Yes, you can buy it plastic-packed and super-chilled all year round in the supermarkets, but consider how many days it has been hanging around, and that's just in airports. Purists argue that asparagus should be eaten within one hour of cutting (a bit extreme; three days is fine). Like garden peas, that sublime sweetness ticks away with every minute.

As a kid, asparagus never entered our house. Even as a young chef, the closest I got to it was Jolly Green Giant tins of strange-looking vegetables. (That being said, tinned asparagus has its uses. It's not unusual for me to make asparagus soup out of the 'sprue' – thin, straggly or immature pieces – and bulk it out with a few tins.) My next encounter came at 16, when I was working as an apprentice in a so-called fancy restaurant. I remember having to lay limp, soggy, shrivelled green spears across the tops of quasi-classic French dishes, with names such as *Escalope de Veau Parisienne* or *Suprême de Volaille Princesse*, in what was meant to be an attempt at culinary sophistication. I was still not impressed.

It was only when I got a placement at the Hotel Bellevue in Baden-Baden in Germany that I began to appreciate asparagus. I arrived just before Easter. Within days the whole town had exploded into *Spargelzeit*, the Festival of Asparagus. It was everywhere, on market stalls, in shopping bags, on every restaurant menu. This was the real deal. I became so caught up in this asparagus whirl that I went out and bought a fancy, expensive asparagus peeler, which I still have to this day.

Peeling asparagus is a perennial debate. It's a question of size and quality. I peel if I'm serving them in the restaurant, but not when eating at home. If you are troubled by it, try this little test. If a bit of the outer skin comes away easily with your thumbnail, you might want to peel them.

There are two varieties of asparagus (three, if you want to be pedantic, but the third is merely a difference in growing technique): green and white. The growing tips of white asparagus are trenched every day – kept under the soil – to keep them blanched. It is big, bland and common in mainland Europe. The green is what we grow in Britain. To my mind, it's sweeter, more subtle and has greater depth of flavour – particularly when grown in the north, which I put down to the colder climate necessitating a more leisurely growth.

Fresh asparagus should be firm, glossy, and springy. When pressed gently with your thumbnail, a little moisture, the sap, should rise to the surface. Deciding where to trim is easy: bend it, and where it snaps is the point at which to cut.

Cooking asparagus is dead easy too. Far too much nonsense is talked about using fancy tall pans with perforated inserts. All you need is a large pan with lots of salted water, about 20 grams per litre. Thoroughly wash the asparagus to remove any grains of dirt that might be caught in the tight buds of the tips. Bind equal-sized spears with fine string into bundles, to keep the spears intact and to keep cooking times the same, and plunge them into the boiling water.

Don't pack the bundles in too tight; they need the luxury of lots of water. Stuffing the pan causes the water temperature to drop dramatically and you will lose vital vitamins and nutrients through the longer cooking time. This, incidentally, is true of all green vegetables. Cover the pan and surface of the water with a clean, damp tea towel

to ensure all the bundles stay submerged. After 3–4 minutes, squeeze the base end of a spear to test for tenderness.

What about chargrilling, I hear you say. When blackened vegetables were all the rage on fashionable menus in the late '90s, I turned up my nose at it. A silly fad, I thought, with no taste benefits. I hold my hands up; I was wrong. Chargrilling is great. Drizzled with olive oil and a generous scattering of sea salt, you get that fantastic contrast between the crunchy bitterness of the caramelized skin and the tender sweetness inside. But be warned; it's easy to get carried away and overcook them.

Asparagus is good in an omelette, great in quiche and fantastic in risotto. Use the peelings and trimmings for the risotto stock, add the tips right at the end and go steady on the cheese. At home, we often have asparagus with potato gnocchi, browned sage butter and Parmesan.

But the finest way to eat asparagus is to lift them straight out of the pan onto a plate. Squeeze a wedge of lemon over them, sprinkle with sea salt, pick up with your fingers and dip into a pot of melted butter. There's something almost decadent and definitely sensual about eating asparagus in this way.

Tips

To prepare ahead:

Drain the cooked asparagus, plunge under cold water, dry and lay on a plate covered with a cloth. To re-heat, place them in a single layer in a large, flat saucepan with a scant 3 or 4 tablespoons of water. Add a knob of butter, pinch of salt and pinch of sugar. Boil for 3 minutes or until most of the liquid has evaporated and the asparagus is glossy and coated with a buttery emulsion.

Great with:

Butter, chervil, cured ham, crabmeat, eggs, fried breadcrumbs, hollandaise sauce, lemon, mushrooms (any sort but particularly morels), olive oil (extra virgin), Parmesan cheese, sea salt.

Cooking green vegetables:

Never cook in a pan with the lid on. Green vegetables contain volatile acids, which are released as they heat up. A lid traps the acids in the pan, where they will break down the natural chlorophyll in the vegetables, causing them to lose their fresh, green colour.

ASPARAGUS TART

(Serves 8 as a first course, 6 as a light main course)

250g	shortcrust pastry
1kg	asparagus
250ml	Jersey cream
250ml	milk
4	free range eggs
	salt and pepper
1	egg white

Roll out the **pastry** to about 3mm thick and use to line a 28cm, loose-bottomed tart tin. Refrigerate for at least 20 minutes, to allow pastry to relax. Meanwhile, preheat oven to **200°c.**

Place a sheet of greaseproof paper inside the pastry case and fill with baking beans. Bake blind for 15 minutes before removing the beans and the paper. Return to the oven for another 5 minutes. Remove and, whilst still hot, brush out the inside of the tart shell with beaten egg white. Reduce oven temperature to **160°c.**

Trim and discard the woody ends from the **asparagus.** Cook in boiling, salted water until just tender. Drain and refresh in iced water. Drain again.

Cut the tips of the asparagus to 7½cm lengths and reserve.

Place the remaining asparagus ends into a liquidizer with enough milk to cover. Process until very smooth, then force the resulting purée through a conical strainer into a bowl. Add the remaining **milk, eggs** and **cream** and beat until smooth. Season well.

Pour the asparagus cream into the tart case and arrange the tips attractively on top. Return to the oven and bake for 35–40 minutes until the custard is set and golden brown. Remove carefully from the oven and allow to cool for 5 minutes before attempting to cut.

Serve warm.

SEARED WILD SALMON WITH COLD ASPARAGUS CREAM

(Serves 4)

24	asparagus spears
2ltrs	water
40g	butter
1tsp	sugar
90g	crème fraiche
4 x 80g	fillets of wild salmon
	salt and pepper
½	lemon

Garnish

	A little curly endive
6tbsp	vinaigrette
	chervil sprigs

Peel and trim the **asparagus**, cut off the woody ends.
Bring the water to a boil with butter, salt and sugar.
Cook the **asparagus** and refresh in iced water when tender.
Trim 12 nice tips from each, about 1½" long, and set aside.
Liquidize the remaining asparagus to a purée and rub
through a fine sieve.

Mix with **4tbsp crème fraiche**, season with **salt and pepper** then
chill. Wash and pick the **curly endive** into bite-sized pieces.
Toss the asparagus tips in a little **vinaigrette**. Dress the **endive**
also. Season the **salmon** with salt and pepper, then quickly
sear in a very hot, dry, non-stick frying pan for 1 minute
on each side. Add a little squeeze of **lemon** and remove to
a plate to keep warm.

Assembly

Arrange three pools of **asparagus cream** on each plate with an
asparagus tip between each. Place a piece of **grilled salmon** in
the centre. Garnish with **curly endive and chervil**.

ASPARAGUS SOUP

(Serves 4)

2	leeks (white part only)
1tbsp	soft butter
1	onion, chopped
2	garlic cloves, peeled and sliced
750ml	chicken stock
1	medium floury potato (Dunbar Rover or similar), peeled and sliced
2 bunches	asparagus, cut into ¼" rounds
	coarse salt and milled pepper
1 pinch	caster sugar
110g	spinach, stemmed, washed and coarsely chopped
25g	unsalted butter

Chop the **leeks** and wash well. Sweat together with the **onion**
and **garlic** in the butter. Season with **salt, pepper** and a tiny
pinch of **sugar**. When soft, add the **chicken stock** and **diced
potato**, bring to the boil and cook for 5 minutes. Throw in
the **asparagus** and season. Simmer for 12–14 minutes until
the asparagus is very tender. Stir in the **chopped spinach** and
cook just until it wilts.

Liquidize immediately, pass through a fine sieve or strainer
and cool on ice in order to retain the colour. Reheat when
needed but do not allow to boil. Stir in the **unsalted butter**
to thicken and emulsify. Serve.

WARM SALAD OF ENGLISH ASPARAGUS, POTATOES AND WILD SALMON

(Serves 4)

300g	Pink Fir Apple or La Ratte potatoes
250g	English asparagus, peeled
500g	wild salmon fillet
50g	small salad leaves and herbs (oak leaf, wild rocket, curly endive, watercress, red chard, flat-leaf parsley and chervil), washed and spun dry
50g	unsalted butter

Vinaigrette

3tbsp	white wine vinegar
2tbsp	tarragon vinegar
5tbsp	sunflower oil
6tbsp	asparagus cooking water
	black pepper and sea salt

Mix together everything for the vinaigrette with a whisk. Scrub the **potatoes** and cook in boiling, salted water until tender.

Drain, leave until cool enough to handle and cut into 4mm thick slices. Keep warm.

Cut **asparagus** into 1½" lengths and cook in boiling, salted water until tender. Drain and allow to cool, retaining **6tbsp cooking water** for the vinaigrette. Cut the salmon into bite-sized pieces, and stew very gently in a non-stick frying pan, with the **butter**, over a low heat.

Remove from the heat and season with **salt, black pepper** and **lemon juice**. Carefully mix the **salmon, asparagus, potatoes** and **6tbsp vinaigrette**.

Arrange nicely on plates with the salad leaves. Spoon the **vinaigrette** over and around. Serve whilst still warm.

Soft-boiled, free range hens eggs with asparagus soldiers

(Serves 4)

*Be vigilant when grilling asparagus; a minute's overcooking will cause them to collapse and lose texture.
Remember, the fresher they are, the quicker they cook. If you are in a hurry, or perhaps aren't in an 'egg mood',
the asparagus are great served straight from the grill and drizzled with vinaigrette, made from best quality olive oil
and aged balsamic vinegar. Shave the Parmesan, rather than grating it, and scatter generously over.*

4	large free range eggs
16	asparagus tips
8	slices air-dried ham (Parma, Serrano or similar)
4 tbsp	grated Parmesan cheese
2 tbsp	extra virgin olive oil
	coarse sea salt
	milled black pepper

Peel the **asparagus** and trim any woody ends. Drizzle with **olive oil** and season with **sea salt** and **black pepper**. Heat a ridged, iron grill pan and char grill over a high heat for 3 minutes. Turn and grill the other side for 30 seconds. Remove from the grill and divide between plates, season with coarse sea salt and a grind of black pepper.

Split each **ham slice** in half lengthways and sprinkle each piece with grated Parmesan cheese. Roll an asparagus spear tightly in each, making sure that you leave the tip exposed. Reserve.

Bring a pan of salted water to the boil and cook the **eggs** for 3 minutes. Remove and transfer to egg cups. Slice the tops from the eggs with a sharp, serrated knife, exposing the soft yolk. Season with coarse sea salt and black pepper. Arrange the asparagus soldiers alongside and accompany with some good quality, unsalted butter.

Iain Alexander
Senior Beat Keeper, Raby Estates

Game

"Unlike farmed venison, where deer are treated as any other stock, the Raby Park deer are only ever handled once in their lives, when they are tagged as new-born calves or fawns. They are left to their own devices when it comes to foraging, which obviously means that they are getting no additives or antibiotics."

Another visit south today, the 'far south' for most Northumbrians, since we will be in sight of North Yorkshire. We're visiting Iain Alexander, the Senior Beat Keeper looking after the deer at Raby Castle, near Staindrop, County Durham.

Raby Castle is home to Lord Barnard, and has been home to his family since 1626, when his ancestor, Sir Henry Vane the Elder, bought the estate from the Crown. They had seized it from the banished Nevill family, who were in trouble for their involvement in the Rising of the North in support of Mary Queen of Scots. Good Queen Bess could be as ruthless as her father when it came to dealing with people who opposed her, so the Nevills were lucky it was banishment and not a block booking on Tower Hill. Since 1131 only two families, the Nevills and the Vanes, have owned Raby Estate.

The present Lord Barnard's family is linked to the Nevills through Dorothy Nevill, a daughter of John, 4th Lord Latymer, who married the 1st Earl of Exeter (one of the Cecils of Burghley). The present Lord Barnard's grandmother, the 9th Lady Barnard, was a daughter of the 3rd Marquess of Exeter.

The Castle was built mainly in the 14th century. Fortunately it was little damaged in the Civil War, although besieged by the Royalists on at least two occasions, as it stood out for

Parliament. Interesting that Raby Castle came out in support of Mary, but stood against her grandson, Charles I. This was largely because of Sir Henry Vane the Younger, who had converted to Puritanism and was a leading Member of Parliament. Although later, Sir Henry distanced himself from Cromwell (who imprisoned him), he was executed after the Restoration, despite promises given to the contrary by Charles II.

In the eighteenth century, major alterations were carried out to the medieval structure and the result is a stunning interior in Gothic Revival style. In the nineteenth century, the Octagon Drawing Room, the grandest room in the castle, was built. It was designed to impress, with gilt ceiling

and silk damask wall coverings. Recently it underwent a major restoration, and now shines brightly again as one of the jewels of Raby's treasures. Of which there are many: Meissen porcelain, fine furniture and art works which include paintings by Van Dyck, Reynolds and De Hooch. Raby welcomes thousands of visitors each year, to view its sumptuous interior, the gardens and the 200-acre deer park. Which brings us to why we are here.

I turn in through the gates and drive through the park, making for the home of Iain Alexander, Senior Beat Keeper, at Kennel Cottage. Not surprisingly, it is on the site of the old Raby Hunt kennels, which housed the Earl of Darlington's hounds.

Iain Alexander *Senior Beat Keeper, Ruby Estates*

Game

I arrive as Iain is passing over a couple of ferrets to a visitor. There is a brief, silent-comedy moment as the wee beasts play 'revolving door' and refuse to stay in the box together. Order is restored and they are off on their way. And so are Iain and I as we jump in the Land Rover (the back full of a motley crew of dogs) and are away to see the deer in the park.

Iain is, as you might have guessed from the spelling of his name, a Scot, from the Irvine Valley in Ayrshire. He worked for ten years as a keeper for the Marquis of Bute: both the present ex-Formula 1 driver Johnny Dumfries and his father. He came to Raby some three-and-a-half years ago as a beat keeper, and has since become Senior Beat Keeper.

Now there are wild deer on other parts of the Raby land, but in the park, the animals we're driving to see are red and fallow deer. Iain slows, and edges the Landrover forward as quietly as possible.

"There they are," he points, handing me his binoculars.

They are indeed. A magnificent sight it is too. With Raby Castle as a backdrop, I can see two separate herds of deer, but all are at the moment standing stock-still and facing our way. Despite the distance of several hundred yards, and

Iain's efforts at arriving surreptitiously, they have their guard up. The antlers of the stags and bucks rear up above the rest of the herd. Someone has given the signal 'heads up'.

It takes quite a while for them to relax and begin to go back to feeding.

As we sit and watch them, Iain fills me in. "There's been deer in the park since Norman times. Some of these we see here are their descendants. The early deer park was a very practical measure. It was a ready source of fresh meat for the house; it's only later when it is seen as part of the decorative landscaping. The larger animals are the red deer. The others are fallow and black fallow… although they're more dark grey-brown really. There are some mottled ones and we have some plain white fallow, just a few. There's one!"

There is indeed. I focus the glasses on where it stands, just beyond the small herd of Longhorn cattle, which also grace the park.

"They're not albino", continues Iain, "just a white gene. We wouldn't want too many," says Iain. "There are complete white herds, but I can't see why anybody would want a complete herd of deer that look like goats."

the deer, and should circumstances deem it necessary, then a sick or injured animal will be dealt with promptly and humanely.

Let's get this right; fallow deer are called bucks and does, whilst red are stags and hinds. Red deer have calves, fallow deer have fawn and roe deer have kids. Both herds are left to their own devices, their own social order and their own, often violent, power struggles. In the rutting season the older males fight to establish harems, and then defend them against interlopers chancing their arm.

The fallow deer decide that enough's enough and scatter.

"Aye," confirms Iain, "the fallow are more flighty than the red, they are easier upset. The wind or some walkers might have 'em off in a corner somewhere. Look, there's a late youngster."

"Oh yes, so there is" I agree, trapping what I think is a small one in the ring of binocular vision.

"No, over there," corrects Iain, and under his direction I manage to focus in on one which is indeed tiny. "It's unusual to have one like that this late in the season. Something's not gone quite as it should earlier in the year. If we get a very hard winter, that one might struggle a bit."

It's worth pointing out that these park deer, whilst confined by the barriers of the park, are to all intents and purposes wild. Unlike farmed venison, where deer are treated as any other stock, the Raby Park deer are only ever handled once in their lives, when they are tagged as newborn calves or fawns. They are left to their own devices when it comes to foraging, which obviously means that they are getting no additives or antibiotics. However, a close watch is kept on

It can be a fierce, wounding and sometimes fatal battle. These guys can punch their weight. The red stag is the largest wild, British, land mammal. They start to grow their antlers the spring after they are born. They increase in size each year, until at four years old a stag is known as an 'eight pointer'; each antler has four points or prongs. In spring they shed their antlers and start to grow new ones. Until this new set is fully grown, the antlers are covered in red-brown hair and the stag is said to be 'in velvet'. The fallow bucks develop similarly, but the mature antlers are palmated (which the uninitiated might describe as clubbed), rather than pointed. It's a canny sight, whether pointed or palmated, but they can't half get stuck in with the things.

The main food of the red is grass and foliage. Fallow too eat grass, but are also partial to young shoots, forest fruits, chestnuts and acorns. In winter the diet of both herds is supplemented with hay, clover and carrots, turnips or beets. "Whatever's cheapest," says Iain.

The venison which Raby sell, via game dealers such Yorkshire Game and Stephen Morrell, comes from the 100–150 animals culled in the park each year. They're taken at one year old for the table, although older animals are shot too,

either for humane reasons or to maintain the numbers and stability of the herd. There are statutory seasons for both red and fallow, with different dates for the males and females. Iain wanted to make it clear that at Raby, only the keepers shoot the park deer. Highly trained and skilled marksmen. Indeed, it is Iain himself who mainly does the job, with a 243 rifle. The priority is to make sure that the herd is as little stressed as possible, as few times as possible, so he's experimenting at the moment with a sound-moderating rifle. There is no question of these park animals ever being stalked for sport.

The venison goes off to be processed and then it's off via the game dealers to restaurants, hotels and the dining table. Some of the meat comes back to Raby to be sold in the shop during the time the house is open, and before Christmas when the rise in demand for the festive season fortunately coincides with the open season.

Iain and I move off now, back towards the house. He laughs dryly. "That photographer of yours, Duncan…spent ages trying for the best angle…'Can you get them 100 yards to the left?' he says to me. I thought 'I'll try, but I'm no a sheepdog'".

On the journey back, Iain tells me about the other game.

"Throughout Raby we don't rear game. We've pheasant, grouse, duck and partridge, none of which are reared. There's predator control and management of habitat for game, but we don't have the rearing-field side of things here."

He very much enjoys his work, that's obvious. "I love the life. I was once a plumber and, as you know, the money is good, but I have a much better life now. I definitely get to see better places."

I take one last look around at Raby Castle, with its park and gardens, and I have to say that a better place it is indeed. And one that produces some first class venison from those herds of deer grazing the park.

I take my leave and head back north.

As I drive home, I can't help wondering if that chap has tried taking the ferrets from the box yet. I bet they won't come out!

Game

Iain Alexander *Senior Beat Keeper, Ruby Estates*

It may be colder than the south, more open to Siberian winds and woefully short of football trophies, but one thing the north east can claim over the south is an abundance of fresh game on its doorstep. Pheasant, partridge, quail and guinea fowl are reared in large quantities these days, but are often disappointing. The best of the local game, to my mind, is grouse and venison.

People can be nervous of game, perhaps because it still clings to an élitist image of plus fours and shooting party lunches. It would be a pity to let this put you off. Game is not complicated to cook – venison is one of the easiest roasts in the cookbook – an excellent source of protein and low in fat. So, healthy and tasty.

As we sit plum in the middle of grouse country – the region stretches from Scotland down to Yorkshire and across into Lancashire – it would be a crime to ignore one of our few, truly indigenous products. Every year, predictably, in the run-up to the Glorious Twelfth, the market is whipped into a frenzy, with gloomy predictions of a poor season and low numbers. Surprise, surprise, prices soar. Funnily enough, come September, prices always drop. I wonder why.

Grouse is probably our richest game bird. Feeding largely on heather, it's a nimble, quick-witted bird that flies high and fast. As a result, it has virtually no fat and its meat is dense, hence the strong, almost musky taste. Because the bird has effectively done all the work in producing the flavour, it's pointless – indeed, unhelpful – to try and add anything further.

With young birds, I would never attempt to do anything other than roast them and serve in the traditional way, with bread sauce and redcurrant jelly. This is a doddle. Cover the breast with a couple of rashers of bacon – you will need two birds per person – and roast at 220°c for no more than 15 minutes. If you can be bothered – and it is worth the effort – quickly bone and carve the bird, toss the carcass back into the roasting tin, add a little red wine and water, simmer for 10 minutes, and there's your gravy.

Grouse, undoubtedly, has a true gamey flavour, but it's a popular misconception to think all game is big, brassy and coming out fighting. Venison, particularly our local deer, is far more delicate, although still satisfyingly complex. Roe deer are smaller than red and fallow deer and are completely wild. Tricky to find, they may be glimpsed at daybreak foraging around the edges of pine forests, where they love nothing better than a breakfast of tender young pine shoots.

It's this pine needle diet which gives their finely grained meat a distinctive flavour. When I worked in Baden-Baden at the Hotel Bellevue, the Head Chef, Herr Jäckel, would sometimes send us out in the morning to collect young pine shoots from the Black Forest. Back in the kitchen, we liquidized them in grape seed oil, and added them to a sauté of wild mushrooms. This gave a delicious intensity to the earthy flavour of the mushrooms.

Most people only get as far as roast venison, which is a pity. It's a hugely versatile meat. The best joints can be pan-fried or braised. Shoulders can be stewed or minced and made into burgers, sausages, terrines or game pie. Venison can even be eaten raw, as carpaccio, or quickly seared, Japanese-style, as tataki.

The prime joints are the saddle and haunch. The saddle can be roasted whole or divided into steaks or cutlets for grilling or pan-frying. The haunch can also be roasted or diced to braise. Venison is naturally tender, but if braising, it's worth marinating in the traditional way. The wine in the marinade gives both a deep flavour and a deep rich colour, but

marinate for no longer than 24 hours. For roasting, a lighter marinade of olive oil mixed with juniper berries, coriander seeds, orange zest and pepper adds an extra flavour dimension, without overpowering the natural flavours.

When roasting, start at a high heat – 200°c – turning down to 160°c after ten minutes. The joint needs to be well seasoned, but the traditional French method of studding the flesh with extra fat to aid the cooking is unnecessary. You're not aiming to cook it through; you want the middle to be rosy pink. Just keep it basted with oil or butter, but it needs to be watched. Precisely because it lacks natural fat, venison – unlike beef or pork, where you can be more relaxed – is unforgiving. Overcook it and you've got an expensive piece of shoe leather on your hands.

A small saddle – around two and a quarter pounds, ideally on the bone – is perfect for six people, and should take

no longer than 16 - 18 minutes. To make the gravy, get rid of the excess fat in the roasting tray, add a glass of red wine, 2 tablespoons of soured cream, a serious grind of black pepper and a knob of butter. Stir for a couple of minutes until the liquid has boiled and reduced a little. Because it's so rich, the accompaniments are kept simple – noodles, braised red cabbage, a few fried wild mushrooms. For a bit of sweetness, you could add a poached pear and a spoonful of redcurrant jelly.

These accompaniments work equally well if you're pan-frying. This is so simple, you've got to try this one at home. Roll a couple of venison steaks in crushed peppercorns and cracked coriander seeds. Pan fry them in butter - keep the heat high, so you get a little caramelization going on - add a glug of cognac and two tablespoons of crème fraiche. That's it, job's done. More interesting than fillet steak, that's for sure.

1	small deer saddle, about 1.5kg
20g	butter
20g	olive oil
	salt and pepper

Marinade

750g	strong red wine
20	juniper berries
10	white peppercorns
10	black peppercorns
3	cloves
1	cinnamon stick
1	thyme sprig
1	bay leaf
1"	ginger root, sliced
1tbsp	cranberries
1tbsp	olive oil

Vegetables

2	carrots
2	leeks
1	celeriac
12	button onions
50g	butter
	salt
	sugar
1tbsp	chopped parsley

Sauce

125ml	whipping cream
	cayenne pepper
	lemon juice
30g	butter

ROAST SADDLE OF VENISON

(Serves 4)

Trim the **venison** clean of all skin and sinew. Place the saddle, together with the trimmings, in a deep tray. Add the **wine, juniper, peppercorns** and **spices**, together with the **cranberries** and **1tbsp oil**.

Cover with a sheet of oiled, greaseproof paper and refrigerate for half a day.

Wash and peel the **vegetables**. Cut into ½" dice. Preheat the oven to **220°c**. Remove the venison from the marinade and pat dry with kitchen paper. Heat a heavy, cast iron roasting tray on top of the stove, add **butter, olive oil** and the **seasoned venison saddle**. Colour gently on the flesh side, turn and transfer to the hot oven. Roast for 15 minutes, basting regularly as it cooks.

Remove from the roasting tray and set aside in a warm place to rest.

Strain the marinade and retain the trimmings. Put the trimmings into the roasting tray and colour lightly on top of the stove. Add a little of the marinade and cook until reduced to almost nothing. Continue adding marinade in small quantities and reducing until all has been used. Add the **cream** and simmer gently until you have a sauce consistency. Strain through a fine sieve and keep warm.

Place the vegetables in a large, shallow pan in a single layer. Cover with water and season with **salt** and a **pinch of sugar**. Cover with a lid and cook until tender. Remove the lid and turn up the heat until the moisture has evaporated and the vegetables are lightly caramelized.

Place the venison saddle on a large serving dish, scatter the vegetables around and keep warm. Reheat the sauce, check the seasoning and swirl in the **butter**. Add **a squeeze of lemon**.

Present the venison family-style, to be carved at the table, and serve the sauce separately.

GROUSE PATE WITH FOIE GRAS

(10 portions)

750g	grouse flesh, trimmed of all fat, skin and sinew
750g	fatty pork shoulder (needs to be 50% or more fat)
125g	foie gras
125g	chicken livers
45ml	dry white wine
2tbsp	cognac
2	juniper berries, finely chopped
2tbsp	vegetable oil
	leaves of 1 thyme sprig
100g	button mushrooms, finely sliced
40g	chopped shallots
1tsp	finely chopped garlic
2tbsp	salt
½tsp	pepper
1 pinch	ground cloves
1 pinch	ground nutmeg
400g	pork caul fat

Cut the **grouse flesh, pork shoulder, livers** and **foie gras** into 2cm dice. Season with **salt, pepper** and **spices**, pour over **cognac** and **white wine**. Mix in the **thyme leaves** and **juniper**. Cover with cling film and refrigerate for 24 hours.

Drain the meats, discarding any marinade. Sweat the **shallots, garlic** and **mushrooms** in **vegetable oil** without allowing them to colour. Chill.

Push all of the meats through the coarse blade of a well chilled mincer, along with the shallot and mushroom mixture. Cover and chill again, without mixing, for 1 hour.

Preheat the oven to **150°c**. Line an oiled, 1ltr terrine with **pork caul fat**. Mix the minced meat lightly by hand – it must remain quite coarse – and spoon into a terrine mould. Pack in firmly, fold over the pork caul, cover with tin foil and place in a roasting tray containing 2 litres of boiling water. Transfer to the preheated oven. Cook to a core temperature of **65°c** (approximately 1½ hours).

Remove from the oven, allow to cool for 20 minutes and place a board and a 1kg weight on top. Cool before refrigerating overnight.

Serve with winter salad leaves in walnut oil dressing, pickles and crusty bread.

Iain Alexander *Senior Beat Keeper, Raby Estates*

GAME PIE

(Serves 8)

This dish is best made a couple of days in advance, to the stage before the pastry is added,
in order to allow the flavours to mature.

700g	game meat in 2cm dice: venison, hare, pheasant, pigeon, grouse or partridge
	vegetable oil
½tbsp	tomato paste
40g	plain flour
	salt and pepper
225g	button mushrooms
1tbsp	redcurrant jelly

Marinade

50ml	strong red wine
1½	carrots, peeled and sliced into 2cm rounds
12	button onions
2	celery sticks, peeled and cut into 2cm chunks
15	juniper berries
6	black peppercorns, cracked and tied in muslin
1	bay leaf
1	thyme sprig

To Finish

350g	puff pastry
1	egg yolk

Bring the *wine* to a boil, remove from the heat, add the *vegetables, herbs* and *spices*. Allow to cool to room temperature and add the *game*. Cover with a sheet of oiled, greaseproof paper and marinate for 24 hours.

Next day, preheat the oven to *130°c*. Drain the meat, reserving the marinade. Dry the meat and vegetables in a cloth. Heat a large, heavy, cast iron casserole, season the meat and colour in the hot *vegetable oil*. When nicely browned, add the *butter* and *vegetables*, cook a little more until the vegetables soften a little. Drain off any excess fat, then add the *tomato paste* and cook for another 3 minutes. Sift in the *flour* and cook for another 2 minutes whilst stirring. Pour in the wine from the marinade and enough water just to cover the meat. Add the herbs and spices from the marinade, bring to the boil, skim and cover with a lid. Transfer the casserole to the oven and braise for 3 hours.

Just before the meat is cooked, stir in the *mushrooms*. Check the seasoning and the consistency of the sauce. Stir in the *redcurrant jelly* and allow to cool. At this stage, the dish may be left for a couple of days for the flavours to mature, and then finished as follows.

Roll out the *pastry* 3mm thick. Transfer the meat and its sauce to a pie dish. Brush the rim of the dish with beaten *egg yolk* and place the pastry lid on the top. Press down well on the edges to get a good seal.

Brush the top with the remaining egg yolk. Bake @ *200°c* for 35–40minutes. Serve with mashed potatoes and red cabbage.

ROAST GROUSE

(Serves 4)

The traditional accompaniments for roast grouse are bread sauce, fried breadcrumbs, potato crisps, redcurrant jelly, watercress and gravy. The bread sauce and redcurrant jelly are crucial, the breadcrumbs, potato crisps and watercress optional and the gravy not really needed if the grouse are young.

These days restaurants would generally remove the grouse from the bone before serving. It certainly gives a better presentation and makes eating more manageable, but I do feel it takes some of the fun away.

4	young grouse, hung for 3 days
	salt and milled white pepper
8	rashers streaky bacon
1tbsp	oil
3tbsp	soft butter
12	chicken wings, each chopped into 3 pieces
½	onion, chopped
1	celery stick, chopped
1	small carrot, chopped
85ml	red wine
300ml	brown chicken stock

Ask the game dealer to eviscerate the **grouse** for you. Season it inside and out with **salt** and **milled pepper**. Smear the grouse breasts with **soft butter**. Lay the **bacon** over the breasts and tie loosely with kitchen string.

Preheat oven to **220°c**. Heat a heavy roasting tray with the **oil** and **1tbsp butter** and seal the grouse quickly on all sides. Transfer to the hot oven and roast for 5 minutes on one side, then turn over and roast for another 5 minutes. Turn the grouse onto their backs and roast for a further 5 minutes. Remove from the oven and keep warm.

Tip the fat from the roasting tray and replace with **1tbsp butter**. Add the **chicken wings** and the **chopped vegetables**, turn them to coat in butter and place in the oven. Cook until nicely browned. Remove the tray from the oven and add the **red wine**. Place over a medium heat and simmer until reduced by half. Add the **chicken stock** and simmer gently for 15 minutes. Strain through a fine sieve into a small saucepan and allow to settle for 15 minutes before skimming off any fat lying on the surface. Check for seasoning and adjust if necessary.

Cut the string from the birds and remove the bacon.

Serve the grouse on nice large plates, accompanied by the bacon, a small bunch of watercress, bread sauce and some redcurrant jelly.

GAME SOUP

(Serves 8)

This is very much a winter, lunchtime soup; not the sort of thing to serve as a first course at a dinner party.
It's quite a bonus if you can find an old bird. The flavour will be a lot more pronounced.
It can be made equally well with grouse or partridge.

2 tbsp	butter
2 tbsp	smoked bacon, cut into small dice
1	old pheasant
	livers and hearts from several other birds
1	carrot, sliced
1	medium onion, cut into ½" dice
1	leek, white only, washed and sliced
1	garlic clove, crushed
1 tbsp	diced celeriac
1½ ltrs	chicken stock
45g	soft butter
45g	flour
40ml	sherry
150ml	cream
1 pinch	cayenne pepper
20g	wild mushrooms
2 slices	white bread
	a little whipped cream

Clean the **mushrooms**, cut into smallish pieces and sauté in butter. Set aside. Remove the crusts from the **bread**, cut the slices into dice and fry in butter until golden. Set aside on an absorbent towel to drain.

Place a heavy saucepan on a medium heat. Melt the **butter** and, when the foam subsides, add the **smoked bacon**. Sauté for a minute or so before adding the pheasants' **livers and hearts**. Brown well on all sides. Add the **vegetables** and roast until also browned. Pour in the **chicken stock**, bring to the boil, skim and simmer gently for 1½ hours. Remove the pheasant, lift off the breast and reserve. Strain the stock through a fine sieve.

In another pan, heat the **soft butter** until melted and beginning to foam. Add the **flour** and stir over a low heat for 15 minutes. Remove from the heat to cool slightly, about 5 minutes. Return to the heat and begin to add the **stock** slowly, 1 ladle at a time, until it is all incorporated. Simmer gently for 20 minutes before adding **sherry** and **cream**. Check the seasoning and adjust. If necessary, sharpen with a **pinch of cayenne pepper**. Strain the soup through a fine sieve.

Slice the pheasant breasts finely and add to the soup. Top with a dollop of **whipped cream** and scatter the **wild mushrooms** and **croutons** over.

Tom & Hugh Richardson
Wheelbirks Dairy Produce

Cream

"…standing in the pastures just below the farm, Hugh Richardson and I are surrounded by Jersey cows. Even before his mobile phone rang, they all made a beeline for us, faces raised. They seem tiny to me."

oday we travel to the rolling pastures of the Tyne Valley, to Wheelbirks Farm, home of the brothers Tom and Hugh Richardson and their families. I've journeyed here via a fuel-stop in the nearby town of Corbridge, which is looking very swish these days, with its ciabatta sandwich shops, internet café, coffee shop in the art gallery and design emporium in the square. Leaving Corbridge for Wheelbirks you cross the Tyne and take the famous A68. Its views are magnificent, but the sharp bends, steep crests and hidden dips have taken many an unwary traveller by surprise. Take good heed of the 'Don't Speed' signs if you're heading to Wheelbirks to pick up a pint of milk, or some home-made ice cream.

182

Heed duly taken, I am very soon standing in the pastures just below the farm with Hugh Richardson, surrounded by Jersey cows. Even before his mobile phone rang, they all made a beeline for us, faces raised. They seem tiny to me. Hugh smiles, recognizing my reaction. "People do forget how small Jerseys are compared to the black-and-whites we're more used to seeing". They mill around us inquisitively, except for one who sits smugly in the next field. "She's perfected the trick of crawling under the

barbed wire on her knees," Hugh tells me. "She's never where she's supposed to be." These flighty but personable animals all have pet names, in addition to their breed names, and I can't help thinking that Steve McQueen would be a good one for our Great Escaper, but I suspect Hugh would draw the line. The Richardsons' young daughters all have the honour of cows named after them, including eight-month-old Nelly, who later wakes up and rewards me with the biggest smile I've seen for a good while.

It's a very peaceful vista from here, rolling hills, wooded glades and a monastery just a little way off. You can see what attracted Hugh and Tom's great grandfather here. David Richardson, a nineteenth-century Tyneside industrialist, had taken the train out of Newcastle and walked out into the countryside. He came upon Wheelbirks Farm, semi-derelict with rabbits running in and out of the back door. The previous owner had sunk all his money into developing the place, but things just hadn't worked out. David Richardson was so taken with it, he bought it.

Colin Richardson was told that Jerseys wouldn't thrive in such cold climes, but the doubters were proved wrong. Actually, Jersey cows are probably the most geographically spread cattle in the world, being found from the Arctic to the equator.

184

The Wigham-Richardson family had interests in ship-building. In fact, the large cowshed on the farm was once a shed in the Mermaid Ship Yard. There was an interest in a china factory, and they also owned a leather works in Elswick, from whence bits of leather and part-made shoes seem to have made their way into the soil at Wheelbirks, for they've been regularly turned up by the plough. The Richardsons were and still are a Quaker family, and both Tom and Hugh were educated at Bootham School in York. Notable family members include the meteorologist and weatherman Lewis Fry Richardson, and Hugh also recalls an Uncle Alan being noted for his sculptures.

The Quaker past has a very physical manifestation at Wheelbirks, not only in the sanatorium built for the Richardsons' Tyneside workers, which still stands on the estate, but also in the various inscriptions around the farm left by previous generations:

Live as though you'd die tonight,
Farm as though you'd live forever.

Elsewhere we find:

Be fruitful, multiply and replenish the earth

Wisely improve the present

and

A stone put in the wall will not be left in the way.

(The wisdom of the latter is made apparent on the way home as a large chipping flies up from the road and cracks my windscreen!)

There's also Christina Rossetti's poem *Does the road lead uphill all the way*, and *Come ye into a quiet place and rest awhile.*

Whilst it does have the feel of a 'quiet place', Wheelbirks is not a sentimental place. It's a working farm, run as a business, with lots of attention to detail in all aspects, be it the dairying or the commercial forestry and tree surgery. The Richardson brothers, whilst undoubtedly possessing the calm of their Quaker forebears, also have a little bit of an edge to them that I can't quite place – until Tom tells me that their mum is Australian. Oh yes, that's it: The Old Green Cap would fit. It turns out that both brothers spent time travelling and working on farms in Australia after agricultural college, and both played hockey for a North

Victoria team that contested finals on the state pitches in Essenden.

The Quaker past also has another, major manifestation on the farm: the Jersey herd and their milk and cream. Hugh and Tom's grandfather was Colin Richardson, and his motivation for bringing the Jerseys to Northumberland in 1925 was a genuine desire to improve the milk supply. He felt that milk was an essential for life, and wanted to give everyone the opportunity to have clean milk. His herd was tuberculosis-tested from the outset and the first to be brucelosis-tested. Wheelbirks Jersey milk and cream was soon selling locally and being sent by train as far as Leeds and Edinburgh.

Colin Richardson was told that Jerseys wouldn't thrive in such cold climes, but the doubters were proved wrong. Actually, Jersey cows are probably the most geographically spread cattle in the world, being found from the Arctic to the Equator. Animals from Wheelbirks were soon winning prizes. At the Royal Show held in Newcastle in 1935 (the Show moved about in those days), Wheelbirks Cornelia won first prize in the milking trials and a gold medal in the butter test.

Tom's father, Michael Richardson, took over the running of Wheelbirks from his father Colin in 1966. As Tom says, "Dad really put his efforts into expanding and improving the Jersey herd. He modernized the whole farm, with new buildings, including one of the first herringbone milking parlours in Northumberland. He retired in 1998, but his knowledge is of great help to me and my brother." The sort of knowledge Michael Richardson gained can be seen from the fact that he was Chairman of the Jersey Society in 1982, and Northumberland NFU have just awarded him life membership for all the tremendous work over many years on its behalf, including being Chairman in 1973. As well as helping those sons of his, Michael Richardson can still be found out and about, putting his knowledge to good use, doing insurance assessments for the National Farmers' Union.

So, through thick and thin, the Richardsons have stuck in there with the Jerseys. "There have been times when quality seemed like the wrong bet, " says Tom. "When people were being paid for producing quantity. But maybe the tide has now turned. Seven or eight Jersey herds in Northumberland went under as people took the golden handshake, but we persevered." Hugh is certain that, once tasted, anyone could tell Wheelbirks milk from any other, and that a cook would be able to tell that their sauces were richer and better tasting than if they'd been using what he calls 'white water'. "It's lovely in mashed potatoes, too."

So what makes their milk and cream special?

Jersey milk has a naturally high butterfat and protein content, which ensure its rich, full taste. The Richardsons have worked to improve the herd by carefully studying form and taking advice from breed experts. Recently they have had their herd served by Danish sires, rather than American, to develop an increased percentage of butterfat and protein. The herd is a closed herd (they don't buy cows in), and is carefully monitored in terms of which animals are selected to breed the next generation of milkers. This is done in terms of both quality of yield and ease of management.

"Good looks are a bonus, but we're not breeding for show," cautions Tom.

Good dairy practice is very important at Wheelbirks. The results coming back from the Ministry show that their high standards of cleanliness put them in the very top band for cell count and bacteria scan. Mastitis is impossible to eradicate in any working herd, but its extremely rare appearance at Wheelbirks is impressive. Whilst not wishing to imply that all farmers producing quantity are neglectful of hygiene, Hugh is sure that the emphasis at Wheelbirks on quality means that they don't need to pressure the herd or the labour force. They milk only twice a day, rather than the three times found in the most commercial herds.

What is also important is the animals' feed. The location of the farm does give a natural advantage compared with other areas in Northumbria. The land's better here in the Tyne Valley, and the rainfall is that bit higher. Which means more grass. "We don't farm organically," cautions Tom, "but neither do we chuck chemicals about. That wouldn't do

anybody any good, including me and my family. We don't believe in placebo medication either. There's no blanket cover of antibiotics, and we have tried homeopathic remedies, which does mean daily attention for the animal concerned."

The cows are turned out to grass in summer, and again, there's attention to detail, including eradication of wild oats and thistles. (Tom kicks them out!) In winter, inside, the cows get a combination of silage (fermented grass)

and own-grown 'wholecrop' and lupins. 'Wholecrop' is where a wheat crop is taken almost to maturity and then cut with a forage harvester. This is then laid on top of the silage and covered. This is an important ingredient in the cow's diet, since the dry matter increases the level of acetic acid, which in turn increases the level of butterfat in the milk. The lupins produce a bean, high in protein, which is rolled to break it down so that the cows can use it. Some cake is bought in, but from a GM-free source, and some balancers are used, but again they are all fully traceable. Traceability is our watchword when it comes to producing quality food.

Those of you who didn't get thrown out of biology will remember that the cow has a quadrapartite digestive system, and attention has to be paid to the wellbeing of the micro-fauna , especially in the rumen, the fourth stomach. For those of you who did get thrown out, let's just leave it that the good bugs, working away to help the cow digest its food, need to be fed properly too. The Richardsons have called upon the assistance of nutritional experts, and the dairy herd has a Herd Health Plan drawn up in conjunction with the vet. Wheelbirks has also qualified for the FABBL label, which means that it's 'Farm Assured' for both crops and animals.

Cream and milk are separated, bottled and potted on site. The milk is taken into a plate cooler that takes it down dramatically from around 37°c to 4°c, and it is held in a large tank at a temperature of 3.5°c. Anyone buying milk from Wheelbirks can be sure it's been bottled no earlier than yesterday (more likely today), and that it has not been mixed from various sources, transhipped in tankers and been in the supply chain for three or four days already.

The Richardsons are keen enthusiasts for the benefits of non-pasteurization. They regard it as an adulteration which removes the milk from its natural state. They have never pasteurized since the Jersey herd arrived in 1925. "It destroys vitamin C," Tom tells me, "and also destroys bacteria which are useful to the human diet, and which allows other bacteria to invade." This is why pasteurized milk does its trick of going from being OK to being revolting in an instant. "Non-pasteurized milk has a more gradual decaying process, which is important sometimes for a cook, since the milk and cream can be used on its way to souring to give certain desired effects."

People do come a long way for the Richardson's dairy products. They are sold for drinking and cooking, to individual cheese- and ice cream-makers, and to the Northumberland Cheese Company, whom we met earlier (see chapter 7). Some of the milk – and this has to be pasteurized – goes into the Wheelbirks ice creams, made on site and available from the farm.

Tom had a good try at explaining to me what makes Wheelbirks so different and special. It has to be said that it's not just location, and without being exactly unworldly, it does seems that there is something intangible at work, some kind of Wheelbirks spirit that called to David Richardson on his walk over a hundred years ago. A Jersey cow has just headbutted me behind the knees, nearly cowping me over, as if to say "Divn't be so soft, man".

And the taste of that milk…unless you are addicted to semi-skimmed, just give that taste a try. It took me back to summers on Beacon Rod Farm in the West Riding about forty years ago…I dunno , I'll be hearing a brass band soon.

Live as though you'd die tonight.
  Farm as though you'd live forever.

Cream

Not many of our native products can provoke envy in French chefs, but cream, especially rich, golden Jersey cream, makes them wish they were working this side of the Channel. I can see why. Having worked in European restaurant kitchens when I was training, and where I was often forced to work with something akin to UHT cream, I've come to appreciate the superior quality of our dairy products.

Cream figured big in our household when I was growing up. I remember my mother and sister returning from shopping on Saturday afternoons with a waxed white box from Smythes the confectioners, full of fat, rich pastries to be fought over at Sunday tea: cream horns, meringues, vanilla slices, butterfly cakes. The chocolate éclairs were so thick with cream that, no matter how carefully you bit into them, they squirted a messy moustache all over your face.

But that was for high days and holidays. Most of the time we had 'shaky milk', the little red and white cans of Carnation. I still enjoy a bowl of strawberries and Carnation. There's a hint of sourness to it, which goes perfectly with the juicy sweetness of the fruit.

I suppose my real introduction to the natural wonders of cream came when I worked at the Mermaid Hotel on Jersey. The cream was so thick, so yellow, so rich, it hardly required whisking to make it stand up. Between the lunchtime and evening shifts, most of the staff would escape to sunbathe on the beach at St Brelade's Bay. Without fail, at 5 o'clock, half an hour before we were due back on duty, we would nip across the road to The Cobweb Café for a Jersey cream tea. That combination of fruit scone, strawberry jam and thick cream was hard to beat.

You can do all sorts of fancy things with cream, but often the answer is to keep it simple. Just a dollop on the side of a plate, or the sight of a plain jug of the buttery-coloured liquid, can transform an ordinary scone or a slice of pie into something luxurious, sophisticated and ever-so-slightly wicked.

It's easy to assume that double cream is the best, or that increasing its quantity will improve a dish. Not always so. Whipping cream is often the better option if we want a light end-result. The difference between creams is defined by their percentage of butterfat. The butterfat content is lower in whipping cream, which means more air and volume can be incorporated into it when whipped. Hence it's the better cream to use in mousses or other preparations where lightness and volume is important – and, because it's less cloying, the better accompaniment to tarts and pies.

The golden rule when whipping is to make sure both the cream and the implements are chilled. Stainless steel bowls are preferable to glass, as they keep cool better. Avoid plastic as it has a tendency to hold aromas and flavours. Keep in mind for what purpose you are using the whipped cream. Don't assume everything wants stiff, dry peaks. If making a mousse, for example, you want the cream aerated but still soft and pliable, so keep the whipping gentle. On the other hand, meringues and éclairs benefit from a thick, almost dry layer of cream, so you need to whip more fully.

And please don't assume that more equals better. Too much cream can mask the other flavours. Our tongues are porous and the fat particles in cream are significantly larger than the many tiny holes covering the tongue's surface. Too much cream inevitably means this major taste sensor becomes coated and unable to detect other flavours.

Cream is nature's gift to the cook and food lover. It may be commonplace on the supermarket shelves, but it is very much a luxury product.

VANILLA CREAM WITH FRESH STRAWBERRIES

(Serves 6)

Vanilla cream

500ml	milk
1	vanilla pod
150g	sugar
1 tiny pinch	salt
4	egg yolks
4 leaves	gelatine
300g	lightly whipped Jersey cream

Strawberries

2 punnets	English strawberries
	caster sugar to taste
	juice from half a lemon

Soak the **gelatine** in a bowl of cold water. Pour the **milk** into a small saucepan with the **sugar** and **salt**. Split the **vanilla pod** in half lengthways and scrape out the seeds into the milk. Bring to the boil and whisk into the **egg yolks**. Strain into a clean saucepan and return to a low heat. Cook gently, stirring with a wooden spoon, until it reaches a coating consistency. Remove from the heat, drain the gelatine, squeeze gently and add.

Transfer to a bowl which is sitting inside another bowl of iced water.

Stir until cooled and just beginning to thicken. Gently fold in the **lightly whipped cream** and fill six 250ml Baba moulds with the mixture. Chill for 4 hours before attempting to turn out.

Hull the **strawberries** and select the best for decoration (6 per person). Liquidize the remainder with the **lemon juice** and **caster sugar** to taste. Force through a fine sieve and reserve.

Turn out the vanilla creams by dipping the moulds into hot water for 3 seconds. Invert immediately onto the centre of dessert plates.

Arrange the **strawberries** around and drizzle with strawberry sauce.

Serve with shortbread or a crisp Tuile biscuit.

CREME CHANTILLY

This is basically whipped cream with the addition of a little vanilla. Often badly prepared and with poor ingredients,
Crème Chantilly is a must with a warm fruit tart; pear and almond, or apricot, for example.
It's also fantastic with a good meringue, or with fruit scones and strawberry jam.

300ml	whipping cream, chilled
40g	icing sugar
	seeds from half a vanilla pod

Chill a stainless steel mixing bowl in the freezer. Remove and pour in the **cream** and **vanilla seeds**. Whisk until the cream stiffens and the whisk leaves a trail. Sift in the **sugar** and whisk until fully combined and the cream holds soft peaks. *Do not over whisk and allow to dry out.* Return to the fridge and hold, chilled, until needed.

GOOSEBERRY FOOL

(Serves 6)

The word fool was at one time synonymous with the word trifle, meaning something that was trifling – a thing of little consequence.
Evidently, a fruit purée mixed with cream was considered, in years gone by, to be foolish – a mere trifle.

450g	gooseberries
190g	sugar
	double cream

Place the **gooseberries** in an ovenproof dish. Scatter the **sugar** over and add **100ml water**. Cover the dish with foil. Place in a preheated oven at **150°c**, bake until soft and beginning to collapse. Remove and purée in a food processor. Allow to cool completely.

Measure the purée and then an equal quantity of **double cream**. Whip the cream until slightly thickened and soft peaks appear. Fold the cream and purée together with a rubber spatula. Spoon into glasses and refrigerate for a couple of hours.

Serve with shortbread.

CINNAMON ICE CREAM WITH SPICED WINTER FRUITS

(Serves 4)

Cinnamon ice cream with spiced winter fruits captures the essence of winter: honey, mulled wine, cinnamon, and dried fruits.

Ice cream

Place the **milk, cream, 150g sugar** and the **cinnamon sticks** into a saucepan. Bring to the boil, remove from the heat and cover with a lid to infuse for 1 hour. Strain through a fine sieve into another saucepan and heat once more.

Meanwhile, put the **yolks** and the remaining **sugar** into a stainless steel bowl. Whisk together until pale in colour. Pour on half of the cinnamon-infused milk and whisk until smooth. Tip this mixture into the pan with the remaining mixture of milk and cream. Heat over a gentle heat, stirring continually with a wooden spoon until thick enough to coat the back of the spoon. Strain immediately through a fine sieve into a clean bowl, which is sitting inside a bowl of ice. Stir until cold and then churn in an ice-cream maker.

Fruit

Simmer the **wine, sugar, honey** and **spices** for 30 minutes in a small saucepan. Remove from the heat, cover with a lid and allow to infuse for several hours. Remove 150ml liquid and put the **prunes** to soak in it. Peel the **pears**, cut into quarters and remove the core. Heat the **remaining wine** and add the **pears, apricots** and **other fruits**, poaching for 10 minutes or so at a gentle simmer. Add the **prunes** and their soaking liquid. Reboil, then remove the pan from the heat and allow to cool before refrigerating.

Assembly

Arrange the fruits decoratively on dessert plates, spoon a little juice over and serve a ball of cinnamon ice cream on top.

Cinnamon ice cream		Fruits	
500ml	double cream	½ bottle	red wine
500ml	milk	75g	caster sugar
8	cinnamon sticks	40g	clear honey
8	egg yolks	1	small bay leaf
300g	sugar	1	vanilla pod
		½	cinnamon stick
		1	star anise
		3	coriander seeds
		5	black peppercorns
		2	cloves
		225g	stoneless prunes
		1	ripe pear
		12	dried apricots
		12	walnut halves
		2tbsp	bilberries

CREME BRULEE

(Serves 6)

100g	egg yolks
75g	caster sugar
500ml	double cream
2	vanilla pods
70g	brown sugar

Preheat oven to *140°c*. Place 6 ramekins in a deep baking dish.

Slit the *vanilla pods* lengthways and scrape out the seeds. Heat the seeds and pods in the *cream* with *half of the sugar*. Bring to a boil.

Whisk together the *egg yolks* and *remaining sugar* until light in colour and the whisk leaves a trail. Pour on the cream and mix well. Strain through a sieve into a bowl and discard the vanilla pods.

Carefully ladle or pour the mixture into the ramekins. Using a teaspoon, skim off any foam that forms on top of the surface. Pour enough boiling water into the baking tray to come about half an inch up the sides of the ramekins. Bake until the custards seem firm on the edges and still a little soft in the centres.

Remove from the water bath and chill overnight. Rub the brown sugar through a sieve and cover each custard with a thin layer. Glaze under the grill, with the heat about 2" above the sugar-coated custard.

Don't chill, or the caramel will soften

The Pattinsons
Hotbank Farm

Beef

'Those are the Galloways.'
A greatly admired breed in their own right…
These russet and hairy cattle with ears sticking
up and out like teddy bears are one half of the
Blue-Grey equation. The other half is soon to be
found, hiding in a hollow.

Today the quest sees us travelling west, out along the Tyne Valley. Hotbank Farm is slightly nearer to Carlisle than to Newcastle, and not that far from the Cumbrian border. To get there, we can ignore the dual carriageway and take the Military Road, one of my favourite drives in Northumberland. Following the course of the famous Roman frontier, Hadrian's Wall, the Military Road runs straight as an arrow. It was built in the mid-eighteenth century, just after the 1745 Rebellion. The roads between Newcastle & Carlisle had been so bad that the garrison from Newcastle and their cannon had not been able to move over to the west to block Bonnie Prince Charlie's progress south… so when the dust settled, a new road was built. (There are those who claim that the garrison never actually set off, because it was Newcastle Races that week.)

For a good part of the way, the Military Road is actually in the *vallum*, the wide ditch that would have been behind Hadrian's Wall immediately to the south. From the Military Road you can gain access to the many Roman forts, such as Chesters, Vindolanda and Housesteads, which is only a mile away from Hotbank.

To take a look at Housesteads, which the Romans called *Vercovicium*, you have to take a fifteen-minute, steep, uphill walk from the car park. 'Why did they have to put it up here?' is the question in the mind of many a visitor, trudging wearily up the hill. When they reach the fort, and survey the commanding view both north and south,

the answer is obvious. You could keep your eye on what was happening for a canny few miles from up here. Today the remains of several buildings are clearly visible, including the headquarters and the hospital, and there is a civilian settlement, too, the like of which grew up around every Roman fort.

There had to be a pub. You'd have an awful long walk otherwise.

Some of the best finds dug up at Housesteads, including a figure of Mars, are in the museum at Chesters. That's well worth a visit. You can build up quite a picture of the

people who stood shivering up here on duty on this wall, and dispel a few myths too. Many of the soldiers who were posted here had never seen Italy; they were from all over the Roman Empire, including Africa, and there was a regiment of archers from Syria.

Incidentally, that name, *Vercovicium*. I've seen it in textbooks translated as 'the place of the regiment called The Efficient Fighters'. It doesn't have much of a martial ring to it, does it? I can't see two Roman squaddies sitting in that fort-side pub going

'What mob are you in mate?'

'Me? Oh I'm with the Old Efficients, squire'.

Still, it beats the Old Inefficients, who were a very dodgy mob to have in front of you!

rally car, which scrabbles and bounces over the rocks as we claw our way up to the Pattinson's farm. I clean this tricky test section, and arrive fantasizing about giving Erik Carlson a run for his money. However, the sheep acting as marshals today seem totally unimpressed. What it must be like trying to get up here in a bad winter, I can only guess.

John Pattinson (a very traditional name in this neck of the woods) looks every inch the part; a native Northumbrian hill farmer whose family have been here for generations. Now we know from our experience with Steve Ramshaw that appearances can be deceptive, but this time our assumptions are spot on.

"Have the Pattinsons been here long?" I ask, as we sit down for a chat in the farm kitchen.

One mob that definitely did move into Housesteads after the Romans left were the local brigands and rustlers, who would have used the ancient fortifications to hide their stolen kine. Which reminds me, that's what were looking at today: beef.

Hotbank farm is the home of the Pattinsons, and we're going to have a look at their traditional breed of Blue Greys. Just past Housesteads I turn into the Hotbank track, which snakes up the hillside and passes through a cleft in what look like cliffs from the road. I was forewarned about the condition of the track, and have brought my 1960s Saab

"Aye,"confirms John ," I've allus been here… nigh on thirty years farming Hotbank… my father Joseph had the farm before me."

"Is the farm likely to stay in the family?"

"My eldest lad John-Jo is busy learning, getting set to carry on the family tradition at Hotbank."

"Why Hotbank?" I wonder aloud, thinking that there isn't anything remotely hot about any banks that I can see.

"They think it's from Holtbanks, 'cause the lake just over the hilltop had otters in it, so otter holts on the banks gives us Holtbanks, which turns into Hotbank over the centuries. Something like that, anyway!"

"So why Blue Greys, John?" I ask, and realize that, inside a minute, I've asked four questions of a Northumbrian farmer, which is normally a cue for being told to mind your own business. But John's a gent and gives me my answer.

"Well, my father was a founder member of the Whitebred Shorthorn Association, which was formed in 1962 to protect the identity of the breed. We use the Whitebred bull for the Blue Greys, so I kept them on because of him. They're just the job for a place like this, as fit as lops (Northumbrian for fleas). Their thicker coats help them survive hilltop winter conditions, and they thrive on hill farms where continental breeds don't, as they don't need feeding a lot of barley. They'll pile on fettle just fed on grass. They're smaller and lighter, they can forage on wet land where bigger cattle would bog themselves down. They're an important part of the farm system, keeping down the vegetation so that the sheep can graze. They mature slower, which affects the taste, and the meat has that marbling of fat that the chefs like."

John hesitates, and a look comes into his eyes. He's mentioned chapter and verse about the advantages of Blue Greys, but I know the one thing he won't mention is that the hairy, mottled little beauties are his favourites! You see, I have a mole – his daughter, Louise – and, according to her, he loves the little blighters. Which means that the terrible events of the last few years must have hit the Pattinsons hard.

They didn't have foot-and-mouth themselves, but a nearby farm got a suspect test, so the stock at Hotbank had to be culled. It turned out that the test came back negative,

no foot-and-mouth after all… but by then the convoy had been and gone. Entirely by accident, the Pattinsons had some stock away from Hotbank, at Highshield, which survived and their bloodlines with them. But new stock has still had to be bought in from neighbours and from farmers in Cumbria. A tough time for these tough folk.

So what, actually, is a Blue Grey?

It's a Galloway cow crossed with a Whitebred Shorthorn bull. From the Galloway it gets its hardiness, and from the Whitebred Shorthorn it inherits efficient milk production. Both parents are upland breeds, but being a first cross, the Blue Grey has what's called 'hybrid vigour'. They are a slow-maturing breed, producing an element of marbling in the flesh, essential for flavoured beef.

"Can I take a look at them?" I ask, somewhat warily, because there are no cattle whatsoever in sight. There are plenty of walkers, some of them Pennine Way pilgrims, others just here to walk for a short while alongside the Roman Wall, a section of which forms one of the walls of the Hotbank farmyard. It may actually be the case that Hotbank Farm was partly built, long ago, with stone from Hadrian's Wall. It would have been a handy quarry. But I digress; there are no cattle in sight. We have to take a walk.

This is where I am given a guide to take me out on the hills to look for Blue Greys. John Pattinson has to get back to tending his stock, so my guide for today is daughter, Louise. As we head out of the farmyard she tells me she has an older brother and sister and a younger brother still at school. Louise has just started at Nottingham University, studying pharmacy, which is going to take a good few years. As we start to climb the hill, and I look back at the isolated farmhouse with the wild moorland all around,

I can't help but think that the city of Nottingham must be something of a new experience for her. At least there is one thing of which we can be pretty sure, and that's that a load of strangers won't be tramping through her garden! I'm told some of the walkers hereabouts have been known to open the Pattinson's farmhouse door without knocking, and just walk in.

We head on up over the fields. Now I think you may be able to tell from the photographs that when we say 'field' here, we are not talking about a flat square of lush green grass. This field is undulating hilltops, marshy in places and very open to the elements, although there are a few trees lower down by the lake. Crag Lough, with the massive outcrop of

Steele Rigg standing behind it, is reputed to be the most photographed site in Northumberland, with Hadrian's Wall running high along the very edge of the Rigg.

"Look! Down there by the lake, there's a Blue Grey in that patch of tall grass," points out Louise. I peer and take her word for it, but to be honest, I can only vaguely make out that there's an animal down there. We walk on further up the hill and there are some cattle. Thank goodness, we have found our quarry… but no. "Those are the Galloways," a greatly admired breed in their own right. Indeed, Mrs Pattinson is Secretary of the Cumbria Galloway Group. These russet and hairy cattle, with ears sticking up and out like teddy bears, are one half of the Blue Grey equation.

The other half is soon to be found, hiding in a hollow.

The Shorthorn bull lounges at his ease, surrounded by his harem. He's a young bull, bred on the farm, and is Dad's pride and joy. He's big! OH YES, HE'S BIG!! And were it not for the fact that I am determined to match Louise's insouciance, I would be a lot further away – in the next field, probably.

The Galloways shy away from us quickly, and Louise confirms that they are relatively wild in their behaviour, although the more they are handled the tamer they become. Still no sign of the Blue Greys, and then she points again, and I'm somewhat taken aback, for the face peering out at us from the tall grass, white with black rings around its eyes, appears to be that of a startled lemur. It isn't, it's a Blue Grey calf, and as it moves out of cover I get my first glimpse of this wee beast, with its mottled colour-change running the length of its body.

"There's another," informs my guide, and indeed there is. The markings are different on this one; it's a bit lighter too, but definitely steel blue. This one has the most amazing, almond eyes. There are over fifty of these cattle spread across these hilltop pastures. They will stay out all year, except maybe in a bad winter, when some of the smaller ones might be brought inside. Their diet is completely natural. In winter they will be given silage, which is cut on the farm, and maybe a little beet pulp, but definitely no artificial additives.

Hotbank Blue Grey beef is part of Hadrian's Wall Beef and Lamb, which also takes in neighbouring Bradley Farm, with its Housesteads Aberdeen Angus. Both farms are designated Sites of Special Scientific Interest, and as such are subject to environmental management schemes designed to protect the landscape. Both farms are on land owned by the

National Trust. All this puts severe limitations on what can and can't be done. In partnership with the Trust's Rural Regeneration Officer (funded by the Northern Rock Foundation), the idea was hit upon to come up with an 'added value scheme,' in which Hadrian's Wall Beef would be marketed to the customer who liked the idea of traceable, high quality, environmentally friendly stock. There was a launch in 2002, with Local Food Fortnight, and several local outlets agreed to put Hadrian's Wall Beef on their menu. One of the first such establishments was Café 21, where Terry gave customers both Blue Grey and Aberdeen Angus beef side by side.

It's very hard to farm within the strictures placed on farmers in historically important & environmentally sensitive areas such as Hotbank, and I can't help feeling that they're not quite getting what's due to them. So if you do select Blue Grey Quality Beef at Café 21, or buy it direct from the farm, you'll know you're directly supporting the north east's World Heritage Site, Hadrian's Wall, and the livelihood of upland farmers. Which is no bad thing, as it's not an easy life by any means, even with grit like the Pattinsons'. Mind you, they're known for a sense of humour too, and I bet the story of the writer and the bull is already circulating in the 'crac' in these parts. "You shoulda seen the colour gan from his face when Pattinson's lass took him up close to the bull!"

Beef

If I could only give one piece of advice to anyone setting up a restaurant, it would be to make sure the beef is of the highest quality. It may sound out-dated, even reactionary, but a good percentage of the paying public judges a restaurant by the quality of its steak. The décor may be stunning, the presentation classy and the service faultless, but serve an indifferent piece of beef and you have an unhappy customer.

Ask me to explain why beef is such a restaurant benchmark and I'm not sure I can. But beef is intangibly caught up with things intrinsically British – roast beef and Yorkshire pudding, red-coated Beefeaters, country pubs and Brown Windsor soup. It's solid, reassuring, well-mannered and comforting. Despite the recent buffeting of BSE and foot- and-mouth, there's the feeling the world will be all right if beef is on the menu.

When I was growing up, it was unquestionably a luxury. Roast beef was strictly for special occasions and steak only encountered if you ate out. It wasn't until I worked abroad that I realized there were other options apart from grilled steak and roasts – or, in our household, minced beef and Fray Bentos. In Baden-Baden, I discovered boiled brisket and beef stroganoff. Goulash was a revelation; goulash soup even better, particularly with a dollop of noodle dough dropped in just before serving. I learnt how to slice topside joints into paper-thin escalopes, then flash- fry them with butter and chives. In Switzerland I came across *bunder fleisch*; salted, air-dried beef, fantastically intense. I also ate raw steak tartare, which, at the time, was a scary concept.

Gradually, British kitchens took on these continental approaches. Stew became *boeuf bourguignon*, chicken casserole became *coq au vin*. Pot-roasting, braising and flash-frying became commonplace. Occasionally, we grew a little too clever. Fillet of beef with strawberries, served at a well-known, smart, Newcastle hotel, comes to mind.

Thankfully, we're seeing a return to more common-sense cooking, and an appreciation of the quality of the raw product. I have no doubt this has been driven, in part, by the recent scares which have provided a timely wake-up call to the importance of good husbandry.

One of the difficulties I have is convincing farmers that I need a beast with a high level of fat. The average shopper has been persuaded that lean meat equals healthy meat. It may be ultra-healthy – although, by definition, a balanced diet must include fat – but at the expense of taste. Fat is essential for succulence and moisture. The best piece of beef I've ever eaten was in a New York restaurant (Craft in SoHo). It was a piece of skirt steak – not a fashionable cut – which can be rather fibrous and chewy. But it was Japanese Kobe beef from a Wagyu beast. These animals are raised on a diet of rice and bran, as well as being bottle-fed on beer and treated to a massage four times a day to distribute the fat evenly. And, boy, did it show. The succulence was indescribable – and it was worth every dime of its eye-popping $54.

For our restaurants, we buy organic Aberdeen Angus and Blue Grey, a Galloway-Shorthorn cross. The former is delicate, close-grained and smooth; the latter more masculine, coarse-grained and earthy. Both have a healthy covering of fat. When buying any joint, but particularly steak, the meat should be neither overly red nor overly wet. Both are signs that the meat is too fresh and should have been hung for longer.

Steaks vary widely, so think about who is going to be eating it and what the occasion is. Not surprisingly, given that it's such a hard-working muscle, rump steak has the most strongly developed texture, resulting in a deep, gutsy flavour. Fillet steak is the polar opposite – silky smooth and tender, in both appearance and taste. If you want both texture and

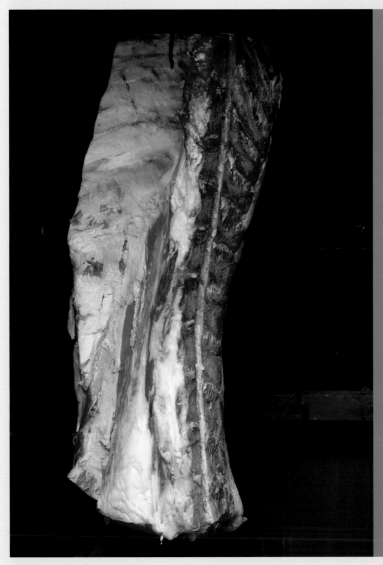

Tips

Ageing/hanging meat:

All meat needs to be hung. During this process, the meat's natural enzymes break down the proteins in the muscle tissues, which helps the meat to tenderise. It also allows any excess moisture and blood to evaporate and the flavours to concentrate. Ideally, beef needs to be hung on the bone for three weeks. Unfortunately, commercial pressures mean that this vital process is often ignored; meat hanging around ties up capital. A quicker alternative is 'wet ageing'. The carcass is cut into joints, which are vacuum-packed and aged in the fridge. This gives tenderness but not flavour, as the moisture is unable to evaporate. Buying at source guarantees you will know how long the meat has been hung. Failing that, try and buy from a reputable butcher whom you can trust. Any butcher who cares about his produce won't mind if you ask how long the meat has been hung.

Finger and thumb test:

Cooking steak at home can intimidate people; the problems generally revolve around not being able to figure out when it's done. Different cuts cook at different rates, and you need to access each piece of meat individually for thickness, internal temperature and fat content. Then there's the temperature of your grill or the type of pan you are using. Professional cooks rely on a touch test. A rare steak should feel like the fleshy triangle of skin between the thumb and index finger of a relaxed hand. A medium steak will feel like the same spot on a clenched fist and if you want it well done, compare it to the tip of your nose. An alternative method would be to use a digital, instant read thermometer. A rare steak will have a core temperature of around 45°c; medium rare 50°c; medium 55–60°c and well-done 75°c.

A point worth remembering is that thicker steaks will continue to cook for a while once removed from the pan.

flavour, although neither will be the tops, sirloin is the ideal compromise. Rib-eye steak (the 'eye' of the fore-rib) is coarser than sirloin, with wonderfully succulent fat, and can be fantastic. Big appetites like the T-bone steak, a cross-cut of sirloin and fillet. For this very reason, however, it's tricky to cook both evenly. The skirt can be sensational; chewy but not tough, with a strong, almost Oxo-like flavour. Although it is not the easiest to handle; it needs to be cooked quickly over a high heat so as not to dry out.

Cooking the perfect steak is not rocket science. The simpler the method and the accompaniments, the better. The truth is, most of the work has been done before it reaches the butcher's slab. All we have to do is take care of it.

Never cook a steak straight from the fridge. Allow it to come up to room temperature (30 minutes for a 250g steak). Some people argue that seasoning the steak while it is raw will draw out the moisture, causing the meat to boil rather than fry. My preference is to season it the second before

you place it in the pan. This reduces the hygroscopic effect and also allows the heat to draw some of the seasoning into the meat.

Heavy, cast-iron pans are the best, as modern aluminium ones cool incredibly quickly. Ridge grill-pans are ideal if you want to char the meat. Use a combination of oil and butter; oil for a high heat, butter for flavour. The only sure-fire way to tell when steak is cooked is the finger and thumb test. Nothing equals the reliability of touch. And don't make the mistake of thinking a well-done steak is easier to pull off. There is a huge difference between well-done and overcooked.

As for accompaniments, my repertoire is very small: peppered sauce, Béarnaise sauce, Bordelaise sauce (red wine with sliced, poached bone marrow) and a simple red wine sauce with very finely chopped raw shallots. I may make a flavoured butter, with chopped parsley, a tiny bit of garlic and some chopped shallots cooked in white wine. And chips, of course. That goes without saying.

SLOW-COOKED SHOULDER OF BEEF IN RED WINE

(Serves 8)

2½kg	beef shoulder, ideally feather blade, in one piece
	salt and milled white pepper
	flour
	olive oil
50g	butter
500g	onions, peeled and cut into large dice
1tbsp	tomato paste
200ml	red wine
500ml	veal stock
1	bouquet garni (thyme, bay, parsley stalks)
12	small carrots, halved lengthways
40	button onions, peeled

Season the *beef* with *salt and pepper*, then dust with *flour*. Colour on all sides in hot oil in a large, cast iron casserole. Remove the meat from the casserole and add the *butter* and *1tbsp olive oil*. Add the *onions* and cook gently until nicely caramelized. Add the *tomato paste* and cook very gently for 10 minutes before adding *50ml red wine*. Reduce the wine away, then add another 50ml. Repeat twice more before adding *stock* and *beef*. Top up with water, bring to the boil, skim and add the *bouquet garni*. Cover with a lid and braise very gently for 3 hours at *140°c*.

Add the *carrots* and *button onions* to the casserole and continue cooking for another hour. Lift out the carrots and button onions and reserve. Lift out the beef. Strain the sauce through muslin and simmer until reduced to a coating consistency.

Assembly

Cut the beef into thick slices. Serve with mashed potatoes alongside and garnish with the carrots and button onions. Pour the sauce over and serve piping hot.

STEAK AND KIDNEY PUDDING

(Serves 6)

I ate the best steak and kidney pudding ever, six years ago in the chef's office at Claridge's. My friend John Williams (now at The Ritz) was executive chef there and he gave me this recipe. When the pudding is cooked, the paste should be a golden brown colour and have slightly caramelized. John makes his own consommé to use in the pudding, but I've tried it several times using a canned product and always had a good result. John is a great chef and a great human being. If you ever get the chance to have lunch in John's office, take it!

Paste

125g	fresh, soft breadcrumbs
125g	suet
185g	plain flour
1dessertsp	salt
110ml	cold water

Filling

1kg	diced chuck steak, with a little fat attached
125g	diced veal kidneys
125g	diced ox kidney
200g	chopped onions
250g	quartered button mushrooms
1 ltr	canned beef consommé
50g	Marmite yeast extract
1½ tbsp	English mustard
	Worcestershire sauce to taste
	salt and milled black pepper
10g	flour

Mix **all of the dry ingredients** together. Slowly add the **water** and mix carefully until the ingredients come together. **Do not overwork.** Wrap in cling film and refrigerate for half an hour to relax.

Roll out on a floured board 3–4mm thick. Line a 2-litre pudding basin with the paste and cut a disc the size of the mouth of the basin, to use as a lid.

Place the **beef** and the **kidney** in a large bowl and season, then coat the meat with **flour**. Add the **mushrooms** and **onions**. Mix well.

In a separate bowl mix the **consommé, Marmite, mustard** and **Worcestershire sauce**, season with **salt and pepper**. Pour the mixture over the meat and mix thoroughly. Taste for seasoning and adjust if necessary. Fill the lined bowl with the mixture, taking care to distribute it evenly. Brush the suet paste lid with cold water and cover the pudding, moistened side down. Crimp the edge to seal.

Place buttered greaseproof paper over the top and then cover with a piece of clean muslin cloth. Tie with string and steam for 4 hours. (Oysters may be popped in the top of the pudding for the last half hour of cooking.)

Turn out, cut into 6 portions and serve with mashed potato.

OXTAIL SHEPHERDS PIE

(Serves 6)

This demands a lot more effort than the traditional pub version, but the end result is worth the trouble.
Oxtail has an unsurpassed depth of flavour, and not having to mess around with the bone is an extra bonus.
It can be made a couple of days in advance – in fact I think that it actually benefits from a maturation period.

Oxtails

1	oxtail, cut into joints
1	large onion
2	carrots
3	celery sticks
½	head garlic
2tbsp	tomato paste
2tbsp	flour
1	thyme sprig
1	bay leaf
1ltr	strong red wine
	salt and milled black pepper
100ml	red wine vinegar
50ml	vegetable oil

Topping

1kg	floury potatoes (Yukon Gold or Dunbar Rover)
3	parsnips
2 heads	celeriac
60ml	double cream
2tbsp	unsalted butter
3–4tbsp	Parmesan cheese

Peel the **onion, carrots** and **celery** and cut into ½" dice. Trim any excess fat from the **oxtails**. Place the **vegetables, meat** and **herbs** in a large bowl. Pour the **wine** over, cover and marinade overnight in the refrigerator.

Next morning, drain in a colander then strain the wine through a very fine sieve or a piece of muslin. Transfer to a saucepan and bring to the boil. Remove any scum or impurities that rise to the surface, then simmer until the wine is reduced by half. Set aside.

Dry the oxtails on a clean cloth and season well. Heat the **vegetable oil** in a large casserole dish and colour the oxtails on all sides. Discard any excess fat then add the **butter** and vegetables to the casserole. Cook until nicely caramelized. Add the **tomato paste** and cook for another 5 minutes, stirring. Add the **flour** and stir in with a wooden spoon, cook slowly for 5 minutes before pouring in the **vinegar**. Cook for 5 minutes until evaporated completely

Add the reduced wine and enough water to cover the oxtails. Bring to the boil, skim, add the **herbs** and cover with a lid. Braise in a low oven (**130°c**) for 4 hours.

Remove from the oven and leave until cool enough to handle. While waiting, make the topping. Peel the **potatoes, parsnip** and **celeriac** and cut into 2" dice. Cover with cold, salted water, bring to the boil and simmer until tender. Drain, dry and force through a food mill.

Heat the **cream** in a small saucepan. Stir in the hot cream and **butter**. Set aside and keep warm.

Remove the oxtails from the cooking liquid and strain the liquid through a fine strainer into another pan. Retain the vegetables but discard the herb sprigs. Reheat the liquid, skimming off any excess fat and impurities. Boil to reduce to a nice sauce consistency.

Remove any fat from the oxtails and strip the flesh from the bones.

Mix the diced carrots, onion and celery with the meat and bind with a little of the reduced sauce. Spoon the mixture into 6 individual ovenproof dishes and cover with the topping, creating a layer ½" thick and leaving a ½" border. Sprinkle with the **Parmesan**.

Bake at **180°c** for 20 minutes until golden and bubbling.

THAI BEEF SALAD

(Serves 4)

A great way to use up the tail ends of beef fillet, which are relatively inexpensive and fabulously tender.

Dressing

1	garlic clove, puréed
2tsp	finely chopped lemon grass
2tsp	finely chopped coriander stalks
2tbsp	light soy sauce
1tbsp	lime juice
½tsp	fish sauce
2tsp	demerera sugar

Salad

500g	beef fillet in 4mm thick slices
1tbsp	vegetable oil
12	cherry tomatoes
2	large red chillis
½	small red onion, peeled
½ coffee cup	mint leaves, in perfect condition
½ coffee cup	coriander leaves, in perfect condition
100g	toasted peanuts

To make the **dressing**, mix everything together and set aside.

Halve the **tomatoes**, then slice the **chilli** into thin strips. Halve and slice the **red onion**. Place in a bowl with the other salad ingredients.

Heat the **vegetable oil** in a heavy, cast iron frying pan. Season the **beef fillet** and fry quickly on each side, leaving it very rare. Slice into 4mm strips, add to the salad ingredients and spoon on the dressing. Toss gently and divide between 4 plates. Scatter the **peanuts** over and serve.

TOURNEDOS ROSSINI

(Serves 6)

6	fillet steaks, 160g each
3tbsp	vegetable oil
3tbsp	soft, unsalted butter
6 slices	white bread
100g	clarified butter
6 slices	fresh foie gras, 80g each
1	black truffle, cut into 6 nice slices, the remainder chopped
	a little black truffle oil
	salt and milled black pepper
150ml	Madeira sauce

Madeira sauce

150ml	dry Madeira
4tbsp	port
300ml	brown chicken stock
75g	cold, diced, unsalted butter
	a drop of lemon juice

Pour the **Madeira** and the **port** into a small saucepan, bring to the boil and simmer until reduced to about 2 tablespoons. Add the **chicken stock** and continue cooking until reduced by half. Add the **cold butter**, a couple of pieces at a time, and swirl the pan around to incorporate the butter into the sauce. Season and sharpen with a drop of lemon juice.

Cut a disc from each slice of **bread** with a 3" pastry cutter. Heat the clarified butter in a non-stick frying pan and fry the discs until golden on both sides. Set aside.

Heat the **vegetable oil** and the **soft butter** in a cast iron frying pan over a high heat. Season the steaks generously with salt and pepper and fry 2 minutes each side for rare, 5 minutes for medium and 8 minutes for well done. Remove from the pan when cooked to your liking, season again and set on a small plate upturned on top of a larger plate. Cover loosely with foil and hold in a warm place.

Gently warm the **Madeira sauce**. Heat a small frying pan over a medium heat. Season the slices of **foie gras** with **salt and pepper** and fry for 45 seconds on each side. Remove from the pan with a palette knife and place one piece on top of each steak.

Reheat the croutons and place each in the centre of a warmed joint plate.

Sit a fillet steak on top, place a **slice of truffle** onto each piece of foie gras and spoon the Madeira sauce over. Drizzle with a little truffle oil.

Serve with fried potatoes, creamed spinach and maybe some sautéed wild mushrooms.

PEPPER STEAK

(Serves 4)

4 x	284g (10oz) dry-aged Sirloin or fillet steaks
3tbsp	black peppercorns
3tbsp	white peppercorns
2tbsp	coriander seeds
1½tsp	fine sea salt
2tbsp	vegetable oil
2tbsp	soft butter
100ml	cognac
200ml	brown chicken stock
180ml	double cream
2tbsp	soft green peppercorns in brine

Coarsely grind the **black and white peppercorns**, together with the **coriander seeds**. Transfer the crushed peppercorns to a sieve and shake to release and discard any pepper dust. Roll the **steaks** in the crushed pepper, pressing firmly to embed them into the meat. Set aside at room temperature.

Heat a large, heavy, cast iron frying pan over a high heat. Add the **vegetable oil**, season the steaks with **salt** and place carefully into the frying pan. (It is vital that the pan is very hot at this stage, as the addition of the cold steaks will cool the pan, resulting in the meat stewing rather than frying if not hot enough.) Cook for 2 minutes over a high heat and then add the **butter**. Continue cooking until blood rises to the surface. Turn the meat over at this point Cook for another 2 minutes for rare, 4 minutes for medium rare, or continue until blood rises again to the surface, which indicates that your steak is medium.

Remove from the pan when you are happy that the cooking is to your liking, and transfer to a plate that has a smaller, upturned plate on top. This is to help collect any juices that may be released whilst resting the meat and whilst the sauce is being made. Leave to rest in a warm place, above the stove or on the open door of a low oven.

Discard any excess fat from the frying pan and swill out with **cognac**.

Return to the heat and boil until reduced to 1 teaspoon, before adding the chicken stock. Boil until reduced by half and then pour in the cream. Simmer gently until reduced to a coating consistency. Strain through a fine sieve into another small saucepan and stir in the soft green peppercorns. Check the sauce for seasoning and set aside to keep warm.

Transfer the steaks to warm serving plates, tip any collected juice into the sauce and spoon the sauce over the meat. Serve with vegetables or salad and good, crispy chips.

Martin Charlton
*Mushroom Collector
(And anything else growing
wild that's edible!)*

Wild Food

"'Aye, here we are', Martin stops us and points. There lies a long-fallen trunk, and all the way along it, in layers, are growing mushrooms. They're oyster mushrooms. Martin calls them wood trumpets, but to give them their Latin name they're from the genus *Pleurotas*. They're also sometimes known as 'shellfish of the woods'."

In

most of these chapters, I've started off by trying to give you an idea of the Northumbrian whereabouts we're visiting. Not this time. Oh no. Our location is secret.

I've given my word.

We're in a wood. That much I'm prepared to disclose. *But no more.* So don't ask. OK?

It's a wood covering the steep sides of a gully, down which I'm scrambling, somewhat precariously. I'm following Martin Charlton as he 'breaks trail' for me, pushing aside the brambles and nettles. Well, not all of the nettles; some he picks and gives me to eat. "Rub them between your fingers to get rid of the sting," he instructs, demonstrating the correct technique. "There, try that." Gingerly I have a go, and have to admit it's not at all a bad taste. "I'm coming back to pick some of those later, to make some soup," confides Martin. "Watch your step."

I must indeed watch my step, and carefully. I make maximum use of the footholds pointed out by my guide, as we pick our way down the steep slope, over the slippery, slimy trunks of ancient, fallen trees. The sodden bark is now

covered with mosses and fungi and that's why we're here. Martin collects wild mushrooms.

This chapter is full of health warnings. "Get the wrong mushroom and you can end on dialysis," cautions Martin. Do *not* try this at home! Not without following a similar, careful path to Martin, who first began his passion for mushrooms some years ago. "You begin by admiring, enquiring, investigating, comparing, checking, eliminating, checking again and then picking," suggests our mushroom man. "You must take into account the time of year and the details of the location, whether it's growing singly or in a group. You ought to make notes, as these will help you identify your find. Compare it with the illustrations in a good mushroom book, and taking photographs would be a good idea. These days you could even go for advice to the internet, using a snap with a digital camera."

Martin also suggests that you should also take spore samples, by placing an example of the mushroom under a glass on contrasting black and white card. The resulting spore pattern, dropped by the fungus and its colour, will give you another indicator to compare with the experts and the reference material. The first time you pick you should use gloves or a plastic bag to handle the fungus. "Take it to someone who has already built up a body of knowledge," warns Martin, "and ask them. Play it safe."

As I stumble along behind him, Martin bounds on down the slope, a real live wire of a 'canny lad'. His sport is wind-surfing, and occasionally he's dropped his career in cooking to follow the wind and waves to world-famous wind-surfing hot spots, such as Vassiliki on Lefkas in Greece, or the sport's Mecca of Fuerteventura in the Canaries. These days, Martin Charlton's a lecturer in catering and cooking in Newcastle, and he's more of a family man, with two young children, but at the weekend he's to be found up the Northumbrian coast on the end of the strings of his kite. Kite-surfers bounding along the waves have become something of a regular sight on the beaches of the Secret Kingdom.

"Aye, here we are," Martin stops us and points. There lies a long-fallen trunk, and all the way along it, in layers, mushrooms are growing. They're oyster mushrooms. Martin calls them wood trumpets, but to give them their Latin name, they're from the genus *Pleurotas*. They're also sometimes known as 'shellfish of the woods'.

Martin gives them the quick once over. Some are too old to pick and some are too small and will have to be left for later, but a fair few of these delicate-looking specimens meet with his approval, and out comes the sharp knife and the plastic bag. As he carefully snips them off, he hands one over to me

for inspection. What a smell! "There's no comparison with cultivated," Martin assures me. "There's such a greater depth of flavour, especially when they're fresh like this."

When we've gathered a handy little crop, Martin decides to extend our search to take in one or two nearby places, where it's likely from his previous experience that there will be other kinds of fungi. The first we come upon is the dryad's saddle (*Polyporus squamosas*). You can see how it got its name, it looks just like a miniature saddle. Not too miniature in some cases, as the weight record for a dryad's saddle is about 20 kilograms, but if they grow too large then they're no good for eating. You could probably sole your shoes with a slice of the 20-kilo monster. Sometimes, in dark locations, dryad's saddles can grow to resemble miniature stag's horns, but you don't see that very often, as even a little light will have them reverting to their more normal shape. Martin takes hold of a small one. "You'd shred this," he demonstrates, with a chef's confident dexterity. "You'd cook it slowly. There would be all kinds of recipes which you could use it in."

We then set off to look for something called chicken of the woods, but before we find it, Martin spots something else. Even when he points out the tree branch in question, all I can see is what looks like a small, old, dry leaf, or even a brown moth. Martin calls this wood ears, but it is also known as Judas' ears. The connection, of course, is Judas Escariot, who is supposed to have hung himself on an elder tree. Some older textbooks will list this fungus as Jews' ears, which is probably just a corruption of Judas, but to avoid confusion let's give it its proper name, *Auricularia auricula*. There is a closely related species in Japan, *Ki Kurage*, which is sold widely and exported in great amounts to China, which also imports masses of the stuff from Tahiti for use in soups and vegetable dishes.

We're off again looking for chicken of the woods. No sign. I begin to wonder whether its been seen off by fox of the woods, but this daydream is brought to a deservedly sharp end by the fact that I've wandered off, entangled myself in brambles and nettled myself badly. The brambles interest Martin greatly. "A good crop of blackberries here later. Worth remembering!" Something else catches his eye and he examines closer. "Look at these!" I look. Wild raspberries,

growing in abundance amongst the tangle. They weren't even visible from the path. "Come back and pick them later?" I venture.

"No, they're definitely worth collecting now." Martin whips out another plastic bag. In they go.

And on we search – and successfully this time, as Martin spots a *Grifola pondrosa*, chicken of the woods, sometimes listed as hen of the woods. It is so named because, somewhat prosaically, it was thought to resemble a hen, squatting in the branches of a tree, with its feathers spread to protect its chicks. I say prosaically, because I can't help liking the Japanese name of *Mai-Take*, the dancing mushroom, which they liken to the waving hands and kimono sleeves of dancing girls. Whatever you call it, it's best cooked and eaten young, as, like a lot of other fungus, the flesh becomes tough and fibrous as it ages.

I am quite taken with the names of mushrooms. For instance, there's hare's ears, jelly babies, lawyers wig, velvet cap, the prince and weeping widow. Quite a lyrical lot, apparently, and then there's the varieties which do what it says on the tin, such as soap-scented toadstool and elm tree mushroom. Then you get the ones to which you'd give a very wide berth, purely on account of their monikers: dead man's fingers, destroying angel, death cap, the sickener, and not forgetting trumpet of death. I can't say that bleeding mycena sounds all that attractive either, but there was no need to be rude about it.

Finding mushrooms is about knowing the right place at the right time. The penny bun and wood blewitt can be found in our wood in autumn, but not now, in early summer. To find the chanterelles and the giant puffball you'd have to look in less dense woodland, or even open ground. Martin has a recipe for pineapple and puffball curry that sounds intriguing.

As we walk back to the car through the woods, our noses are regaled by the pungent presence of a large patch of wild garlic.

"I'll pick some of that later," says Martin.

I enjoyed myself immensely in Martin's company, surfing the massive wave of enthusiasm he exudes for mushrooms and all the other wild foods that he picks. It made me realize, too, that any initial idea I might have had, that picking mushrooms was just easy serendipity, was way off line. Time and effort is needed to build knowledge. Then more time and effort to identify the locations that will provide a regular supply. Then comes the monitoring of your sites so as to maximize the crop. Sourcing wild food is not an easy option.

Whilst I was with him, I also enjoyed hearing about how young people are benefiting from Martin's enthusiasm for good food, from his activities as a chef, particularly at the Beamish Park Hotel, but also with his own restaurant in Jesmond. He has some exciting plans for widening the culinary experience of his students.

Martin's last word on the subject is "Be careful, but enjoy!" As I write this, I've just noticed several mushrooms growing in the field at the back of my house. As Martin would say, "I'll pick them later!"

"there's hare's ears, jelly babies, lawyers wig, velvet cap, the prince and weeping widow"

Wild Food

Gathering wild food gives me a buzz and a tingle of anticipation. Chancing upon a circle of delicate, fairy ring mushrooms, or finding a bush of glossy, sweet blackberries that no-one else has discovered, instantly takes me back to my boyhood. It's not so much the fact that it's free (or stolen, even, if you're scrumping for apples), as the sharp reminder that our countryside is governed by the seasons. To my mind, any cook who has their own garden, or allotment, is a far more savvy cook than one who doesn't. It gives them a very good sense of time and place. A garden also teaches how to shop, as it trains the senses to look for ripeness, vitality and seasonality.

As a kid, my year was divided up into money-making opportunities. In late summer, it was rosehips, found up the Tyne valley at Blayney Row, near Newburn. We took our bags of loot to a big house in Walbottle, where a hand would reach out, grab the bags and give us a pile of coins in exchange. I never discovered what happened to the rosehips; nor, for that matter, to whom the hand belonged. As October approached, excitement mounted for 'blackberry week', which not only meant a week off school, but a potentially dangerous expedition to pick blackberries from beside the railway line. A little later, we would hang around beneath two huge apple trees at Lemington Hospital. The choice was whether to risk scaling the fence to pick them, or play safe but chicken, and throw sticks at the branches.

Later, when I was working as a young chef, I learnt to look for food with a mind more open to its culinary potential than its pecuniary advantages. Herr Rudolph of The Hotel Bellevue in Baden-Baden, dressed in full *lederhosen*, provided my introduction to the scary, fascinating world of the mushroom, by taking us out on foraging expeditions. Later, working at the Fisherman's Lodge in Jesmond Dene,

we would gather wild garlic or nettles for soup; even daffodils, whose flowers we would laboriously crystallize. (Cooking at that time was going through one of its more whimsical phases.)

The downside of gathering wild foods is that there is no guarantee. Someone else may have got there first; the best may be, frustratingly, out of reach; or bad weather may have ruined the crop. Wild food doesn't keep for long – it hasn't had the help of fertilizers and preservatives – and it should be cleaned carefully, particularly anything that has been growing near a roadside. Nettles and wild garlic need to be picked when young and tender – their flavours are too assertive when more mature – and mushrooms when the weather is dry; their sponge-like texture means that they soak up water. And don't pick fruit in the vague belief that it will ripen on a sunny windowsill. Fruit only ripens as it grows. You can make it sweeter, by adding sugar, but that's a far cry from being ripe.

It's important to reinforce Martin's Charlton's warnings about gathering mushrooms. While the majority are safe, there is a small number of varieties that are dangerous and poisonous. It is essential that you can correctly identify them before attempting to eat them. By checking a specimen against the description in the field guide you will go a long way towards establishing its identity. If you are still in doubt, you will need to consult a professional mycologist.

We're lucky that the north east has a plentiful supply of wild mushrooms, encouraged by our dampish weather. Ceps, blewitts, wood hedgehogs, chicken of the woods, magnificent giant puffballs, delicate oyster mushrooms and the bright yellow saffron milkcaps are all to be found – if you know where to look. There's even a crop of fairy ring mushrooms growing close to Bistro 21 in Durham.

The hedgerows are living fences of natural vegetation that chequer our countryside. From summer through to mid autumn they are a treasure trove of wild fruits, nut and berries. Sadly, the bounty is less used now that the fruits are easily available from commercial sources.

Whether gathering for free or buying in shops, contrary to most advice about raw ingredients, you want mushrooms to feel light in weight. If they feel heavy, this may indicate large water content, which not only dilutes the flavour, but also means they will soon deteriorate. For the same reason, try to avoid washing them. Clean with a small brush or scrape with a knife. Once harvested, they begin to lose moisture, starches and sugars. Try to use them as soon as possible, but if you do plan to keep them, store in a paper bag in the fridge.

Chanterelles are notorious for holding water. A good tip is to sauté them briefly, 2–3 minutes with a little olive oil in a frying pan with a lid. This will force the water out. Drain in a colander and wipe out the pan with kitchen roll. Melt some butter in the pan over a medium heat and then return the mushrooms to the pan. Season lightly with salt and pepper and cook for 2 minutes. Remove from the heat and season generously with chopped, flat leaf parsley and milled white pepper.

I generally trim the stalks, rather than remove them altogether, and slice generously. Mushrooms shrink when cooked, so thin slices have a tendency to shrivel up. Cook in a single layer in a frying pan. Too many crowded in the pan releases too much natural juice, and the mushrooms end up stewing, rather than frying and developing their deep, nutty flavours. Avoid seasoning until close to the end of cooking. Again, it draws out the moisture so they end up stewing.

Not all wild mushrooms are interchangeable. Some are gutsy and earthy in their flavours (ceps) while others are more delicate. The pale, fragile, fairy ring mushrooms, for example, would be easily overpowered by gamey or spicey dishes, but pair well with lighter meats, such as chicken and pork, or with firm fish such as Dover sole. The giant puffball is densely textured, almost like a piece of veal, and can take a more vigorous approach. We often cut them into escalopes, which are then bread-crumbed and shallow-fried; a vegetarian take on Wiener schnitzel, served with a simple green salad and sauté potatoes. The escalopes could also be topped with tomatoes and herbs and then glazed with melted cheese.

The most luxurious of wild mushrooms is undoubtedly the cep, or the Italian *porcini*. It has an unbelievable depth and richness of flavour. It can stand up to strong, gamey dishes, but equally, if used sparingly, adds a wonderful subtlety to blander dishes such as pasta and risotto. I sometimes use a bit of dried cep to beef up a meat stock, or grind it in a coffee mill and sprinkle the powder on top of mushroom soup.

It's worth making the effort to do a bit of foraging. Who can deny that a blackberry and apple crumble, made from fruit you've picked yourself, tastes infinitely better than one made from frozen berries, even if you are half scratched to death by brambles?

WILD MUSHROOMS ON TOAST

(Serves 4)

700g	mixed mushrooms (oyster, chanterelles, button, field mushrooms, black trumpet)
2tbsp	olive oil
50g	unsalted butter
50g	shallots
1	garlic clove
	salt and milled black pepper
4 slices	brioche ½" thick
4	free range eggs, poached
12 tbsp	beurre blanc
2tbsp	chopped chives

Beurre blanc

2	shallots, very finely chopped
2tbsp	white wine vinegar
2tbsp	dry white wine
2tbsp	cold water
1tsp	cream
250g	best quality, French unsalted butter, chilled and cut into ½" dice
	juice from 1 lemon
	salt & white pepper

First, make the **beurre blanc.** (This needs concentration: it looks simple, but can turn out a greasy mess.) Place the **chopped shallots, vinegar, wine** and **water** into a small, stainless steel saucepan. Place over a medium heat and boil until reduced to a moist slurry; there should be around 2 tablespoons. Remove from the heat and whisk in the **cream.** Return to a gentle heat and begin whisking in the cold **butter** a couple of pieces at a time. Ensure that each addition of butter is incorporated fully before adding the next. Continue adding butter and whisking until all is incorporated, gradually increasing the heat as you go, as the addition of cold butter inevitably cools the sauce. The process should take about 5 minutes to develop a creamy sauce.

When all the butter has been added, season with **salt and pepper** and 'lift' it with a squeeze of lemon. Strain out the shallots, measure off 12 tablespoons of the beurre blanc and stir in the chopped chives. Keep warm until needed.

Quickly wash the **mushrooms** in cold water, drain and then dry on a clean tea towel. Heat the **olive oil** in a non-stick frying pan and add the **mushrooms.** Sauté over a medium heat for 3–4 minutes, stirring regularly. Add the **butter, shallots** and **garlic.** Cook gently for 2–3 minutes. Season to taste with salt and milled black pepper.

Toast the **brioche** on both sides and reheat the poached eggs in hot water. Scatter the mushrooms over the toasted brioche and place a hot poached egg on top. Drizzle the chive **beurre blanc** over and around and garnish with sprigs of fresh herbs.

WILD GARLIC SOUP

(Serves 12)

4	onions, sliced
12	garlic cloves, sliced
100g	butter
	salt and milled white pepper
480ml	white wine
200ml	Noilly Prat
2.4ltrs	chicken stock
1ltr	double cream
400ml	sour cream
	juice from 4 lemons
	cayenne
100g	cold, diced butter
12tbsp	wild garlic cream
12tbsp	whipped cream

Wild garlic cream

100g	parsley
200g	wild garlic
500g	sour cream

First make the **wild garlic cream**. Wash and dry the **parsley** and **wild garlic**, remove any thick stalks and purée together in a food processor. Pass through a drum sieve, fold into the **sour cream**, cover and chill. Remove and keep for 3 days maximum.

Sweat the **onions** and **garlic** in butter until soft, season with salt and pepper. Deglaze with **white wine** and **Noilly Prat** and reduce by half. Add the chicken stock and reduce by half again. Add the **cream** and **sour cream** and simmer for 15 minutes. Pass through a fine sieve, season with **lemon juice**, **salt**, **pepper** and **cayenne**. Whiz in the **cold butter** and the wild garlic cream with a hand-held blender, then fold in the **whipped cream**.

ELDERFLOWER FRITTERS

(Serves 4)

Elderflowers make the most fantastically light, crispy fritters; almost a sweet, highly perfumed version of Japanese tempura. Elderflowers are found from mid- May through June in gardens, parks and hedgerows. Try to avoid those in roadside areas, as they may be contaminated by traffic. Cut the intensively perfumed flowers with scissors, leaving an inch or so of the stem attached. This acts as a handle to use when dipping the elderflowers into the batter.

8	elderflowers
160g	flour
40g	cornflour
250ml	milk
1 pinch	salt
1tsp	sugar
1	egg
	vegetable oil for deep frying
1tsp	ground cinnamon
3tbsp	granulated sugar

Soak the **elderflowers** briefly in a bowl of water, carefully moving them around to help remove any dust. Remove from the water and spread out on a cloth to dry. Mix the **flour, milk, salt, sugar** and **egg** with a whisk to a smooth batter. Leave to rest for 30 minutes.

Heat the **vegetable oil** in a deep saucepan to **180°c**. Dip the elderflowers, one at a time, into the batter, then lift out, allowing excess batter to drain before transferring to the hot fat. Quickly repeat the process with the other flowers. When crisp and lightly golden in colour, remove and drain on absorbent paper.

Mix the **granulated sugar** and **ground cinnamon** on a plate. Sprinkle each elderflower fritter with the cinnamon sugar and serve immediately, whilst still hot, with crème anglaise and poached fruits.

HEDGEROW JAM

Unlike other jams and preserves this needs to be sieved to remove seeds and pips. Make in the autumn when the wild fruits are plentiful.

2kg	wild fruits (sloes, bilberries, blackberries, elderberries, rosehips)
2	cooking apples
	sugar
	water

Remove any stalks and dry leaves from the **fruits,** cut the **apples** into quarters. Put the fruits into a stainless steel pan and just cover with water. Simmer until soft, about 30 minutes. Force through a sieve and weigh the pulp.

Transfer to a clean saucepan and add an equal weight of sugar. Bring to the boil, stirring to dissolve the sugar, and cook over a high heat until the jam reaches setting point (**105°c**). Remove from the heat and leave to cool for 20 minutes. Ladle into warm, sterilized jars to within ½" of the rim. Wipe off any sticky drips with a hot, damp cloth.

Place a wax paper disc onto the jam surface to seal. Cover the mouth of the jar with cellophane, fastened with an elastic band.

GRILLED DUCK BREAST WITH ROSEHIPS

(Serves 4)

4	duck breasts, 200g each
75ml	olive oil
75ml	light, red wine
1tbsp	rosehip syrup
1	small garlic clove, peeled and sliced thinly
1	tiny rosemary sprig, chopped
1	thyme sprig, chopped
12	white peppercorns, crushed

Sauce

2tbsps	unsalted butter
8	chicken wings, each chopped into 3 pieces
2	shallots, coarsely chopped
1tbsp	rose vinegar
50ml	cognac
500ml	light, red wine
500ml	brown chicken stock
1tbsp	rosehip pulp (see opposite)

Make a marinade by mixing the *oil, wine, syrup, garlic, herbs* and *crushed peppercorns*. Roll the *duck breasts* in the marinade, cover with cling film and refrigerate overnight.

Now make a *rosehip pulp* by cutting a small handful of rosehips in half and putting them into a small pyrex dish with a tablespoon of water. Cover with cling film and microwave for 1½ minutes or until soft. Force the pulp through a fine sieve.

To make the sauce, fry the *chicken wings* in 1tbsp *butter* over a medium heat until well caramelized. Add the shallots and cook for 5 minutes more. Pour off any excess fat from the pan, then deglaze with the *rose vinegar*. Add the *cognac* and boil to reduce until almost dry. Add the wine and boil to reduce by half. Add the chicken stock and simmer slowly for 40 minutes.

Strain, through a very fine sieve, into a clean saucepan. Return to the heat, add the rosehip pulp and simmer to a nice, glossy sauce. Stir in the remaining tablespoon of butter and finish with a tiny splash of rose vinegar.

Remove the duck from the marinade and place on a tray under a preheated grill. Cook for 8 - 10 minutes until the skin is crisp and the flesh medium rare. Remove to a plate and rest in a warm place for 5 minutes. Carve each breast into 7 or 8 slices, divide between 4 hot plates and spoon the sauce around.

APPLE AND BLACKBERRY CRUMBLE

(Serves 4)

3	Bramley apples
30g	unsalted butter
150g	caster sugar
1 pinch	powdered cinnamon
80g	fresh blackberries

Crumble

50g	unsalted butter, diced
100g	plain flour
50g	caster sugar

Peel, core and dice the *apples*. Heat the *butter* in a non-stick frying pan, add the *apple* and sauté gently. Remove from the heat and stir in the sugar and cinnamon. Add the blackberries and fold through gently. Divide between 4 individual, ovenproof dishes.

Preheat the oven to *180°c*. Rub together the *butter, flour* and *sugar* until crumbly. Sprinkle the crumble over the fruit and bake until lightly browned. Remove from the oven and sprinkle with icing sugar.

Serve with vanilla ice cream or custard and clotted cream.

Sauteed chicken of the woods

(Serves 4 as a side dish)

Whichever variety, look for mushrooms that feel moist and spongy. Check the stems for pinholes, which could indicate worms.
Wipe clean with a damp cloth and scrape stems with a small paring knife. Try to avoid washing the mushrooms,
as they tend to absorb water which is released into the pan when cooking, causing them to stew into a soggy mess rather than fry.

4tbsp	olive oil
900g	chicken of the woods, trimmed and sliced thickly
	salt and milled white pepper
2	shallots, peeled and finely chopped
1	large garlic clove, peeled and puréed
1tbsp	unsalted butter
2tbsp	thyme leaves
4tbsp	coarsely chopped parsley

Heat 1tbsp **oil** in a large, non-stick frying pan. Add just enough **mushrooms** to cover the bottom of the pan in a single layer. Fry undisturbed for 2 minutes before seasoning with **salt and pepper**. Turn when nicely browned, add a little soft **butter**, a pinch of **chopped shallot**, a little **garlic** and a pinch of **thyme leaves**. Toss in the pan and continue cooking until the mushrooms are tender. Transfer them to a plate and wipe out the pan with a paper towel.

Repeat the process until all of the mushrooms are cooked.

Sloe Gin

Sloes are tiny wild plums found in the hedgerows. Sloe gin is made in the autumn, ideally after the first frost
which bursts the sloes slightly, and is ready by Christmas.

1ltr	sloes
1ltr	gin
375g	sugar

Prick the **sloes** with a sterilized needle and pack them into a wide-mouthed jar with the other ingredients. Cover tightly and shake from time to time to dissolve the sugar. Leave in a warm, dark place for three or four months before straining. Transfer into bottles, cork tightly and try to keep for as long as possible.

North east producers

Northumbria larder is the regional food and drink group for the North East of England.
Its aim is to encourage develop and support its members to produce the finest food and drink
the region can offer.

Bakers and Confectioners

Burtree House Farm
Burtree House Farm
Burtree Lane
Darlington
DL3 0UY
Tel No: 01325 463521
Fax No: 01325 356608
E-Mail: enquiries@burtreehousefarm.co.uk
Website: burtreehousefarm.co.uk
Contact: Robert or Lea Darling

Produce: *Award winning sauces, traditional
and deluxe Christmas puddings, sticky toffee,
chocolate, ginger, toffee pecan puddings made
with organic butter and cream, gluten-free sticky
toffee puddings, tea loaves 13 different varieties
including non fat and gluten-free, free range
chickens, guinea fowl and Kelly Bronze turkeys
slowly reared – no drugs or GM fed.*

Elizabeth's
13 Fair View
Prudhoe
Northumberland
NE42 6EU
Tel No: 01661 835515
E-mail: tf.miles@btinternet.com
Contact: Rona Miles

Produce: *Homemade bakery products:
sugar-free cakes, gluten-free cakes,
wheat-free cakes.*

FM Foods
Unit 5D
Southwick Industrial Estate
North Hylton Road
Sunderland
SR5 3TX
Tel No: 0191 5480050
Fax No: 0191 5169946
E-Mail: info@fmfoods.co.uk
Website: www.tropicalwholefoods.co.uk
Contact: Karen Hetherington

Produce: *Importer of Fair Trade dried fruits
and manufacturers of snack bars.*

Heatherslaw Bakery
Cornhill on Tweed
Northumberland
TD12 4TJ
Tel No: 01890 820208
Fax No: 01890 820208
E-Mail: info@heatherslawbakery.fsbusiness.co.uk
Website: www.ford-and-etal.co.uk
Contact: Colin Smurthwaite

Produce: *Cakes and biscuits.*

Heatherslaw Corn Mill   2
Cornhill on Tweed
Northumberland
TD12 4TJ
Tel No: 01890 820338
Shop: 01890 820488
Fax No: 01890 820384
E-Mail: tourism@ford-and-etal.co.uk
Website: www.ford-and-etal.co.uk
Contact:

Produce: *Wholemeal, rye, barley flour,
muesli, oat flakes, oatmeal, oat bran,
toasted barley flakes, pearl barley, wheat germ.*

Jenkins and Hustwit Ltd
Farmhouse Fruit Cakes
3B Laurel Way
Bishop Auckland
Co. Durham
DL14 7NF
Tel No: 01388 605005
Fax No: 01388 605005
E-Mail: enquiries@jenkinsandhustwit.com
Website: www.jenkinsandhustwit.com
Contact: Hilary Jenkins or Anne Hustwit

Produce: *Farmhouse fruit cakes, low sugar fruit
cakes, luxury fruit cakes and Christmas puddings.*

Katie's Kitchen
11/12 High Street
Sedgefield
Co Durham
TS21 3AR
Tel No: 01740 629356
Fax No: 01740 629356
E-Mail: smjohnson@farming.co.uk
Website: www.katies-kitchen.co.uk
Contact: Liz Wilkinson

Produce: *Farmshop and deli. Pies, quiches,
cakes, ready meals, home-reared meats.*

Mason & Graham Gourmet Treats
470 Old Durham Road
Low Fell
Gateshead
Tyne & Wear
NE49 5DR
Tel No: 0191 4915341
Alt No: 0191 4201344
E-Mail: masonandgraham@blueyonder.co.uk
Contact: Morella Graham and Suzanne Mason

Produce: *Sweets, oils, biscuits, vinegars, nuts
and preserves.*

Mrs P's Country Kitchen Ltd
Unit 2A
Stainton Grove Industrial Estate
Barnard Castle
Co Durham
DL12 8UJ
Tel No: 01833 695508
E-Mail: enid4@btinternet.com
Contact: Enid Pilcher

Produce: *Traditional style cakes, pastries
and rich fruit cakes. Handmade loaf cakes,
biscuits and cookies.*

Nichol & Laidlow Ltd
Bridge End Bakery
Bridge End Industrial Estate
Hexham
Northumberland
NE46 4DQ
Tel No: 01434 600111
Fax No: 01434 600979
E-Mail: sales@nicholandlaidlow.co.uk
Website: www.nicholandlaidlow.co.uk
Contact: Stephen Laidlow or Louise Thomson

Produce: *Individual and multi pack cakes,
tray-bakes, muffins, brownies, flapjacks, country
cakes. Bespoke and product development.*

North Country Lass
11b Oakway Court
Meadowfield Industrial Estate
Meadowfield
Co. Durham
DH7 8XD
Tel No: 0191 378 0838
Fax No: 0191 378 9829
E-Mail: northcountrylass@btconnect.com
Contact: Ian & Margaret Grainger

Produce: *Game pies and gateaux.*

Northumberland Cake Co.
14D Airport Industrial Estate
Kenton
Newcastle upon Tyne
NE3 2EF
Tel No: 0191 2714170
Fax No: 0191 2714170
Contact: Michael Parrish

Produce: *Traditional hand-baked cakes.
Tray bakes, quiche and sundry pies.*

Northumbria Fudgery
2 Hallimond Road
Escomb
Bishop Auckland
Co. Durham
DL14 7SS
Tel No: 01388 664003
E-Mail: hallimond@escomb.fslife.co.uk
Contact: L. McRae or L.C. Readman

Produce: *Quality fudge, 42 flavours
including vanilla, chocolate, maple and walnut,
rum and raisin.*

Proof of the Pudding
Heckley High House
Alnwick
Northumberland
NE66 2LQ
Tel No: 01665 602505
Fax No: 01665 606945
E-Mail: rlgreen@heckley.fsbusiness.co.uk
Contact: Susan Green

Produce: *Chocolate puddings, sticky toffee
puddings and sauces.*

Thomson's Bakery
385 Stamfordham Road
Westerhope Village
Newcastle upon Tyne
NE5 5HA
Tel No: 0191 2869375
Fax No: 0191 2869381
E-Mail: janian@geordiebakers.co.uk
Website: www.geordiebakers.co.uk
Contact: Ian & Jan Thomson

Produce: *A family-run bakery. A speciality bread
range with the flagship Newcastle Brown Ale bread.
Breadbuns, flatties and scones. Meat pies, pasties,
sausage rolls, biscuits, cakes, traybakes, fresh cream
cakes. Sandwiches and wraps. Celebration and
wedding cakes. Christmas cakes, puddings
(including Brown Ale), sweet mince pies, stollen.*

Tyne Valley Fudge
8 Mount Pleasant
Stocksfield
Northumberland
NE43 7LP
Tel No: 01661 844294
E-Mail: amacklam@yahoo.com
Contact: Angela Macklam

Produce: *Homemade luxury fudges made with
handmade jersey farm butter. Various flavours.
Supply to farmers' markets at Hexham, Alnwick,
Berwick and Tynemouth. Also supply retail outlets.*

Beverages

Lanchester Fruit　9
Brockwell Farm
Lanchester
Co. Durham
DH8 9EX
Tel No: 01207 528805
Fax No: 01207 528805
E-Mail: bevemmerton@hotmail.com
Contact: Beverley Emmerton

Produce: *Farm-pressed English apple juice.
Pick-your-own fruit and farm shop when
in season.*

Pumphrey's Coffee Ltd
Bridge Street
Blaydon
Tyne and Wear
NE21 4JH
Tel No: 0191 4144510
Fax No: 0191 4990526
E-Mail: sales@pumphreys-coffee.co.uk
Website: pumphreys-coffee.co.uk
Contact: Stuart Archer

Produce: *Freshly roasted coffee and locally blended
tea. Coffee machines and services available.*

Redburn Brewery
Roselea
Redburn
Bardon Mill
Northumberland
NE47 7EA
Tel No: 01434 344656
Fax No: 01434 344656
E-Mail: redburnbrewery@btinternet.com
Website: www.redburnbrewery.co.uk
Contact: Charles and Christine Sandford

Produce: *Bottle-conditioned and cask-conditioned
Real Ale. Bottled and draught beer.*

Seaton Spring Water
The Waterworks
Seaton
Seaham
Co. Durham
SR7 0NF
Tel No: 0191 5131234
Fax No: 0191 5130600
E-Mail: info@seatonspring.co.uk
Website: www.seatonspring.co.uk
Contact: Andy Grantham

Produce: *Spring Water and water coolers.*

Dairy Produce and Eggs

Acorn Dairy
Garhorne Farm
Archdeacon Newton
Darlington
Co. Durham
DL2 2YB
Tel No: 01325 466999
Fax No 01325 464567
E-Mail: organic@acorndairy.co.uk
Website: www.acorndairy.co.uk
Contact: Gordon or Graham Tweddle

Produce: *Organic dairy produce including
milk, cream, yoghurt, cheese, eggs and butter.
Organic bread, cereals and fruit juices.
Mineral waters (full range of sizes and flavours).*

Artisan Foods
Unit 12
Blaydon Business Centre
Cowen Road
Blaydon
Tyne and Wear
NE21 5TW
Tel No: 0191 4141180
Fax No: 0191 4146680
E-Mail: sales@beckleberrys.co.uk
Website: www.beckleberrys.co.uk
Contact: Ian Craig

Produce: *Hand-made fresh cream ice creams
and real fruit sorbets in over 30 flavours.
Traditionally produced patisserie products
including mousses, truffles, cheesecakes,
gateaux, tarts and cakes.*

Doddington Dairy Ltd.
North Doddington Farm
Wooler
Northumberland
NE71 6AN
Tel No: 01668 283010
Fax No: 01668 283033
E-Mail: enquiries@doddingtondairy.co.uk
Website www.doddington-dairy.co.uk
Contact: Jackie and Neill Maxwell

Produce: *Award-winning luxury farm made ice
creams, traditional mature cheeses from their own
unpasteurised cow's milk; Doddington, Cuddy's
Cave, Berwick Edge. List of outlets on the website.*

Northumberland Cheese Company　7
Make Me Rich Farm
Blagdon
Seaton Burn
Northumberland
NE13 6BZ
Tel No: 01670 789798
Fax No: 01670 789644
E-Mail: enquiries@northumberland-
cheese.co.uk
Website: www.northumberland-cheese.co.uk
Contact: Mark Robertson

Produce: *Pasteurised cheese using vegetarian
rennet. Cow's Milk: Chevington, Cheviot,
Coquetdale, Hadrian, Kielder, Northumberland-
Chive, Chilli, Garlic, Nettle, Original, Smoked,
Reiver, Tynedale. Sheep's Milk: Redesdale.
Goats Milk: Brinkburn, Elsdon.*

Mark Toney
12 Wesley Drive
Benton Square Industrial Estate
Newcastle upon Tyne
NE12 9UP
Tel: 0191 266 1879
Fax: 0191 270 2294
E-Mail: enquiries @marktoney.co.uk
Website: www.marktoney.co.uk
Contact: Anthony and Ann Marcantonio

Produce: *Ice creams and sorbets in all sizes
of tubs, both retail and catering.*

Wheelbirks Dairy Produce　11
Wheelbirks Farm
Stocksfield
Northumberland
NE43 7HY
Tel No: 01661 843378 or 842613
Fax No: 01661 842613
E-Mail: enquiries@wheelbirks.co.uk
Website: www.wheelbirks.co.uk
Contact: Tom & Hugh Richardson

Produce: *Jersey milk and cream, Jersey milk ice
cream. Produce can be bought at the farm.*

Farm Shops

Larberry Farm Shop
Larberry Pastures
Longnewton
Stockton on Tees
TS21 1BN
Tel No: 01642 583823
Fax No: 01642 582249
E-Mail: larberry@farmersweekly.net
Contact: Ken Wade

Produce: *Organic beef and eggs.*

New Barns Farm Shop
New Barns
Warkworth
Morpeth
Northumberland
NE65 0TR
Tel No: 01665 710035
Fax No: 01665 772531
E-Mail: doreen.forsyth@btinternet.com
Contact: Doreen Forsyth

Produce: *Meat, fruit pies, cakes,
ready-made meals, soups, sausages and
home cured bacon. Meals in coffee shop.*

Fish

Swallow Fish Ltd
2 South Street
Seahouses
Northumberland
NE68 7RB
Tel No: 01665 721052/720580
Fax No 01665 721177
E-Mail: wilkin@swallowfish.co.uk
Website: www.swallowfish.co.uk
Contact: Patrick J. Wilkin

Produce: *Smoked salmon, cod, haddock,
kippers, crabs, lobsters, prawns and homemade
speciality pâtés.*

Fresh Produce

J. Craig's Ltd
Tritlington Hall
Morpeth
Northumberland
NE61 3ED
Tel No: 01670 790944
Fax No: 01670 790520
E-Mail: joannacraigs@aol.com
Contact: Joanna Craigs

Produce: *Raspberries, strawberries, winter
vegetables; potatoes, turnips, cabbage,
asparagus and leeks.*

The Herb Patch
Brockwell House
Newlands
Ebchester
Co. Durham
DH8 9JA
Tel No: 01207 562099
E-Mail: herbs@brockwell01.freeserve.co.uk
Website: www.brockwell01.freeserve.co.uk
Contact: David Potts

Produce: *Herb plants, herb mixes, jellies and
stuffings. Farm shop and tea room.*

North East Organic Growers

Earth Balance
West Sleekburn Farm
Bomarsund
Bedlington
Northumberland
NE22 7AD
Tel No: 01670 821070
Fax No: 01670 821026
E-Mail: neog@care4free.net
Website: www.neog.co.uk
Contact: Alasdair Wilson, Marc Walker

Produce: *Organic vegetables, herbs and salads.*

Carroll's Heritage Potatoes　3
Tiptoe
Cornhill-on-Tweed
Northumberland
TD12 4XD
Tel No: 01890 883060
Fax No: 01890 883060
E-Mail: info@heritage-potatoes.co.uk
Website: www.heritage-potatoes.co.uk
Contact: Anthony Carroll

Produce: *Heritage potatoes, varieties that
were bred pre-1950 and are no longer
commercially available.*

Meat, Poultry & Game

Broom Mill Farm
West Auckland
Co. Durham
DL12 9QP
Tel No: 01388 834564
Fax No: 01388 834564
E-Mail: broommillfarm@aol.com
Website: www.broommillfarm.co.uk
Contact: Matthew & Tracy Betney

Produce: *Home-bred pork, traditional dry cured
bacon, smoked and unsmoked, gammon slices and
joints. Homemade speciality pork sausages and
seasoned pork.*

C & D Rayson
Herding Hill
Shield Hill
Haltwhistle
Northumberland
NE49 9NW
Tel No: 01434 320668
Contact: Debbie Rayson

Produce: *Home-bred rare breed Dexter cattle;
pigs and sheep.*

Hadrian's Wall Beef & Lamb　12
Shield on the Wall
Haltwhistle
Northumberland
NE49 9PH
Tel No: 01434 320583
E-Mail: lamb.beefsales@nationaltrust.org.uk
Website: www.hadrianswall-beef-lamb.co.uk
Contact: Clare Oliver

Produce: *Beef and lamb, direct sales.*

Middle May Lamb
Middle Coldcoats
Ponteland
Newcastle upon Tyne
NE20 0DC
Tel No: 01661 872825
E-Mail: carron@craighead.freeserve.co.uk
Contact: Carron Craighead

Produce: *Fresh spring lamb: lamb cuts, joints,
koftas, chops. Ready made Middle May Moussaka.*

232

Moorhouse Farm Shop
21 Station Road
Stannington
Morpeth
Northumberland
NE61 6BX
Tel No: 01670 789016
Fax No: 01670 789016
E-Mail: ian@ivypigs.fsnet.co.uk
Contact: Ian and Victoria Byatt

Produce: *Fresh lamb, pork and beef, dry cured bacon & gammon, full sausage range and burger range, ready meals (10 varieties), cooked meat, range of meat pies, pâtés, home-baked cakes. Farm shop and coffee shop.*

Northumbrian Quality Meats Ltd   **1**
Monkridge Hill Farm
West Woodburn
Northumberland
NE48 2TU
Tel No: 01434 270184
Fax No: 01434 270320
E-Mail: steve@northumbrian-organic-meat.co.uk
Website: www.northumbrian-organic-meat.co.uk
Contact: Steve Ramshaw

Produce: *Award-winning organic Aberdeen Angus Beef and Blackface Lamb. Rare breed organic pork. Organic sweet cured bacon, gammon and sausages. Organic chickens and eggs. In season wild Northumbrian game.*

Piperfield Pork
The Dovecote
Lowick
Berwick upon Tweed
TD15 2QE
Tel No: 01289 388543
E-Mail: grahampeterhead@yahoo.com
Contact: Graham Head

Produce: *Top quality Middle White pork sausages, dry cured bacon, air-dried chorizo, streaky bacon, glazed hams.*

Ravensworth Grange Farm   **8**
Ravensworth Grange
Kibblesworth
Gateshead
NE11 0HX
Tel No: 0191 4877221
Fax No: 0191 4877221
E-Mail: ann@gray8984.fsnet.co.uk
Contact: Ann Gray

Produce: *Rare breed pork and lamb in a vast range of joints; chops, steaks, mince, diced, stir fry strips and sausage, including their homemade traditional and Cumberland sausage using an age-old recipe.*

Teesdale Game and Poultry   **10**
82 Galgate
Barnard Castle
County Durham
DL12 8BJ
Tel No: 01833 637153
Fax No: 01833 637153
E-Mail: teesdalegame@aol.com
Website: www.teesdalegame.co.uk
Contact: Stephen and Alison Morrell

Produce: *Fresh local game: grouse, pheasant, mallard, partridge, hare, rabbit and woodpigeon. All cuts of venison, venison sausages, venison mince, homemade game pies, and smoked products.*

Well Hung and Tender
Baldersbury Hill Farm
Berwick upon Tweed
Northumberland
TD15 1UY
Tel No: 01289 386216
Fax No: 01289 386157
E-Mail: info@wellhungandtender.com
Contact: Donald & Sarah MacPherson

Produce: *Prime Aberdeen Angus beef produced on the farm. All naturally reared and grass fed. Hung 'on the bone' for a minimum of 3 weeks. Normally pre-packed and can be cut to customers' requirements, fresh and frozen.*

Westholme Farm Meats
Westholme Farm
Marwood
Barnard Castle
Co. Durham
DL12 8QP
Tel No: 01833 638443
Contact: Martin Bell

Produce: *Teesdale raised beef, lamb, sausages and burgers*

Preserves and Honey

Chain Bridge Honey Farm   **4**
Horncliffe
Berwick upon Tweed
Northumberland
Tel No: 01289 386362
Fax No:
E-Mail: info@chainbridgehoney.co.uk
Website: www.chainbridgehoney.co.uk
Contact: Willie Robson

Produce: Pure honey products and by-products: Tweedside honey, clear, heather, aromatic and clover, honey mustards, pure beeswax candles and polish. Cosmetics: creams, ointments and soaps. Visitor centre.

Wynbeech
Wynbeech
Church Road
Wylam
Northumberland
NE41 8AU
Tel No: 01661 852593
E-Mail: wynbeech@btinternet.com
Website: Under construction available November 2003
Contact: David Appleby or Jayne Appleby

Produce: *Superior quality preserves, marmalades, curds, chutney's, relishes, sauces, flavoured mustards, herb and spice flavoured oils and vinegars, herbal and spiced hand creams, using their own or locally sourced produce. Traditional and gourmet ranges all made with no artificial additives.*

Ready Meals

Fresh Element
Unit 3
John Buddle Work Village
Buddle Road
Newcastle upon Tyne
NE4 8AW
Tel No: 0191 226 7323/ 0191 285 7112
Fax No: 0191 226 7324
E-Mail: pete@freshelement.co.uk
          andy@freshelement.co.uk
Website: www.freshelement.co.uk
Contact: Pete Hunt, Andy Ross

Produce: *High quality meals using local produce delivered to your home or office.*

Associate Members

The Butler's Pantry
14 Front Street
Wolsingham
Bishop Auckland
Co Durham
DL13 3AA
Tel No: 01388 527224
Fax No: 01388 528056
Contact: Elaine Ridley

Also in this book

Lindisfarne Oysters   **5**
West House
Ross Farm
Belford
Northumberland
NE7Q 7EN
E-Mail: enquiries@lindisfarneoysters.co.uk
Website: www.lindisfarneoysters.co.uk
Contact: Chris & Helen Sutherland

Produce: *Oysters.*

L. Robson & Sons   **6**
Haven Hill
Craster
Nr. Alnwick
Northumberland
NE66 3TR
E-Mail: sales@kipper.co.uk
Website: www.kipper.co.uk
Contact: Neil Robson

Produce: *Crabs, lobsters, kippers, smoked fish.*

Northumbria Larder. Tel: 08454562340 **www.northumbria-larder.co.uk**

This project received funding from One NorthEast.

www.onenortheast.co.uk

The Development Agency
for the North East of England